HC

Anders Lassen
VC, MC, of the SAS

Odin's creed, if we disentangle the real kernel of it, is true to this hour. A man shall and must be valiant … Now and always, the completeness of his victory over fear will determine how much of a man he is. It is doubtless very savage that kind of valour of the old Northmen … They thought it a shame and misery not to die in battle.

Thomas Carlyle
On heroes, hero-worship and the heroic in history
1841

Anders Lassen
VC, MC, of the SAS

The story of Anders Lassen and the men who fought with him

Mike Langley

Foreword by
William Langley

Pen & Sword
MILITARY

First published in the UK in 1988 by New English Library
This edition published in Great Britain in 2016 by
Pen & Sword Military
an imprint of
Pen & Sword Books Ltd
47 Church Street
Barnsley
South Yorkshire
S70 2AS

Copyright main text © Mike Langley 1988
Copyright foreword © William Langley 2016

ISBN 978 1 47387 951 5

Typeset in Ehrhardt by
Mac Style Ltd, Bridlington, East Yorkshire
Printed and bound in the UK by CPI Group (UK) Ltd,
Croydon, CRO 4YY

Pen & Sword Books Ltd incorporates the imprints of Pen & Sword
Archaeology, Atlas, Aviation, Battleground, Discovery, Family
History, History, Maritime, Military, Naval, Politics, Railways, Select,
Transport, True Crime, and Fiction, Frontline Books, Leo Cooper,
Praetorian Press, Seaforth Publishing and Wharncliffe.

For a complete list of Pen & Sword titles please contact
PEN & SWORD BOOKS LIMITED
47 Church Street, Barnsley, South Yorkshire, S70 2AS, England
E-mail: enquiries@pen-and-sword.co.uk
Website: www.pen-and-sword.co.uk

Contents

Maps

Plates

Foreword, by William Langley

I first became aware of my father's interest in Anders Lassen when I returned from a working stint in New York to find him practising knife-thrusts in the family kitchen. "Keep it low," he hissed. "Aim upwards." Dad, for his part, had recently been in Crete where, so I learned, he had been researching the life of a World War Two soldier I had never heard of, and, in my mildly exhausted state, wasn't terribly interested in.

Over lunch, with the knife safely restored to routine carving duties, he began to tell me of his new interest in an extraordinary Danish warrior; a man of apparently sophisticated tastes and primitive instincts, skilled in the arts of both seduction and killing, who, despite being one of the most highly decorated soldiers of the war, was virtually unknown to the public.

Today, the myth of Andy Lassen – awarded three Military Crosses and the only Victoria Cross ever won by the SAS – is steadily growing. Historians credit the blue-eyed Dane with everything from providing the inspiration for James Bond (Ian Fleming, on attachment to the Special Operations Executive, would have been well aware of Lassen's debonair-but-deadly exploits), to being some kind of prototype ideal of European co-operation.

Keen as he was for Lassen's achievements to be recognised, I'm not sure Dad would have endorsed such theorising. This book, first published in 1988, presents Lassen as the man his comrades, family and friends knew. Its great value as a biography is the first-hand nature of its sources, almost none of whom are alive today. Important figures in the story, such as Earl Jellicoe, Lassen's commanding officer in the Special Boat Squadron, opened doors to others, whose reminiscences led to others. Mike Langley, with his practised reporter's skills, was able to track down and interview a wide range of the people who actually knew and fought with Lassen.

It was a natural story for him. Dad, although a few years younger than Anders, had also been in a wartime naval special ops unit, landing at Juno Beach on D-Day, later fighting his way north into Belgium. Like many servicemen of his generation, he didn't talk much about what he had done or seen, but as he grew older his interest in the war stirred, and when he stumbled on the story of Lassen he felt it was one he had to tell.

The only biography then in existence was by Suzanne Lassen, Anders's mother, published in Danish and out of print for several years. Understandably, this was more of a eulogy to a lost son – heavy with memories of family life at the Lassens' country estate in southern Jutland – and sparse in its chronicling of the violent events that led to Anders' death in April 1945. In effect, Dad was starting from scratch.

An early realisation was that Lassen was no Boys' Own hero. Mateyness and team spirit, as your average British squaddie might understand them, were not his thing at all. He could be detached, obsessive, lecherous, brutal, cold and impervious to the basic disciplines of warfare. Many recollections of him included variations on the image of the "coiled spring". No one really knew what Lassen would do next, or particularly wanted to be around when it happened.

I think my father finished the book liking Lassen less than he had expected and admiring him more. This was an important distinction, for it is hard to read of Lassen's incredible feats of bravery without feeling that this was a man who cared very little for himself. There were things he did care about though – particularly those who served under him and his family; and he was exceptionally patriotic, even for an era when national pride was not considered suspect. The war was personal to Anders.

It was never his intention to become a soldier, and without the German invasion of Denmark in 1940 he might have remained in contented obscurity as a merchant seaman, perhaps finishing his days sipping akavit in a bar on Copenhagen's quayside. It took the war to unearth the fearsome qualities later summed up by Col. David Sutherland of the Special Boat Squadron: "In my opinion Anders caused more damage and discomfort to the enemy over five years than any other man of his rank and age …"

For all his ferocity, Lassen was no mere killing machine. He was creative, fastidious and carefully chose his weapons to suit the occasion. The knife, as my father explained that day, was a particular favourite. "It never runs out of ammunition."

William Langley, 2016

ACKNOWLEDGMENTS

This first British biography of Anders Lassen, VC, MC and two bars, springs from my slight connection with the only Swiss decorated for bravery in World War Two. Arturo Fanconi ran through a German minefield to the rescue of three comrades wounded and trapped near Utah Beach in Normandy; he treated and helped to extricate two of them and died still dragging himself towards the third with both feet blown off and his medical kit scattered by explosions.

He was awarded the very last Albert Medal in Gold which, had he lived until 1971, would have been translated into a George Cross. I knew of Fanconi's deed for we served in parallel units; four small groups of Royal Marines and Royal Navy ratings on special service ashore in Normandy with mobile radar and the earliest VHF radios.

Switzerland, though, did not know of Fanconi and it was my pleasure to inform Swiss TV in 1984 that the land of neutrality need not feel left out of the fortieth anniversary of D-day; they could honour the hero – a pastry cook from Ilminster by way of the Grisons – of whom they had never heard. This was done in a full-length documentary, *Arturo Fanconi's Longest Day*, and it was while researching British awards to Continentals that I stumbled upon the name of Anders Lassen.

His story, I soon discovered, was unknown to the general public here and becoming forgotten even in Denmark, as I found through a flying visit to Copenhagen and by inquiring among Danish friends. Suzanne Lassen's biography of her dead son was long out of print and, by 1985, classed as "very scarce" on bookfinders' lists and so, despite my admiration for the quality and thoroughness of the mother's work, I felt that the life of Anders Lassen ought to be re-told for a modern audience and from a British viewpoint. With this in mind, I sought an interview with the founder and first commanding officer of the Special Boat Squadron, Earl Jellicoe, KBE, DSO, MC, PC.

He invited me to his offices by London Bridge on a morning when

9

a former chairman of some gigantic concern – either Shell or ICI, I cannot remember which – waited in another anteroom while Jellicoe, moving at the cracking pace remembered by SBS old-timers, organised an official luncheon at the Mansion House for Mikhail Gorbachev and conducted a running conversation on the telephone with the chairman of Sotheby's.

I offered to return another day; I said that my query could wait, it wasn't important. Jellicoe stayed me with a gesture. "Nothing," he said, emphasising the word, "is more important to me than my memory of Andy Lassen." He paused before delivering the sentence which provided the impetus for this book: "Andy Lassen was the most extraordinary person I have ever met."

Earl Jellicoe, by providing contacts and suggesting avenues of inquiry, opened the first doors for me and I am deeply grateful to him, as I am also to Henrietta March-Phillipps for the use of her radio script: "If Any Question Why We Died", which uncovered for me details of OPERATION POSTMASTER (Lassen's first raid) that would otherwise remain secreted in Ministry of Defence files until the next century. Henrietta also pointed me towards survivors of the Small Scale Raiding Force, the unit that was founded and led by her valiant father, and this guidance put the enterprise fully under way.

There are other ladies to thank for their help: Henrietta's mother, Marjorie, Lady Marling; Varinka Muus; Mrs G. S. Capon for Danish translations; Ayalah Caplan of the Jewish National Fund and, especially, my wife Barbara, for painstaking transcriptions of many taped interviews and her unfailingly sensible proposals for improving the text.

Most of my helpers, though, were men and, among them, I am particularly indebted to Kammerherre Frants Lassen for his interest and advice over the years, as well as for entrusting me with the treasured photograph of his brother for the jacket. In alphabetical order, while saddened that some have not survived to see the finished product, I thank the veterans and other interested parties who gave so freely of time, recollections and knowledge to make this book:

Freiherr Axel von dem Bussche; Chris Dodkin of the SAS Association; Jack Doyle of the Eighth Army Association; Dr R. J. L. Ferris, MC; Norman Fidler; Raymond Fletcher; HH Prince Georg of Denmark; Tony Grech; Fred Green; E. R. Hancock, Peder C.

ACKNOWLEDGMENTS

Hansen; Col. Terry Hardy; Tommy Heard of the Commando Association; Professor André Heintz of Caen University; Gordon Hogg; R. J. Holmes, MM; Baron Howard of Penrith, DL; Patrick Howarth; Charles Howe; Ray Iggleden; J. J. B. Isaac of Anderson Manor.

Porter Jarrell, GM, provided one of the last, and most revealing, interviews and thanks are also owed to Manoli Kanakais, BEM; Col. J. N. Lapraik, DSO, OBE, MC, TD; Robert Wilkinson-Latham and Wilkinson Sword Ltd; Gregor McBain; Jan Nasmyth of the original *Maid Honor* Force; J. T. Nicholson, DCM, MM, TD; Kenneth Parker; Barrie Pitt; Bryson B. Rash of the Washington (DC) Press Club; W. A. Reeves; Alan Sanders, and to Sven Seehuusen of the Danish War Veterans' Association.

Commander Adrian Seligman, DSC, was the first of almost sixty interviewees; I acknowledge also the help of Jim Slater, National Union of Seamen; Brian Spray; Leslie N. Stephenson, DCM; Hugh W. Stowell, DSC; Col. D. G. C. Sutherland, MC and bar; A. R. Trafford; the Rev. Canon Arthur Walter; Gerry Walter; Ian R. Warren, MC; Paddy Webster; David Williams, DCM, MM; James Williamson; Thomas W. Winter, MM; Douglas Wright, MM, and Les Wright, DSM, CGM.

Finally, my thanks to the most helpful staffs of the Commonwealth War Graves Commission, the Imperial War Museum, the Military Secretary's branch of the MoD, and to the Scottish Meteorological Office for being able to tell me the weather was crisp and dry at Oban on Christmas Eve 1940, when the British part of this story began.

MIKE LANGLEY, 1988

PROLOGUE

One day in the spring of 1941, Sergeant Tom Winter of Special Operations Executive waited at St Pancras Station. Newly transferred to the quaintly named *Maid Honor* Force, his first task was to meet the morning train from Market Harborough and escort three Danish volunteers back to the unit's base at Poole in Dorset. Railway terminals in wartime Britain were caverns of gloom where the steam from locomotives stayed trapped beneath the heavy tarpaulins and boards that blacked out and protected the great glass roofs. Winter waited at the barrier where he was joined by Ernie Evison, a Londoner reporting for duty as the unit's cook. Trains in 1941 were rarely punctual but the delay to the Leicester stopper was brief; she chugged in and decanted three blond young men, obvious Scandinavians, carrying their belongings in suitcases, not kitbags or webbing packs. Their khaki was loose fitting and unpressed, enlivened only by the red and white of the Danish flag, stitched beneath shoulder-flashes bearing the single word "Denmark". They were a wireless operator, a trainee navigator and a seaman, but Winter hadn't time to ask who was who. An officer was approaching.

"He was a captain," Winter recalls, "Geoffrey Appleyard, or Apple as we all knew him later. He walked towards us smiling. I had just left a crack outfit, so I did what I'd been used to . . . I called my little group together and saluted." Evison snapped his heels together, stretching his thumbs down his trouser seams in the approved manner. Two of the Danes shuffled into positions of approximate rigidity, but the third Dane was caught on the hop.

"I hadn't noticed that he was smoking. He spat out the cigarette. His face was a picture. I looked at him and his mates, all so green, and wondered who the hell I was joining. Apple read my thoughts and said quietly: 'It's all right, Sergeant. I'll tell you about it later.'"

13

On the short journey across London to Waterloo, the smoking Dane lit another cigarette and studied his new British comrades through eyes that were unnervingly steady and of the palest blue. Winter knew without asking that this young foreigner was a virtual stranger to parade grounds and had somehow escaped the basic training that, as well as teaching the folding of blankets, marching in step and smoking only with permission, instils some fear of authority into the most fractious recruit.

He wondered how the strict rules governing transfers from reserved occupations to the forces had been breached to let this ex-sailor dress as a British soldier instead of being sent back to sea and told to stay there. Winter weighed him up. "At least 6 feet 1 inch tall, if only he stood up straight and stopped slouching. A bit spare across the shoulders, yet looks strong enough. But what's he doing with us?"

The young man was Anders Lassen, private 234907, a former Ordinary Seaman transferred from the Merchant Navy. He would rise to the rank of Major, win an MC and two bars, and go on to become the only member of the SAS to win the Victoria Cross.

1

BUTCHER AND BOLT

Britain was on the defensive. Since the fall of France in the summer of 1940 its people had been gripped by a mood of militant isolationism, telling themselves that allies were unreliable and that, "We'll do better on our own."

The Hurricane and Spitfire pilots of the Royal Air Force had swept the Home Counties skies clear of daylight raiders throughout July, August and September, but the Dornier, Heinkel and Junker bombers still came in force by night, the pulsing, unsynchronised beat of their engines terrifying whole towns and cities into fleeing for shelter in tube stations, garden dug-outs or coal cellars.

What Churchill had said in July 1940 still held true for the British: "Hitler knows he will have to break us in this island or lose the war." He was addressing an officially darkened land of identity cards and gasmasks for all, a land without signposts where silvery barrage balloons warded low-level bombers away from targets without a name, a land ill-equipped to withstand the full, invasive onslaught of Hitler's Operation Sealion.

Royal Navy destroyers, supplemented by paddle steamers, pleasure boats and flotillas of weekend yachtsmen, were still ferrying 388,000 troops off the Dunkirk beaches when Churchill, belligerent and foresighted, instructed his Chiefs of Staff to prepare ceaseless raids on the enemy coast by training, "Hunter troops for a 'butcher and bolt' reign of terror."

Gus March-Phillipps and Geoffrey Appleyard were two officers of exactly the type in Churchill's mind. Their natural thirst for action had been heightened by the reverse at Dunkirk where they first met, most informally, while under fire on the dunes. Appleyard, whose letters home never ceased to show a blithe disregard for Army censorship, wrote: "I was crouched alone in a sand-hole when suddenly sent sprawling by something hitting me in the back. My mouth was full of sand; I thought, 'This is it, they've got me' when a voice in my ear said, 'I say, I f-f-feel a b-b-bloody coward. How about you?'"

March-Phillipps of the Royal Artillery was thirty-two, Appleyard of the Royal Army Service Corps was only twenty-four but they took to each other and agreed to team up permanently at the first opportunity. It came less than three months later, in the August of 1940, when March-Phillipps, a vigorous string-puller with a wide field of Army contacts, was put in command of B troop, No. 7 Commando, one of the first ten Commandos that were being raised from "Volunteers for special duties", and trained at Newmarket, in Suffolk.

Appleyard volunteered as his second section leader, an appointment confirmed by the War Office on March-Phillipps' strong recommendation. An epic partnership had begun and soon Appleyard's letters rang with a hero-worship of the older man: "M-P is a keen naturalist, a great lover of the open air, of country places and, above all, of this England of ours and all its unique beauty and life. He was at Ampleforth and is the first Army officer I have met who kneels down by the side of his bed for 10 minutes before he goes to sleep."

These letters, collected into a slim, paper-rationed volume just after the war, were addressed to his parents, John and Mary Appleyard, at The Manor House, Linton-on-Wharfe, a prosperous village of substantial stone houses just outside Wetherby in Yorkshire. The Appleyards owned the largest motor business in Leeds, a company still quoted on the Stock Exchange under the family name. Geoffrey, the eldest son, had been educated at a Quaker school and that background, allied to first-class honours in engineering at Cambridge University, his friendly, gentle manner and natural eye for detail may have misled the Army into seeing him at first as an organiser of transport and fuel dumps rather than a leader of small combat teams. Strangers could easily make a mistake about Appleyard; they might not spot that this apparent stereotype of the quiet Englishman was naturally competitive, as well as sturdy, strong, and agile. Appleyard had been a university skier, confident enough to challenge the Norwegians on their own slopes.

The camera hardly ever caught Geoffrey Appleyard without the forage cap that concealed his widow's peak of dark, thick hair. In the same way, the stock photograph of March-Phillipps, a passport picture that he liked to say "was intended to frighten the Germans", does no justice to a remarkable man for it shows a face that could belong to any young officer in the *Country Life* set. All the props are there. The jutting chin, slightly cleft. The trim moustache and the peaked cap, with the Royal Artillery badge, pulled over the eyes and shading the nose. Nothing indicates that the moustache hides the scar of a lip severed by a nervous horse and that the nose had been broken in a hunting fall, nor does the pose reveal that the eyes are those of a writer and visionary. His widow remembers another feature: "A lovely shaped head. Very high, rather bony and with a lot of back to it."

He was, wrote Geoffrey Appleyard in a letter home, "A great worshipper and disciple of the Knights of Old who believes the spirit of Drake and Raleigh, of Robert the Bruce and of Cromwell is the spirit that will save England . . . And I'm sure he's right."

Henrietta March-Phillipps said in her 1971 BBC radio programme on the father she never knew: "Sometimes I wondered if Gus and Apple were really true. They were so very idealistic. Above all, so very patriotic. Looking back from now, it would be easy to laugh."

Laughter would not survive the facts. March-Phillipps was killed on the coast of Normandy in 1942 when leading his own creation, the Small Scale Raiding Force. He was a DSO and an MBE. Appleyard vanished on a reconnaissance flight in Sicily in 1943. He was a major in the Special Air Service Regiment with two Military Crosses and the DSO. They were no armchair patriots and March-Phillipps was serious in yearning to raid Honfleur on Crispin's Day; Harfleur, his first and more appropriate choice, now lay deep inside the dock installations of Le Havre and beyond the reach of a small seaborne force. March-Phillipps in 1942 also talked of pedalling an underwater bicycle into a Norwegian fiord to sink the German battleship *Tirpitz* with limpet mines; indeed, he began training for this operation which was cancelled only when the *Tirpitz* moved into an inaccessible hiding place.

"Phoney war" was the newspapers' jibe about the long, opening lull to hostilities in France from September 1939 to May 1940. March-Phillipps was there, earning his MBE as a staff officer with the British Expeditionary Force while hungering for action. He used a Christmas leave to go on ski-training with the Chasseurs Alpins in the High Savoy and, with other restless officers, lobbied for selection should Britain form a force to assist Finland against Russia in the Winter War of 1939–40. France was March-Phillipps' second taste of the Army, his first had been as a regular in India.

He found the life humdrum and escaped by resigning his commission at twenty-three and auctioning his kit and accoutrements to pay the passage home. March-Phillipps drew on these experiences for the third of his three novels, *Ace High*. *The Sunday Times* said of *Storm in a Teacup*, his first book, "It will delight anybody who has ever sailed a boat." He followed it with *Sporting Print*, published in 1937 and set in the country of the South Dorset Hunt where March-Phillipps in top hat and grey coat had been a regular rider and an occasional unpaid whipper-in. Victor Greenwood, "toasted as the greatest amateur huntsman of his day", is the main character and has elements of March-Phillipps as seen by wartime companions.

Greenwood uses the March-Phillipps catch-phrase, "You bloody little man", in a tirade against his groom only to reprimand himself later: "Lost my temper again. Can't keep my temper. Never could." The same was said of March-Phillipps by Tim Alleyn who shared a Thames Valley cottage with him after the return from India: "Gus had a violent temper. He would sulk and turn absolutely white if you disagreed with him sometimes. And when he was very cross, his bad stammer got much worse."

It has been suggested that the stammer handicapped the career of March-Phillipps in the regular Army, but men who served under him in the war tend to agree with the comment, "Gus turned the stammer into an offensive weapon." He also compensated for it, as far as possible, by unusual smartness of dress and bearing.

Gordon Winter, another of his pre-war friends, thought: "Gus never lost his army mannerisms. He thought it important to get on with things quickly and to do everything well. He had a built-in dislike of slackness and a great scorn of anybody who was carrying an ounce overweight." Yet March-Phillipps, in the persona of Victor Greenwood, felt the need for a balancing partner with a more controlled and mollifying nature; he saw himself with prophetic clarity in this passage contrasting Victor with Tom, his whipper-in:

> Victor had something of the poet, the visionary about him. Tom something of the devotee. Victor's love for his hounds ran through him like a flame. Tom's feeling found its expression in rigid attention to discipline and detail without which nothing much can be accomplished. Apart, these two would have fallen into the inevitable pitfalls of their creeds – thoughtfulness and forgetfulness on the one side, lack of initiative and inspiration on the other. But together they were an ideal combination, Victor a genius at breeding and training, Tom a genius at organisation and management.

Geoffrey Appleyard, as the record shows, was his own man but he also played "Tom" to March-Phillipps' "Victor" and this role of Appleyard's is illustrated by the long list of requirements for a voyage under sail from Dorset to West Africa. Everything on the list is in Appleyard's handwriting, except for one word added by March-Phillipps: "Cheese".

Commando officers received a daily allowance of thirteen shillings and fourpence to feed and lodge themselves, twice as much as the other ranks who were paid six shillings and eightpence a day. These sums were attractive supplements to Army pay and much mourned whenever lost through a return to general duties, but money did not figure in the motivations of March-Phillipps and Appleyard. This was recognised by Sir

Colin Gubbins, the executive head of SOE, when describing them as: "Full of initiative, bursting to have a go, competent, full of self-confidence in their own personalities which they had every right to be, and quite determined to get into the war just as soon as they could."

Gubbins, a wiry little Highlander, had written instructional pamphlets on guerilla and partisan warfare. His fancy was caught by a paper, approved and forwarded by March-Phillipps, which discussed means of keeping troops hidden and self-maintained behind enemy lines. The author was Jan Nasmyth, a member of B Troop who had been wounded at Dunkirk – "and, after recovery, was frightfully bored, as everyone was then, until I heard that Gus was raising a troop at Newmarket".

An SOE historian described March-Phillipps memorably as having, "A fiery, disdainful manner that left an unforgettable impression of force." Old comrades quibble with "disdainful" and suggest its replacement by "high-handed", particularly in reference to his methods of recruitment.

"If Gus wanted a man, then Gus got that man," said Tom Winter, his sergeant-major. The methods could be as unconventional as the enlistment at Newmarket of Nasmyth who said:

Gus was out riding with a girl on a beautiful summer evening in peaceful English countryside. It's very hard to describe but Gus seemed to live an almost inspired life at times when he reached some sort of balance within himself.

I always remember him on that horse. He seemed part of the evening, part of everything and perfect in a way that you don't often see perfection in a lifetime. I said that I had only one eye and asked if that mattered. He said: "Do you ride a horse – and can you judge a distance from a fence when you are going to jump it?" I said that I thought so and he said: "That's all right, then. You'll do."

Nasmyth was slightly taken aback by the suddenness and informality of his recruitment; it didn't accord with his experience of an Army which was still entangled in pre-war red tape and unable to implement even minor decisions without form-filling and circumlocution. His new commanding officer, noting the surprise, leaned down from the horse and, twinkling with glee, whispered, "I have absolute powers." A few days later, the transfer went through.

March-Phillipps, as suits a rider, was lightly framed and of medium height. Every ounce, though, was fighting-weight and as taut as whipcord. He wanted his fifty Commandos to be as trim as himself and, in this quest for fitness, sent them on mile runs before breakfast, on daily swims, on cross-country races and on high-speed marches through the Suffolk lanes. They then left for winter training on the west coast of Scotland where a compulsory whip-round – "Not less than 10 shillings a head", said March-Phillipps – raised thirty-five pounds to buy a yawl from a fisherman. She was *I'm Alone*, a solid 5½ tonner with an auxiliary engine; her length was 32 feet and her beam was 9½ feet. The measurements come from Appleyard, writing of her on New Year's Eve: "A magnificent dirty-weather craft. Today, in pouring wet and high winds, was a real test for the mast which we made ourselves from what, a week ago, was a pine tree. It stood the test wonderfully."

B Troop's enjoyment of *I'm Alone* lasted for little more than a month; it was ended by Gubbins summoning March-Phillipps to London and authorising him to form a small special service unit which would be based in Poole Harbour under the direction of SOE. This group became known as *Maid Honor* Force.

Above all, the new unit needed experienced seamen, and Appleyard remembered a young neighbour from Linton-on-Wharfe who had crewed his way round the world in the Finnish sailing ship, *Pommern*. He was Graham Hayes from the Border Regiment who, in his turn, sent for Tom Winter, qualified as both an aircraft pilot and parachutist. Winter recalls:

Graham and I were together in the first 50 paratroops, part of No. 2 Commando and a nucleus of SAS. I put up my parachute wings in October 1940 and did 150 jumps

21

enjoying none of them. We dropped through a hole in a Whitley bomber but, despite modifications to the plane, couldn't follow each other out quickly. I made one of the first tethered jumps at Ringway near Manchester. Part of a Whitley's fuselage had been strapped round a barrage balloon. The straps began slipping. What guinea pigs we were!

Anyway, Graham left the outfit which grew to battalion strength and became the 1st Battalion, Parachute Regiment; then a letter and two telegrams arrived from Graham asking if I would like to join him again. Gus accepted me. It was much later that I found out he'd had a helluva job obtaining my release.

Winter's first task for *Maid Honor* Force had been to meet the next new recruit, Anders Lassen. Lassen had come a long way to meet him.

2

The Persistent Volunteer

A moving little ceremony in London some three months earlier led to Lassen reporting for active service in khaki, instead of the RAF blue on which his heart was first set. Fourteen young Danes had signed these joint and individual oaths in the soft cover of a pocket Bible:

> In the year 1941 on the 25th of January, the undersigned Free Danes in England swore, sword in hand, to fight with their allies for Denmark's liberation from a foreign yoke.
>
> I hereby swear that I will stay true to my king, Christian X. I also swear that I am ready to serve loyally whatever authority is working against the enemy that occupied my Fatherland. I swear that I will never disclose whatever military secrets are entrusted to me.

The volunteers signed alphabetically, Lassen being the ninth. Today the Bible is on permanent display at the Freedom Museum in Copenhagen and his signature is identical with two in the register of the *British Consul*, an oil tanker that brought him on the last leg of his long journey to the war.

On Christmas Eve 1940, Lassen landed at Oban in Argyllshire, one of Britain's loveliest harbours, encircled with hills and a screen of scattered, green islands. The authorities, hardly surprisingly, failed to perceive an approaching hero. They saw in twenty-year-old Lassen only an unshaved, unwashed alien who, far from being embraced as a glorious volunteer for the fight against Hitler, needed reminding to report to the police and not to stay out of doors after midnight on peril of a one-pound fine. Lassen and his sixty crewmates were bristly and grubby, cold and stiff from a blanketless night on bare boards. They were all hungry; as

23

one man, they asked about train times and the nearest canteen breakfast.

Oban, stirring itself behind the black-out curtains, was about to face two problems. How to dispose of a boatload of dead horses slopping around the inner harbour as victims of a twilight bombing raid that had kept the *British Consul* penned overnight in a safer anchorage? How to cope with a Christmas rush by home-going sailors, some of whom had a year's pay in their money belts? McKerchar's Stores awaited the crew with shelves of Glenforsa whisky at sixteen shillings and sixpence a bottle. Joints of venison were displayed in the butchers' shops, labelled enticingly, "No ration coupons required." And the Fifty-Shilling Tailors, true to title, offered to fit all-comers on the spot with suits that for a time and from a distance looked equal to anything stitched together for six pounds by made-to-measure craftsmen. Scotland in those days paid little heed to Christmas, an English holiday to be acknowledged rather than celebrated and, at best, useful only as an overture to the serious revels of New Year's Eve. Nothing in this indifference to Christmas, or in its purely commercial interest in disembarking crews, distinguished Oban from any other small Scottish port.

Lassen found himself in Scotland largely by chance after a nine-month journey marked by rebuffs and obstacles. He could have been put ashore in a neutral or enemy port if the captain of his previous ship had heeded the orders of the owners rather than the demands of his crew. Captain P. V. J. Pedersen of the Danish tanker *Eleonora Maersk* was off the coast of Oman and approaching the Persian Gulf on April 9, 1940, when the wireless operator hurried to him with long-dreaded news. German troops, including 2,000 of them hidden in colliers berthed at Copenhagen, had seized both the capital and the country in a morning.

Lassen's determination to hit back dates from this day. His resolve to join "the big war" withstood arguments and threats by Captain Pedersen and remained steadfast against the discouraging evasiveness of the British. Whitehall was trying to decide if Denmark under occupation was an ally, a neutral or a Nazi puppet.

He and the *Eleonora*'s wireless operator were turned away in Colombo when trying to volunteer for the Royal Air Force. "Foreigners are not required," they were informed, an excuse which ignored the Polish and Czechoslovakian squadrons in training for the coming Battle of Britain. Lassen shrugged off the rebuff. He rejoined his ship for passage to Cape Town and another attempt at becoming one of the comparatively few Danes, 467 to be exact, allowed to enlist in Britain's fighting forces.

The *Eleonora* joined the Allies within a day of Denmark's fall, a decision taken after a noisy meeting by the ship's company who voted on three proposals. These were to stay in neutral waters while awaiting developments, as the New York office recommended; to put into an Italian, a German or a neutral port as the owners instructed under Nazi pressure, or to sail immediately to the British-held island of Bahrain.

Bahrain won unanimously and everyone, including cadet Lassen, signed the log accordingly to provide the captain with evidence of duress to safeguard his position with the line and their new, unwelcome controllers. Lassen, in a hunting log that he used as a diary, wrote "Mutinied in the Persian Gulf" although "mutiny" over-dramatises what was more accurately a passionate, non-violent debate similar to the meetings held across the oceans in more than half of Denmark's merchant fleet.

Some 5,000 Danish seamen, although technically neutral, voted for five years of exile and service in a deadly yet frustratingly passive war. Wartime merchant seamen lived under threat from mines, torpedoes, surface raiders and aircraft without ever enjoying the satisfaction once promised by General Montgomery to his Eighth Army. Civilian sailors never hit the enemy for six.

Sitting-duck was not the role that Lassen wanted to play, but he feared it might be forced upon him if he failed to find a staging-post to the action. Bahrain, Colombo, Singapore, Borneo and Durban slipped by in the *Eleonora*'s wake without even the offer of a services medical examination or any training beyond a short course in firing the 4.7 inch gun fitted by the Royal Navy to the *Eleonora*'s quarter-deck. Only Cape Town was left before the tanker returned to the Gulf and away from the main war. Lassen decided that he could wait no longer.

He provoked quarrels with Captain Pedersen as the tanker neared Cape Town. He demanded to be paid off. He gave no reason. Confidences were never Lassen's style. "He was not the kind of man to tell the rest of us his intentions," said the second mate after the war. There is little doubt, though, that Lassen remained set on service in the Royal Air Force, then being glamorised as a carefree life of sing-songs round the mess piano in between shooting down flights of Messerschmitt 109s. Pedersen refused to release Lassen, objecting that he was bound by a contract of cadetship until September 22, 1941, his twenty-first birthday. Fine-print arguments of that nature always ran the risk of being brushed aside by Lassen for reasons stated by an exact contemporary who knew him well as a teenager; this was Prince Georg of Denmark, a great-grandson of King Christian IX and after the war, in which the Germans held him prisoner for four months, the Danish Military Attaché in London. Prince Georg said:

Anders Lassen was our house-guest on a couple of occasions when home from the sea before the war, but he wasn't a comfortable visitor because he was aggressive and would pick fights at any time, especially when drunk – although that wasn't often. He was always going to be boss, never the No. 2. He sometimes frightened people – and he was a complete loner, although fond of his parents, sister and brother.

The most remarkable aspect of Anders Lassen was the strength of his self-belief; indeed, it was rather more than mere belief. At an age when the average boy is uncertain of himself, Anders Lassen was rare in not only knowing his own mind but then in carrying out whatever course of action he had decided on.

Bred-in-the-bone patriotism and his own fiercely headstrong, tenacious nature combined to convince Lassen that a ticket to the war was worth any breach of discipline; so he malingered, he absented himself from duties and met threats of three weeks' confinement in the tanker's almost airless cells with the challenge, "Right then, jail me!"

Captain Pedersen, ever the realist, saw no advantage in continuing to carry such a determined rebel. He paid off Lassen in Cape Town at the end of September 1940, and turned the *Eleonora* back to the Gulf; the 16,500-ton tanker had been transformed into a typical wartime merchantman – camouflaged, degaussed against magnetic mines, equipped with armour-plate for the ammunition store and fitted with machine-guns as well as the 4.7 inch gun that was capable of bringing down aircraft or sinking a U-boat. These defences were of no avail. Some six months later, in April 1941, she was caught with full tanks off Crete by German bombers blasting the path for a successful airborne invasion; they left the *Eleonora* beached and blazing in the mouth of Suda Bay. Blackened bodies bobbed under the flames for five days.

Lassen, by then, was well on the way to an active war. He had been accepted by March-Phillipps and, as a foreigner in a unit comprised mainly of Englishmen, must have been grateful for the introduction to British attitudes provided by two months aboard the *Consul*, where not the least of his difficulties was attuning to a dialect. He thought the crew were Scots; in fact, they were largely Tynesiders and their sing-song speech must have made Lassen feel, as Geordies say, that he had strayed into a cage of humming-birds.

The *British Consul*, a 10,300-ton tanker, left Cape Town on October 26, 1940. Lassen's presence went unremarked, an oversight which the master, Captain J. D. "Dusty" Miller from South Shields, regretted to Lassen's mother after the war: "If I had known at the time that I had a future VC on board, I would have remembered every last thing about him."

Former Ordinary Seaman Norman Fidler says categorically: "Andy Lassen had no dealings with the deck crew working the ship. Indeed, I have no recollection of a Danish seaman, although he may have lived amidships with the officers and been put on ship's articles as an ordinary seaman just to keep it legal, which was not uncommon."

On the other hand, it's not difficult to overlook someone when working watches on a blacked-out two-decker of 430 feet length. Lassen himself fell into that trap when claiming in his diary: "I am the only Scandinavian on board", unaware that two Norwegians, Sigmund Lundberg and Hauriths Pedersen, had also joined at Cape Town as Ordinary Seamen.

The ship's register shows that supernumeraries were described as such and that their pay was entered as "nil", but Lassen had signed to work for five pounds sixteen shillings and threepence a month and must have carried out duties; for instance, as a bow look-out which, his diary records, was his post in an air attack.

"Lord Haw-Haw", the Nazi radio propagandist William Joyce, had wrongly announced the sinking of the *British Consul* shortly after her departure from Smith's Docks on the Tyne on January 22, 1940. The Germans meant her sister-ship, *British Councillor*, which had left at about the same date on the same run to Abadan in the Persian Gulf, both vessels sailing from the North Sea by the "Scottish route" because the Straits of Dover had been made too dangerous for tankers by German gun batteries and dive-bombers. The *Consul*'s crew shut their minds to the outcome should they, too, need to lower the ship's aluminium lifeboats; fragile craft that showed signs of powdering corrosion. Norman Fidler remembers:

Consul and *Councillor* were typical of British Tankers' fleet of some 120 ships. They crawled with cockroaches. There was no running water or shower for the crew, but only a hand-pump fed from a tank of rust-brown water. We had no freezer but only an ice-box which kept food fresh for a week at best; after that, we lived on tinned and barrelled food such as salt pork. Except for our dry tea and condensed milk, the diet couldn't have been much different from the *Mayflower*.

The crew slept in bunks contrived from scrap wood, strips of orange boxes and sides of tea chests which were nailed across the bed frames; but, at last, they had been supplied with mattresses instead of rough, straw palliasses – the "donkey's breakfast" for which British shipping companies charged their lower decks a sum of two shillings a man until the outbreak of war.

Conditions aboard were spartan even by the standards of Geordies from two-up, two-down terraced homes with outside lavatories and no bathrooms, but Lassen, raised in a country mansion standing amid hundreds of pleasant acres, took the discomforts in his stride. Cockroaches couldn't bother him; in two years at sea, he had seen thousands. He had roughed it from the start as a cabin-boy and dishwasher aboard the passenger-steamer *Fionia* to Bangkok; more muckily, he had scraped and hosed thick deposits of sand and oil from the *Eleonora*'s tanks on voyages spanning Mexico and Bahrain. He considered the *British Consul* average for the time and noted in the diary: "The Englishman is not damned dirty"; he meant not dirty in comparison to a Greek ship that had also offered him a working passage from South Africa to the war. The route to Britain was dangerous along the whole length of West Africa and then into the North Atlantic, but the risks were known to be greatest at three particular points. First, Freetown, the British naval base in Sierra Leone, where U-boats lurked constantly outside the harbour. Further north, the Vichy French – sworn enemies of the British – were suspected of aiding the submarines from their base at Dakar in French Equatorial Africa. Finally, the convoy had to brace itself for attack by German aircraft based on the French mainland. All these perils were negotiated successfully and the *British Consul* arrived undamaged at Oban only to find that her last night would be the most uncomfortable of the two-month voyage. Norman Fidler explains:

Board of Trade officials came aboard with the new crew but the air-raid sirens sounded as we were being paid off, whereupon our liberty boat sailed and didn't return until morning. That left the new crew, mostly Scousers, entitled

29

to take over the cabins while we of the old crew were left to wander the decks or sleep anywhere we could lie down. We couldn't complain. The new crew were signed on, we were signed off. They had the right.

Lassen stepped ashore with nineteen pounds fourteen shillings and twopence, two months' pay doubled by war bonuses. His neat, clear signatures on the register – one for his money, the other against a home address of 63, Nyhaven, Copenhagen – are the only remaining proof of his time on the *British Consul* among a crew who swept into Oban on a tidal wave of cash. The ship's donkeyman, a forty-year-old Londoner signing himself "D. James", set off home with £206 in notes, easily enough in those days to buy and partly furnish a workman's house. Six others, including the first mate, drew sums of more than £100. Norman Fidler, with almost sixty pounds in his money-belt, bought presents and a Christmas chicken for his mother. The big spenders inquired about taxis for the twisting, four-hour drive to Glasgow; the rest returned to the railway station and hoped to be home on Tyneside before the pubs shut that night at ten.

They were all civilians but dressed in a way tantamount to a uniform – double-breasted, belted, navy-blue raincoats; grey or light-blue suits with turn-ups on the trousers; trilby hats for the men, peaked caps for the officers, and white silk scarves for nearly everyone. Their luggage was almost identical: tiny attaché-cases of fake brown leather, small duffel-bags stencilled with their initials, and the invariable suitcase covered in light-green canvas and protected at the corners by buffers of thick leather.

Lassen in denims, the usual duty-free cigarette tucked in the side of his mouth, tagged along with the crowd to the city they extolled as paradise. Newcastle-upon-Tyne became his home for nearly three weeks, a lively destination with two dozen cinemas, six theatres, five dance-halls, numberless pubs, and the outstanding attraction of a mission for Danish seamen where he could relax among companions who addressed him correctly as "Anners", and not "Andy" as the British had it.

30

He established his credentials as a resident alien by enrolling in the National Union of Seamen, but service in the RAF remained his aim. Again, the recruiting office turned him away although more politely than in Ceylon. Lassen and the RAF might have been ill-matched. A ground-staff posting would have been unendurable for someone burning to strike a personal blow at the Germans, but the requirement of secondary mathematics ruled him out of consideration for aircrew. His maths were weak for the same reason many of his school subjects were not up to scratch. "He absorbed very little of his schooling. It didn't interest him," says Prince Georg. "He should have been a poacher. There was not a lot he didn't know about the behaviour of animals, wild or domestic." Lassen's younger brother, Frants, amplifies that verdict: "He was very good at physical training as well as at nature studies. He was also keenly interested in history – but miserable and bored by mathematics, by both German and English grammar, and he hated writing essays."

In short, Anders Lassen was one of those millions of boys who treat their teachers' efforts as irrelevant and who tolerate confinement in the classroom only by summoning up their most cheerful good nature. Herlufsholm, where he was sent at eleven, is a renowned boarding school founded in 1565 and standing in a park outside Naestved, some forty miles south-west of Copenhagen. A hall in memory of Lassen was endowed at Herlufsholm after the war but as Prince Georg recalls: "It was fairly well known, even among non-Herlufsholmians like myself, that the school had not been sorry to see Anders Lassen go, for he had a cruel humour at times and had been in some scrapes."

One of these escapades revealed outrageous disrespect for the school uniform that, in Lassen's day, made the pupils resemble the Vienna Boys' Choir. It was a seaman's square-rig, comprising blouse, loose shorts, a spreading blue collar with three white stripes, a black ribbon in a square bow; this ensemble was topped off by a sailor's soft cap whose band bore the school name. Lassen was wearing this outfit when he jumped into the adjoining River Susa one day to win a bet, a packet of chewing-gum.

The brothers left Herlufsholm when Anders failed his third-year examination after being in hospital for six weeks with a serious inflammation of the kidneys. Frants explains: "But as he'd never been a very good scholar in his short time there, the school advised our parents to remove him. By that time we were in the same class and so, maybe for reasons of economy, it was decided that we should both leave for a school that allowed us to live at home."

They transferred to a private secondary school at Lundby, only eight miles away, and Lassen's attainments there are summed up in his mother's story of hearing loud outbursts of cheering from the playground as she waited outside on the day that results were announced of the leaving examination . . . "Shortly afterwards a big crowd of boys appeared, carrying Anders shoulder-high; everyone was laughing and shouting and Anders looked extremely pleased with himself." He had passed. Somehow.

On New Year's Day 1941 the Newcastle *Evening Chronicle* published the photograph that symbolised Britain's embattled isolation, the famous picture of St Paul's Cathedral ringed by flames. Lassen was among a people fighting alone in Europe, except for the Greeks heroically clearing their mountains of Mussolini's invaders. The Germans now controlled the Continental coastline from North Cape to the Pyrenees. The Russians were neutral, so were the Americans. The United States government was helpful and friendly, but a Gallup poll after Dunkirk had revealed that only 32 per cent of Americans believed that Britain would win the war.

It must have seemed a curious, depressing irony to Lassen that a country desperately short of fighting men, a country that now placed courage, fitness and decisiveness above any paper qualification, should reject him for what was no more than a failure in "matriculation". Suddenly, as he did so many things, he left Newcastle at "half an hour's notice" to join the Danish volunteers in London. He travelled with Mogens Hammer, a Merchant Navy officer who had opened Lassen's mind to the possibility of Danes striking their own blows against Hitler, instead of leaving the fighting to the Allies. A need to do something, if no more than state an intention, exercised the huge majority of Danes, after ten months of Nazi occupation, and was felt most keenly by the men who had come to Britain – only to be kept at arm's length from the action.

At that time, the BBC's Sunday broadcasts of Allied anthems included neither of Denmark's national songs, "There is a Lovely Land" and the Royal Anthem. In Denmark, new words were sung softly to the tune of "God Save the King" – "Churchill will win the war", but in London, a Reuters' correction to a Churchill speech deleted Denmark from the list of countries for whose freedom the British were fighting. In Helsinki, the British Embassy told 300 Danish volunteers to go home.

The oath-taking, the signing in the Bible, was the first step towards changing British attitudes and establishing a Danish force. Werner Iversen, the former Army captain who had called the young men together, added his own vow: "To be true and loyal to the men who are fighting for Denmark's freedom and whose leader I am. Their welfare and conditions shall always be my first concern above all personal matters."

Iversen studied the group once more: Borge Frank, an architect and the donor of the Bible; M. Steincke, the son of a former Foreign Minister; Karl Kurstien, who would serve in the Buffs; Mogens Hammer, Lassen's friend, who would be killed in Germany late in the war as a captain in Special Forces. Then there was the newly qualified doctor Carl Johan Bruhn, the last to arrive at the ceremony but the first to die – as a special agent in Denmark before the year was out.

Iversen's eyes rested on Lassen; he must have wondered how this shy, wild boy would turn out. The shyness may have puzzled Iversen who had been a planter in Malaya, where Europeans were quick to embroider their social back-grounds. Here was a reversal of the pattern, someone whose voice was measured and refined, who bore himself proudly and yet who mentioned no career ambition beyond promo-tion to able seaman.

Throughout the war, Lassen never discussed his origins or family with his comrades in arms. Lord Jellicoe, his commander in the Aegean, says: "We knew nothing about him except that we realised he came from what, by Danish standards, was a rather grand background." Even his close friend Porter Jarrell, an American who won the George Medal in 1943 while serving with Lassen in the Special Boat Squadron, was given no inkling that Anders – the man after whom he intended to name his first son – was himself part-American. The brown Bible and the register of the *British Consul* are the proof that Lassen began as he meant to go on; in both cases, he signed simply, "A. Lassen". He chose not to unfurl his full set of upper-class initials: A.F.E.V.S., standing for Anders Frederik Emil Victor Schau.

3

A WILD CHILD

Lassen was the son of an adventurous extrovert, Captain Emil Lassen of the Danish Lifeguards. On visits to London after the War, Captain Lassen liked to arouse Knightsbridge by standing on the steps of the Hyde Park Hotel and summoning his chauffeured Rolls-Royce with a blast on a hunting horn. Captain Lassen was a man's man who could be devastating to women in his role of handsome soldier of fortune, although those fortunes fluctuated whenever he paid more attention to war than to managing his businesses and estates. War drew the father, as it did his elder son. This was a new development in the family's history.

The Lassens had supplied a line of Lutheran parsons to Jutland and Zealand from the end of the Thirty Years' War in 1648 until the late 1860s. The break with tradition was made by Axel Lassen, Anders' grandfather and the son of a rural dean, who chose plantations instead of the pulpit and went to the Dutch East Indies. He returned with a fortune from tobacco and married Ebba Schau, the posthumously born child of a war hero. Emil Victor Schau was killed in 1864 at Dybbol, the lost, last battle against Prussia. His name was bestowed on great-grandson Anders Lassen as a reminder that no Danish family sacrificed more than the Schaus in the wars of 1848 and 1864. Dragoon Colonel Schau sent his six sons to fight the Prussians. None returned.

"The Schau strain seemed to inject a passion for fighting into the genetics of the Lassen family" in the view of Baron Axel von dem Bussche, the German first cousin of Anders Lassen. It began to show when Emil, in joining the Lifeguards, became the first Lassen to put on uniform and when Emil's sisters entered into military alliances – Jenny Lassen (von dem Bussche's mother) and Estrid Lassen were both swept down the aisle by dashing young German officers before the First World War.

Emil, itching for something more active than ceremonial duties in Copenhagen, set off for the Spanish Civil War of 1936–39 but found only a non-combatant role in the international commission enforcing an arms blockade. He tried again, at last successfully. A volunteer Danish brigade fought for the Finns against the Soviet Union in the fierce, short Winter War of 1939. Emil joined and was proud of being wounded in this anti-Communist cause. He returned with a fund of stories, told like a master, about hunting wolves in Finland. Finally, at an age when even dare-devils should be thinking about their pensions, Lassen senior left for South America and became an honorary captain in the Chilean Air Force.

Suzanne Lassen, mother of Anders, was a writer whose tales for children were popular throughout Scandinavia. *The Naughty Caroline*, her biggest success, was modelled on a childhood friend of her sons, a girl who grew up to make her own name in the war as the Danish Resistance agent, Varinka Muus. Suzanne's mother was an American born in Paris, Nina Moulton – the granddaughter of Judge Fay of Boston and the only child of a talented widow whose singing and skating caught the eye of Napoleon III in the 1860s. This was Lily Moulton who, on marrying a Danish diplomat after the death of her American husband, turned to writing and published *The Sunny Side of Diplomatic Life*. Mother, daughter and groom then went to live in Denmark where Nina, a full American, married Count Raben-Levetzau who became Denmark's Foreign Minister. Suzanne was their child.

Anders Lassen, quarter-American, was born on September 22, 1920, at Hovdingsgard, a fifty-roomed house with a domed tower and pillared portico, near Mern in South Zealand. Frants was born two years later and their sister Bente in 1929 shortly after the ten-mile move to the manor most associated with Anders Lassen.

Baekkeskov is a fine country house of uncluttered design that was built for an Englishman, Charles Selby, created a baron in 1796 for his services as an adviser to the Danish monarchy. The great staircase is lined with hunting trophies;

there is a panelled library, tapestries and some forty rooms mostly running one into the other without benefit of corridors. Outwardly, Baekkeskov has not altered since Anders, Frants and Rufus, their Great Dane, were running wild in the woods and parkland. Thick yew hedges, two yards high, enclose the terrace where Suzanne so often stood looking for a wisp of camp-fire smoke to pinpoint her wandering sons. The sea can be glimpsed two miles to the east; this is the Baltic inlet of Praesto where wild swans still glide among the reeds and where dinghies dance at their moorings. A dolmen erected by Emil Lassen is hidden in a forest glade a mile from the house and the names he carved into the four great stones are moss-encrusted now and barely legible – Anders, Frants, Bente and, on the table stone, Suzanne.

Emil's lively personality, Suzanne's reputation as an author and the beauty of their home and its setting combined to install the Lassens on the Danish celebrity circuit. Famous visitors came to Baekkeskov; not least, Thomas Dinesen, brother of Karen Blixen who wrote *Out of Africa*. Thomas was renowned in his own right as the only Continental to be awarded the Victoria Cross in the First World War. He was a private in France with the Quebec Regiment in 1918 and the citation states: "He showed most conspicuous and continuous bravery during ten hours of hand-to-hand fighting. Five times in succession he rushed forward alone and, single-handed, put hostile guns out of action, accounting for twelve of the enemy with bomb and bayonet." There seem to be no photographs of Dinesen meeting little Anders Lassen, the past and the future VCs, but Suzanne Lassen recorded: "I remember how the boys were deeply impressed and full of admiration."

Anders and Frants were more lastingly influenced by a visit from Gregers Ahlefeldt, a renowned archer who came with hunting bows and allowed the boys to accompany him in stalking the estate's fallow deer. Frants Lassen remembers: "We were intrigued by this grown man playing with bows and arrows and shooting the deer. We were thrilled at seeing it done so well." Archery became the new enthusiasm. The brothers read all the instruction books. They lopped pliable branches from the yews to make their own bows. Ahlefeldt was not their tutor, but their inspiration. Anders Lassen, in any case, needed no lessons on hitting a bull's-eye, a running mouse or a gliding owl. He was a natural.

It's impossible to avoid this picture of life at the Lassens' on many days in the mid-1930s . . . Mother immured in the study with a manuscript or illustrations, Father out seeking adventure or an audience, the children running loose with guns, knives, bows and their huge lolloping dog, as well as their unroadworthy, battered Ford that started only when pushed downhill.

The world has always been full of boys, indifferent to their own, or other people's, danger, who would rampage like the Lassens if given the scope and space. Few of them, though, could boast such a marksman's eye as Anders Lassen or the confidence to put it to the test. This was never shown more clearly than by his acceptance of a shooting challenge from Frants at Baekkeskov where Anders had been hitting every target in his own room with a throwing knife. Frants jibed: "That's easy. But what can you do with a gun?" Placing a broken pipe stem between his brother's lips, Anders picked up his .22 rifle, pointed it at Frants, aiming at no more than two inches of white clay – and fortunately didn't miss. Frants spat out a mouthful of fragments.

Anders, to keep his eye in, began taking an air pistol to the new school in Lundby village. He and Frants pedalled there on a tandem, a 16-mile round trip. Frants says:

The front-seat rider does the hard work on a tandem but, although I was the smaller, Anders would never let me sit behind. He had to be the rear gunner, riding along with the pistol to hand. One day he spotted a blackbird on the vicarage hedge. Pop went the pistol and down went the blackbird. We raced on, not knowing that the vicar's wife was in the garden and that the blackbird had fallen at her feet. She looked down the road, recognised us and phoned our parents. We were on the carpet from the moment we arrived. Father sent us back to apologise.

Baron von dem Bussche watched Anders at work with weapons and the memory impels him to say:

> I don't think Anders Lassen would have made a very easy burgher of Denmark in peaceful times. He was what is called nowadays "a little wild". He was a hunter, a scout and full of martial spirit. He greatly impressed me, though, with his ability to fire a bow so accurately on the run that he could drop a deer dead with one arrow from 80 metres. We would also go fishing together, rather brutally with light guns to shoot carp, or trout in brooks. Quite illegal, but requiring good marksmanship.
>
> Traditionally, the Lassens were against German expansionism and so there were always battles between us boys – Anders and Frants, myself and my brother Kuno – over the war of 1864 in which our common great-grandfather, Emil Victor Schau, had been killed. We always fought as Denmark v. Prussia although the von dem Bussches were actually Hanoverians who had seen their own little kingdom of Hanover finished for good by the Prussians.

Baekkeskov could hardly be bettered as a setting for boyish battles; it offered hedges, undergrowth, farm buildings and forest through which Anders ranged, in a servant's phrase, "like a panther". This servant, the housekeeper's husband and referred to only as Magnus in Suzanne Lassen's book *Anders Lassen, VC*, remembered how, "Anders was quick at everything he did; it was incredible how he could go down the main stairs like lightning and without a sound."

Anders Lassen saw Baekkeskov for the last time in brilliant weather at the end of May 1939, the Whitsun weekend. His parents had sold the property and moved to the centre of Copenhagen but Jenny von dem Bussche, long divorced, still rented the forester's house on the estate and the young people gathered there – Anders, Frants, Bente, the two von dem Bussche boys, and Varinka Muus. She remembers:

> He was home from the sea, his first voyage on the *Fionia* – and, although I have a photograph of us taken together as

39

small children in 1926, that was the only time I met him at Baekkeskov. I remember very clearly his incredible beauty, the looks of the perfect hero – but I was repelled by his aggressive, macho behaviour. He had a gun and was shooting gramophone records to pieces, using them as clay pigeons. I much preferred his cousin, Axel.

Axel and Kuno von dem Bussche were already officers in the regular German Army and pessimistic about the chances of peace. Frants Lassen remembers: "Axel said, 'This is the last time we'll meet as a family because next year we'll be at war.' And I'll never forget Kuno's rejoinder: 'Yes, and I'll be a Stuben-führer (a class-leader of recruits) in a mass grave.' Two years later, Kuno was killed in Russia at Odessa."

Back in Copenhagen, Captain Emil Lassen remained as buoyant as ever. He was confident of Hitler's eventual overthrow, as Frants says:

> Father was always telling us: "Hitler's never been to America. He's not seen their power, he doesn't know what he's up against. Once America starts, he hasn't got a chance." Father was saying this long before the Germans began the war by invading Poland; he was saying it a year earlier when the Nazis annexed Austria. At home, we always had a very positive attitude towards the United States.

The war was still ten months away from embroiling Denmark when Anders Lassen, in June 1939, saw his native land for the last time from the decks of the *Eleonora Maersk*. He was looking at a country that feared the worst, a country that had lost rich farming lands to the Germans in the past and that had a fully justified dread of Hitler as the neighbouring bogey-man. These apprehensions were implied in Suzanne's remark about travelling down to Hamburg in August 1939, to wave off Anders again on the *Eleonora*: "I don't know why I cried, there was no reason for it." Anders was smart in grey flannels, bare-headed and smiling shyly. His mother remembered that. She never saw him again. How different from Denmark was the confidence that Lassen found in Britain. Hitler, even on official posters, was depicted as a buffoon and mocked everywhere as a crackpot house-painter addicted to chewing carpets.

Max Miller, the loud-suited Cheeky Chappie, topped theatre bills and earned some of his broadest laughs by holding up a cabbage for inspection by audiences who had already stopped worrying about air-raid sirens interrupting performances. "'Itler's 'ead," declared Max before delving further into a shopping-bag and producing two cucumbers which, in their turn, were proclaimed as, "'Itler's arms". Next, and finally, two large potatoes were pulled out and held high wordlessly. "No," said Miller at last, his tone chiding an audience convulsed by its own imaginings, "King Edward's."

Lassen wrote in his diary: "They don't care a damn about Germans and bombs." December 1940 was headlined as the "Blackest Christmas" in foreign newspapers beyond the reach of the British censors who were busy enforcing the slogan, "There is no despondency in this house". Blackest? Lassen found Britons of his own generation keyed up for a life that they sensed might never be so vivid and intense again. The war had brought change and movement for young people who rarely spent a night outside their own towns from one peace-time year to another; the war had brought jobs for the million unemployed and entitled them to their first holidays with pay. The war had emptied the servants' quarters, for ever liberating girls from dependence on the genteel, and increasingly luckless, advertisers who were still seeking in 1941: "Maid for light duties. No cooking. Fifteen shillings weekly."

Lassen found a Britain stripped for action. Anti-shatter gauze netting was glued thickly to window-panes, walls of sandbags were everywhere and no landing was complete without a bucket of sand and a stirrup-pump to douse fire-bombs. All signposts had been removed, a measure by officials hoping to confound German invaders but, in practice, baffling their own side more.

Night civilian traffic meant buses because comparatively few Britons owned cars or could qualify for a petrol ration.

These buses, in the name of austerity, began to be fitted with uncomfortable wooden seats slatted like park benches. Buses, lorries, cars and service vehicles were all bound by a speed limit of 20 mph which was observed gingerly on moonless nights because the slitted, wartime headlight mask allowed minimum illumination.

Roadblocks ringed main roads into cities and towns; at first, these checkpoints were often only upturned farm carts but soon sections of concrete storm drains were placed vertically and packed with enough cemented rubble to impede a tank. The Home Guard manned these barriers, monitoring the movement of wayfarers, demanding their identity cards and, a common fantasy, hoping to unmask German paratroopers disguised as nuns.

The Home Guard, a part-time and civilian army, had been formed in the early summer of 1940 as the Local Defence Volunteers, LDV – initials which failed to survive the jibe that they stood for "Look, Duck and Vanish". The new title of Home Guard, for all its resonance, brought nothing extra at first in issued weapons. The members were equipped only with initiative; they rummaged everywhere, even in museums and the props room of Drury Lane Theatre, to confront the Nazi war-machine with rusty muskets, assegais and cutlasses.

The majority of working-class Britons had never met or seen Continentals before the war, but now the dreary streets of land-locked towns came alive with strange accents and uniforms; for instance, the red pom-poms of French sailors. That particular novelty wore off quickly for both parties when all but 7,000 of the French went home after the armistice with Hitler. Foreigners who stayed were considered fair game for Home Guards trying to trap spies with their Government-issue pronunciation tests (Wrong, Wretch, Rats). Later on, in the summer of 1941, Lassen himself was detained by the Dorset Home Guard, whose suspicions, aroused by his accent and Teutonic blondness, were strengthened by his claim to be a member of the Horse Guards. By then he was, in fact, a member of the *Maid Honor* Force commanded by March-Phillipps and in March 1943 he would be transferred to the

Buffs, the Royal East Kent Regiment. (This transfer was for administrative tidiness and because the Buffs' colonel-in-chief was King Christian X of Denmark. The King had held the office since 1912 and must have drawn quiet satisfaction from maintaining the link while under German occupation.)

Yet, in the January of 1941, Lassen entered the Allied cause without a regiment. Captain Iversen's Free Danes, which he had joined, were only nominal soldiers who had been issued with British uniforms but given nothing to do. The inactivity irritated Lassen. He sought advice about returning to sea. A posting to the west of Scotland came just in time; the silver-sand beaches of Arisaig had been selected for what the volunteers called Commando training. They did not know that they were really under assessment by the SOE.

4

THE *Maid Honor* FORCE

Britons between the wars observed Marquess of Queensberry rules on their cobblestones as well as in the boxing rings. Fists were the understood sequel to invitations to step outside and weapons were left to criminals who, like the slum gangs of Glasgow's Gorbals, armed themselves cheaply at the barbers with cut-throat razors wielded to frighten and disfigure. Coshes, marketed euphemistically as "life-preservers", and knuckle-dusters circulated in the underworld. Fire-arms were rare. Stilettos and daggers, apart from being generally despised as un-British, were risky to carry in an era when judges, backed by the scaffold and the cat-o'-nine tails, never failed to pass sentences which reflected the public abhorrence of stabbings.

Then, in 1940 from the Far East, there came a voice saying: "In war you cannot afford the luxury of squeamishness." The speaker was William Fairbairn, the assistant commissioner of Shanghai's Municipal Police. Fairbairn, known as "Dan", and his partner Sykes, inevitably "Bill" although christened Eric, had been recalled from China, commissioned as Army captains and given a free hand to teach their specialities of silent killing, unarmed combat and pistol shooting against opponents firing back.

Colonel Rex Applegate, an American counterpart, called them "Battle-scarred veterans . . . who, according to records in Shanghai, had been engaged in more than 200 incidents of violent close-combat". Their appearance belied this toughness; to their young pupils, they looked nondescript and middle-aged. Sykes, who had commanded the Shanghai snipers' unit, was short, portly and with a demeanour that one SOE agent thought would have done credit to a bishop. Fairbairn was taller, thinner, bespectacled. Like Sykes, he wore a moustache.

Early in November 1940 Fairbairn and Sykes arrived by

taxi at the Wilkinson Sword headquarters in Pall Mall on the mission that would make their name. "We want a mass-production knife that will kill swiftly and silently," they told John Wilkinson-Latham of the company. "The grip has to be heavy so that the knife will set well back in the palm. At the same time, the weapon as a whole must not be too heavy. It must be manageable."

Sketches were made, modified and re-modified. Fairbairn and Sykes, when once unable to explain by drawing, resorted to mime to make a point, and Wilkinson-Latham never forgot Fairbairn grabbing a wooden ruler from the desk and then, after stalking Sykes round the office, clasping a hand over his partner's mouth while thrusting the ruler down towards the soft spot between the neck and shoulder-blade.

Hours of talks ended in Fairbairn and Sykes assenting to a design that incorporated these points: a heavy, roughened handle to give a firm grip in wet or damp weather; a cross-guard to prevent hand-slip on the blade; a stiletto blade with two razor edges and a sharp stabbing-point. They shook hands and left on Wilkinson-Latham's promise: "You can see a prototype within a few days." The first batch, including the sheaths, cost thirteen shillings and sixpence each; before the war ended, Wilkinson Sword made nearly 250,000 of them.

This dagger, with its six and seven-eighths inch blade, is known popularly as the commando knife, but war veterans and close-combat experts cling to the original name etched on the ricasso, the squared head of the blade, "The Fairbairn-Sykes Fighting Knife". Fairbairn and Sykes also designed a No. 2 knife, a leaf-shaped weapon resembling a Bronze Age sword and which they called a "smatchet", but the No. 1 knife remained their stock-in-trade and the SOE's Experimental Station 6 was their first and steadiest customer. Station 6 was the cover name for Aston House, a few miles south of Stevenage in Hertfordshire, where Fairbairn and Sykes set up shop as silent killing instructors until Fairbairn was assigned in 1942 to Camp Richie, Maryland, a training centre for American spies and agents of the Office of Strategic Services, the transatlantic version of SOE.

Fairbairn and Sykes taught also at Achnacarry, the Commando school hidden away in Inverness-shire, but Aston House was the cradle of their methods and there is no reason to disagree with an American view that: "Perhaps more than any other of the SOE's thirty-odd special training schools, this was the real school for bloody mayhem." Sykes was the master of soundless strangulation and Fairbairn, as well as demonstrating wrist and thumb holds, showed how a man could be knocked unconscious by a match-box concealed in a fist. The "Bronco Kick", one of their attacks, is so brutally lethal that it is never seen in film fight-sequences, presumably because the stuntmen find it impossible to fake. Fairbairn said his methods had been developed "through experience and observation in dealing with the ruffians, thugs, bandits and bullies of one of the toughest waterfront areas in the world".

But the inspiration for No. 1 knife may have been European, not Asian. Deep penetration and repeated thrusts was a technique of Florentine assassins, who also knew what Fairbairn imparted to his Commando and SOE classes: "If a main artery is cleanly severed, the wounded man will quickly lose consciousness and die." He advocated left-hand draws from a hidden sheath and daily practice for speed in the manner of Hollywood gun-fighters. "At close quarters, there is no more deadly weapon than the knife," said Fairbairn, adding, "And it never runs out of ammunition."

Fairbairn and Sykes catalogued vulnerable points of the body only to discover later that they had not taken into account some peculiarities of German uniform. The Wehrmacht's water-bottle protected the wearer's kidneys and the leather junction of his thick braces shielded a target point on the spine. The subclavian artery was pinpointed for attack in the quickest, quietest way to kill. Raiders were trained to creep up on sentries and then, hooking a hand round the victim's chin, to tug the head sideways and expose the shoulder to a powerful, downward thrust of the Fairbairn-Sykes knife. In two seconds, the sentry would be unconscious. In three and a half seconds, dead. Drowned without a murmur in his own blood. That was the theory. The practice, as experienced by one holder of the Military Medal, was nightmarishly different: "Killing a sentry silently usually required two men. One holding, the other knifing. It's a hateful job. I don't like to think about that. It's a sad story with me, the filthiest fighting I know. For months after the war, when what I had done came back to me, I had to take pills to help me overcome the remorse."

The Commando badge displays an F-S knife pointing skywards. The SAS badge features a winged sword pointing down. In both groups, the blade is largely emblematic. The men trained with fighting knives but, except in extremities, few used them for anything apart from opening tins, thus conforming to the British belief that stabbing people isn't cricket.

Anders Lassen had never been exposed to this convention and, like Captain Fairbairn, would have considered it squeamish. Lassen had grown up with knives as both a throwing weapon and a hunter's tool; as a boy, he thought nothing of gutting a slain buck. So it was a knife that Lassen drew in the steep, bleak hills of South Morar when presented with the opportunity that determined the course of his war. Arisaig, even today, is a remote area of empty beaches and single-track roads just over the mountains from the sheer plunge of Loch Morar, at 987 feet the deepest inland water in Britain. Here was complete seclusion for sixteen Danes under assessment for a return to their homeland as spies and saboteurs. They were sent on forced marches and rock-climbing exercises. They were taught to strip and load weapons in total darkness. They practised bad-weather landings on the rocky coast. The legend of Anders Lassen began when they were out map-reading, as one of the party told Suzanne:

> We had been out all day working in small groups but joined up to go home together. Suddenly we saw two red deer at a distance of about 50 yards. The ground was covered by small patches of bushes and Anders, first to react, was already threading through them. We knew he was a hunter and, seeing one animal move off, we left him to it. He ran

round the bushes, got up close and stabbed it with his knife. It was a fine, big stag and for the next few days we had lovely roasts.

It was a remarkable feat for a twelve-stone man – Lassen never lost his boyhood knack of moving like a ghost. While the Danish volunteers tucked into venison, another young serviceman with a knife set out to supplement the rations of Royal Marines in a tent outside Plymouth. Les "Red" Wright finished the war with a Distinguished Service Medal and a Conspicuous Gallantry Medal but his first exploit, when aged seventeen, was only to kill a sheep. He said:

Stealing a sheep from the flock in the field behind us began as a dare. I'd said longingly, "Wouldn't one be nice roasted"; then the rest of the tent egged me on until I agreed to do it.

Two of us cornered a sheep and I cut its throat; that was nothing new for me because I was used to helping my father, a butcher who did his own slaughtering. The only hassle was in carrying the carcase back by its hindlegs and over the wire fence into camp. I was covered in blood when I took the sheep to the Cook-sergeant, telling him, "Make sure that we get our share" – which we did a few days later.

But the word got round and reached the commanding officer, a major. I was sent for at the double, I thought I was in the Rattle. Instead, the CO left me with two strange officers; I wondered if they were from Intelligence or, more likely, Military Police. They asked how I'd killed the sheep and I said: "With a knife, my old Boy Scouts' knife", whereupon they opened a case from which they produced a knife, an original F-S knife which they threw to me.

As I caught the knife, they asked, "What do you think of that?" I told them that it looked very nice and they began talking seriously about knives, leading me round to the question that I realised was the purpose of the interview: "Would you use a knife on a human being?" I said, "Yes, I might." They then dismissed me and, from that moment, I did no more Royal Marine duties but was sent for again by the CO. He asked, in a tone suggesting that I was suited to the company of lunatics, if I would like to join Special Operations. I said I'd volunteer for anything; with that I was sent to SOE headquarters at 98, Horse Guards and then to *Maid Honor* Force.

There is no evidence of Anders Lassen undergoing a similar interview after his own spectacular use of a knife, but the inference can be drawn from SOE's choice of Lassen for the *Maid Honor* unit within weeks of him killing the stag. His selection came when, once again, he was fretting at the inactivity of the Danish volunteers who had left Scotland for a holding camp at Gumley Hall in Leicestershire. The group, now doubled in size and permitted to wear red-and-white Denmark flash on their shoulders and the Dannebrog flag on their sleeves, were kept marking time while SOE considered their individual suitability for undercover operations. Lassen could not have failed to meet the requirements of personal courage and fierce motivation against the enemy, but SOE also considered prudence a most desirable quality in the spy; on that score, there must have been a query against Lassen whose restlessness had begun to present Captain Iversen and the training officer, Captain J. Starup, with problems similar to those faced earlier by the captain of the *Eleonora Maersk*. He was contemptuous of their drill sessions, never missing a chance to complain that, "I came to fight, not parade." Inversen could not post him elsewhere, in the British way, because no parallel unit existed, neither could disciplinary proceedings be considered advisable or justified against a volunteer whose offences sprang only from his powerful urge for action. The transfer to *Maid Honor* Force proved a satisfactory solution for Iversen and his fractious recruit. A memo to March-Phillipps assessed Lassen as: "A professional seaman. Skilled with weapons. Aggressive enough to lead a boarding party."

Lassen the Lutheran found honourable leaders in the Quaker Appleyard and the devout Catholic March-Phillipps; as Tom Winter recalls: "With Gus, I never had to worry about

49

anything, he was dead straight." The same could have been said of Appleyard who also shared Lassen's yearnings for an unregimented war, as he revealed in a letter about being accepted for the Commandos:

It's absolutely terrific – the grandest job in the Army that one could possibly get. No red tabs, no paper work, none of all the things that are so cramping and infuriating and disheartening about the Army. Just pure operation, the success of which depends principally on oneself and the men one has picked to do the job with you.

March-Phillipps and Lassen had more in common than they realised. Just as Lassen had been christened Emil Victor Schau after a family hero, so had March-Phillipps been named Gustavus after his uncle, a posthumous VC. Lieutenant Gustavus Hamilton Blenkinsopp Coulson, DSO, brother of March-Phillipps' mother, was killed in South Africa at the age of twenty-two when fighting a rearguard action with the King's Own Scottish Borderers against the Boers in 1901. He rode through heavy fire to rescue an unhorsed corporal; when his own horse was hit, throwing both men to the ground, he ordered the corporal to remount and ride to safety alone, saying: "I'll look after myself."

Lassen met his new commander for the first time at Poole Harbour, where Appleyard had led Evison, Lassen and the two other Danes from St Pancras to quarters that signified their complete break with things regimental. *Dormouse* and *Yo'n'Jo* were house-boats of a kind that Jan Nasmyth, one of the unit's founder-members, called "Playthings for rich men of the 1930s". The same could have been said of the auxiliary ketch that gave the unit its name. *Maid Honor* was 70 feet long with a 16 feet 6 inch beam, headroom of 6 feet 3 inches in the saloon and a draught of 7 feet 8 inches. Requisitioned from Major W. Bertram Bell of Ashton Keynes in Wiltshire, a member of the Royal Yacht Squadron, she had been built in 1925 or 1926 for Charlie Howe, fishing out of Brixham, and named for his daughter Honor. Her brother, also named Charles, remembers the ship well:

Brixham smacks were extremely strong, with planks four inches thick on the outside, cement up to the waterline and three skins. Her tonnage was a fraction over thirty-nine and a half. Her summer sailing rig was a mainmast of about forty feet with a topmast of about another thirty feet, a mizzen-mast and a bowsprit. She had a mainsail, a topsail, a mizzen-sail, a jib out on the bowsprit and a foresail running up the bow of the ship. They were good sea boats, and long lasting. The smacks were speedy, too, as is shown by *Maid Honor*'s time when winning the cup in the 1936 regatta. The course was three times round Torbay which, give or take a mile, meant 30 miles from start to finish. We went over the line in quite a strong breeze at 10.15 in the morning and were back on our mooring, lowering the sails, at one o'clock. Thirty miles in less than three hours. They did go! Major Bell had the *Maid* brought into Brixham harbour for gutting and converting into one of the best-ever trawler yachts. The *Maid*, as was common with Brixham smacks, had no engine but only an Elliott-Garrard steam boiler to drive the capstan and heave her fishing gear up and down. Major Bell, though, put in a four-cylinder auxiliary engine, as well as engaging a Devon artist, J. A. Lake, to paint the owner's cabin with panels depicting various stages of the *Maid Honor*'s victory in the regatta.

These decorative panels were still in place when Lassen first saw the *Maid*. She was moored in Poole Harbour – at 15 square miles, one of the world's largest natural harbours – at a spot that remains secluded to this day. It was Russell Quay on the wooded, north side of the Arne peninsula. The *Maid*'s acquisition had shown March-Phillipps at his most high-handed; in the opinion of Major Leslie Prout, a sergeant in the unit's early days, "Only Gus could have got away with it. Although having no authority to proceed, he calmly requisitioned the *Maid Honor* and her skipper Blake Glanville to sail her from Brixham to Poole."

Glanville, a solid, gently spoken man in his fifties, proved a willing captive and patient tutor of his motley crew of novices. He would busy himself in the *Maid*'s cabin in the evenings when the young men went ashore; those who stayed were rewarded by spell-binding yarns of trawling days and instruction in tying such perplexing knots as the Turk's Head and the Matthew Walker.

A sharp turn in the High Street shelters the Antelope Hotel from winds off Poole Harbour. It is a squarish, brick coaching inn whose sign, the life-sized model of an antelope, looks poised to bound off the portico into the street. March-Phillipps chose the Antelope for his shore headquarters because it combined a convenient location with historical associations: the Duke of Wellington, when plain, young Arthur Wellesley, was reputed to have stayed there, doubtless warming himself before a bar fireplace that is a yard deep and some 500 years old. What Appleyard and March-Phillipps were planning was a form of piracy: they alone knew that the *Maid* was not a training vessel or potential Channel raider, but an unorthodox warship whose prey lay 3,000 miles away in West Africa. Her intended loot was two ships, the small German tanker *Likomba* and the veteran 7,600 ton Italian liner and merchantman *Duchessa d'Aosta,* which had taken cover at the Spanish colonial island of Fernando Po, when Mussolini joined forces with Hitler in June 1940.

The *Duchessa* and *Likomba* had remained at anchor for a year without showing signs of venturing from their neutral hideaway, yet they continued to worry the Admiralty and the SOE as "a supply fleet in being" able to venture out at any time to aid German surface raiders or, more probably, the U-boats which had turned the approaches to Freetown into the death-trap of the South Atlantic. The planners saw an extra role for the *Maid* as a spy ship. Outwardly harmless, posing as a mail carrier or fishing boat, she could reconnoitre the estuaries and creeks suspected of being secret Axis bases north and south of Freetown.

These adventurous possibilities could not have occurred to anyone seeing her moored at the so-called quay, a place that Jan Nasmyth recalled as: "Just sandbanks covered with heather and a little sandy cliff that we used for a firing range." Appleyard was more lyrical: "Out in the wilds, very quiet and lonely but very lovely. Thousands of all kinds of waders and seabirds are around, especially shelduck, herons and curlews."

In these early days of *Maid Honor* Force, the men were encouraged to believe that their craft's innocent appearance might help them escape detection if she were employed on a cross-Channel raid. Sail also did not seem incongruous for a unit commanded by a man whose hero was Sir Francis Drake; as Jan Nasmyth said: "Gus believed in the sailing boat because he believed in traditional things. He didn't believe in aeroplanes. He thought the air was an unnatural element to man, and no doubt he thought power-driven vessels were an unnatural element on the surface of the sea. When in doubt, he reached back into his instinct and said: 'This is the right thing, this is what I'm going to do.' "

The romance of March-Phillipps' expedition did not infect Lassen and his fellow-Danes who, although moving into the house-boats with the rest of the unit, kept slightly aloof. Nasmyth noted: "All three Danes were vaguely aggressive in the sense of resenting authority. They had never been under military discipline before, but their distaste for it took the form of caustic comments rather than physical violence."

Brawling, in any case, was not one of Lassen's regular pursuits although he is said to have been embroiled in a violent argument with civilians once in a Bournemouth café. Police were called before Lassen was forced to reveal himself as an opponent best avoided – not only a heavy puncher, as he would demonstrate some years later in the Lebanon, but also possessed of a fierce ruthlessness that would make him eventually an ideal trainee in SOE methods of "fighting without a tremor of apprehension, able to hurt, maul, injure or kill with ease". The police at Swanage, as well as Bournemouth, also knew Lassen, having detained him and the other Danes as suspected spies after an arrest at the Black Bear at Wareham.

No *Maid Honor* personnel were present to vouch for Lassen and his comrades when an Army officer challenged them in the Bear's bar. Lassen was nearly always improperly dressed in the Army sense, even after rising to major in 1944, so he was enough to arouse anyone's suspicions when garbed in the chaotic informality that passed for uniform at Russell Quay. Jan Nasmyth remembers:

> We wore such uniforms as we possessed which, in my case, meant that I was dressed as an officer cadet having just come from an Officer Cadet Training Unit. Some of Gus's men were in naval gear and others, who had been nothing in particular, wore plain battledress. One evening I was called to the Black Bear where an Army officer said he had seen three foreigners in the bar in uniform but obviously not soldiers. When he asked for proof of identity, instead of an Army Book 64, they showed him documents marked "98, Horse Guards". He said to me: "I was bloody sure they weren't Horse Guards, so I detained them and called the police." The police, in due course, called me and I went round (I think it was to Swanage) and collected Andy and his friends.
>
> The three of them were picked up again at Wareham. This time by the Home Guard. They were challenged and arrested after rowing up the Frome but were able to persuade the Home Guard captain of their *bona fides* – and they returned immensely excited by the discovery that the captain was Percy Westerman, an author specialising in sea stories for boys.

Westerman was read widely in Scandinavia and many of his 200 titles – for instance, *Pirate Submarine* and *Under the White Ensign* – had been translated into Danish. He lived on the Frome in a converted barge and, by way of amends for the arrest, invited Lassen and his compatriots to the boat where he presented them with signed copies of some Danish editions.

March-Phillipps, meanwhile, was busy arming and equipping his fishing smack for her long and probably dangerous voyage. Nevil Shute, the author in his wartime role of Lieutenant-Commander Norway, RNVR, examined the *Maid*'s suitability for fitting with a spigot mortar which, mounted on a steel plate in the deck, would launch small, tail-finned bombs at surfaced U-boats. A test firing exposed the risk of using this weapon on a yacht. Red-hot particles of the charge burned holes in the *Maid*'s mainsail. March-Phillipps was furious, always a frightening sight, as Nasmyth says: "because of the mutilated upper lip which had been practically severed by a horse biting him".

March-Phillipps divided his force into two sections: Six to sail with him in the *Maid* to Freetown in Sierra Leone; they would include all three Danes who could lend Scandinavian authenticity to her cover as a neutral Swedish yacht; the rest would go to Freetown disguised as civilian passengers on a Holland-America liner. Lassen was an automatic choice for the *Maid*'s voyage; Appleyard had approved him in a letter home as, "A splendid seaman and a crackshot with any kind of weapon". But Appleyard had also sidestepped the problem of Lassen by handing it to Sergeant Winter with the words: "Be as strict as you can with him, but don't go too far because he's good-hearted and good at everything – even if he does dislike discipline." More than forty years later, Winter could exclaim about that conversation: "And Andy was only a private!"

Maid Honor Force was not a closed shop. Odd candidates for membership flitted in and out of Poole. A Yugoslav called Marco is remembered particularly by Nasmyth: "A very temperamental fellow. If he didn't have a woman once a week, he went absolutely mad. I had to send him back."

Those who stayed the course went to lectures on seamanship and basic navigation at the Board of Trade offices near the harbour. They were also kitted out in batches at a civilian outfitter's in London, the *Maid*'s crew being issued with seamen denims similar to the type worn by Lassen on the *Eleonora*.

The *Maid* herself was fitted with fake crow's-nests as firing platforms; a dummy deck-house of hinged plywood was built to conceal a two-pounder Vickers cannon, and part of the deck was lowered to allow twin machine-guns to fire through the scuppers. Lassen shinned to the truck of the top mast, some 60 feet above the deck, where he nailed aloft a lucky charm that proved as tough as old leather. It was a dolphin's tail. A gift, he said, from a well-wisher.

August 1941 brought clearance at last for the voyage. The Admiralty, after months of objections to proposed raids by the *Maid* in the Channel, allowed itself to be won over to the argument that a wooden vessel sailing alone would not attract U-boats or be vulnerable to magnetic mines. As 578 British trawlers had been sunk by submarines in the 1914–18 War and another 63 had gone down to mines, the consent may have contained an element of cynical calculation; namely that a gamble with a few lives would gain months of respite from March-Phillipps' demands for action. Nasmyth explains:

> The theory was that a sailing-ship without an escort would not be worth a torpedo. But if a U-boat surfaced to attack with a gun, the *Maid* could give an account of herself with the machine-guns and cannon.
>
> The Royal Navy, it was presumed, kept German surface raiders out of the Atlantic and so the main danger lay in attack by air patrols. That danger seemed very considerable and the Vickers cannon, although a dual-purpose weapon, might have been ineffective as an ack-ack gun through being hemmed in by masts and rigging. I should say the *Maid* was entirely vulnerable to attack by air. One just had to hope that the Germans wouldn't notice her.

Freetown – "one-eyed, ramshackle and teeming down in bucketsful" was Appleyard's first impression – had been chosen as the jumping-off point for two separate missions by the *Maid* and her departure was celebrated in style with a farewell lunch at the Antelope. The landlord, Arthur Baker, who answered to "Pop", appeared from the cellar with bottles of champagne, a rare going-away present after two years of war.

"Put one aside for the boat," said March-Phillipps, suddenly deciding on a sea-borne toast as the *Maid* rounded Old Harry rocks, two chalk stacks south of the harbour. She would then be lost to view of the watchers in the pilot boat who included Sir Colin Gubbins, the chief guest at the lunch, and Blake Glanville, who had declined the opportunity to sail to Africa with his pupils because he was past military age with a wife at home and, above all, because he felt it was not his job. He was engaged to teach *Maid Honor* Force, not to perform alongside them.

Appleyard, waiting to lead out the main party later, had no duties that day beyond attending the lunch and saying cheerful goodbyes, a task made easier by the breezy optimism of March-Phillipps who was almost carried away by the thought that his year of waiting had ended. Anders Lassen alone remained impervious to the general high spirits. He sat with Nasmyth at the far end of the table, a picture of misery. "He's mad, our commander," muttered Lassen, to which Nasmyth answered gaily, "Well, you're not the first to think that." The tone of this reply seemed frivolous to Lassen who persisted, "We are doomed. I will never see any of you again." Nasmyth urged him to cheer up, saying, "It's not that bad, Andy. There's a chance." Silver linings, though, were not what Lassen wanted to see that day. He had cast himself in the role of gloomy Dane and so continued with his warnings: "You don't understand because you have not been to sea in the war. I have, and I know. A ship that drops out of convoy is lost. We are sailing without an escort. We haven't a hope."

Lassen's forecast almost came true at the outset under the scrutiny of not only Gubbins, Appleyard, Nasmyth and the others but also of March-Phillipps' aunt waving from the Sandbanks side of the harbour. It was Sunday, August 10, 1941, with the afternoon drawing into evening and March-Phillipps in a fever of impatience. Nasmyth remembers:

He had the engine going full blast but that wasn't enough. He wanted the topsail up, too.

Graham Hayes, the best seaman aboard, was in charge of that complicated operation but made some mistakes and got into a tizzy. Appleyard, who never allowed himself to panic, was amused by seeing Graham get it wrong, and I heard Gubbins saying something caustic, like, "He's going to pile it up". The three of us were on board watching these operations but said goodbye when the topsail was raised at last. We climbed into the pilot's launch at Poole Bar buoy and watched the *Maid* sail out round Old Harry.

March-Phillipps had intended to uncork his champagne at this point; instead, he and the crew were sent sprawling by the full force of the west wind. Nasmyth, who saw this near-disaster, says: "The *Maid* leaned so far over at Old Harry that we thought she might capsize. She was obviously over-canvased. We heard later that nearly everyone had been sick in a rough passage to Dartmouth where Gus put ashore two of the crew and had the two-pounder repaired."

The discarded crewmen were the other Danes, not Lassen whose stomach was usually proof against even the heaviest seas. The 70 miles from Poole to Dartmouth had been enough to convince March-Phillipps that one of them was too inexperienced to be his navigator and that the other, far and away the worst sea-sickness victim, would be a liability as "a chronic puker". The Danes were not offended; they remained part of the operation and were sent back to sail with Appleyard's party from Oban. A reduction of two men eased March-Phillipps' worries about running out of drinking water in what was likely to be a whole month at sea, and so it was with a light heart that he set out again two days later. All was well this time with the *Maid*. Her gun worked again, her red sails glided her along towards the sunset and her log-book recorded: "August 12, 1941. Left Dartmouth at 6.00 p.m., covered 30 miles, average speed five knots."

5

UNDER SAIL

The weather soon turned against March-Phillipps. "Strong winds, little visibility," he logged on the second day, recording also a sighting of Eddystone Light and a further 91 miles covered. A different hand noted: "Drums want their lashings tightened."

Twenty tons of pig iron, the *Maid*'s original ballast, had been replaced partly by lead ingots during the conversion ordered by Major Bell, thus allowing the lowering of cabin decks for extra headroom. March-Phillipps' crew wondered, as the *Maid* wallowed into the Atlantic, how much her trim had been worsened by the combination of the major's alterations and changes required to turn a pleasure yacht into a clandestine warship. Brixham trawlermen regarded their smacks as the world's soundest sailing craft under 100 tons and they believed them capable of withstanding any weather, at least when not encumbered by drift-nets or heavy trawls, but the *Maid* proved less watertight than expected and the sea slopped about the cabins and wheelhouse as well as blackening the contents of the potato locker.

Day Three, in which 110 miles were covered, found March-Phillipps fixing on the Lizard and then Land's End before sighting: "What should be the Scillies – N20W, very faint." Next day he logged: "Hove to, reefed mizzen and set small jib. Wind rising rapidly. Barometer rising. Mean course S60W from 1830 to 2400," and so the *Maid* headed out into the ocean where her first losing encounter with a roller scattered and upturned her captain's midday meal, as well as stores of lime juice and Quality Street toffees. The helmsman was blamed.

March-Phillipps' scarred lip vibrated with rage as he showed the culprit a saucepan lid into which the ruined lunch had been scraped. He threatened: "S-steer s-straighter or you'll eat out of these, not plates." The skipper's mood improved by the sixth day, his first Sunday at sea when, at last, the Atlantic seemed less lonely and he could record (apparently somewhere south-west of Brest): "Sailed right through a tunny fishing fleet, no markings and no flags. Two of them sailed with us for the afternoon, remaining a few miles to windward and then went about. Bright sun, great sailing weather but ship still very wet."

The sea dropped next day and the skipper wrote: "Time to clear ship and dry everything. Much needed." Lassen was also writing, summarising the voyage in a line for his diary: "Only four of us and the skipper on board. Hard job." Six was the peace-time complement of a Brixham smack, so March-Phillipps sailed a man short but his crew enjoyed greater comfort than the old trawlermen who slept, ate and lived jammed together in a cabin not quite 9 feet square and relieved themselves in a slop-bucket emptied over the side.

A number of men who claim to have sailed on the *Maid Honor* did so only in training at Poole or after her arrival at Freetown. There are no grounds for disputing the accuracy of Lassen, Appleyard and Nasmyth who say the ship's company for the historic long voyage numbered only five: March-Phillipps, Graham Hayes as second in command with a crew comprising the 6 feet 3 inch Dennis Tottenham, Buzz Perkins and Lassen himself. Lassen felt no kinship with his two comrades on the lower-deck and wrote dismissively in his diary: "The officers are decent and lively chaps; unfortunately, I can't say the same for the crew."

The tenth day dawned before March-Phillipps felt enough confidence in his navigation to log the *Maid*'s position: "139 miles, average 5.8 knots. Dead reckoning position – latitude 37.46, longitude 15.21." This placed her halfway between the Azores and Cape St Vincent in the far south-west of Portugal and showed the captain's growing competence in handling the instructional notes and diagrams inserted loosely inside the blue hard-covers of the log.

These papers included the Morse code written out twice on a naval message pad; five pages on sun sights; a guide to discovering the bearing and altitude of a star, also notes on moon sights as well as more advice on star sights, starting with: "These are very nearly the same as sun sights."

Lassen had not been alone in doubting the sanity of March-Phillipps' decision to sail so far without protection, without wireless contact and without a specialist navigator, but the skipper proved right in all three gambles, particularly in relying on his own hastily acquired, largely self-taught navigation. Four days after first logging the *Maid*'s position, March-Phillipps was able to write: "Monday, August 25 (after 1,267 miles by patent log) sighted Madeira. Good landfall." What a triumph for a weekend amateur who, according to his pre-war friend Tim Alleyn, once sailed the yacht *Tomato* into Lyme Bay under the impression that it was Poole Harbour nearly 50 miles to the east!

March-Phillipps anchored near the long, hook-shaped mole of Funchal where a Portuguese coastguard launch came alongside, followed by bumboats with welcome replenishments of fresh water, fruit and eggs. Standing Order No. 5 of the *Maid Honor*, written on gunnery-trace paper and underlined for importance, read: "Avoid a fight if humanly possible, but resist capture to the last." The amiable authorities of Funchal gave no cause to invoke it.

They would have seen, if they had bothered to ask, only what SOE wished them to see – civilian passports and the pay-packets of professional yachtsmen who would be unable to go ashore because of their owner-captain's anxiety to make up time lost through a storm.

The two-pounder and the machine-guns went unspotted. This was lucky because neutral Portugal, particularly Lisbon, was alive with enemy agents and March-Phillipps must have feared that Madeira would also have its quota of prying eyes and informers.

Every man in *Maid Honor* Force – the five at Funchal, the main body on the liner to Freetown, the civilians waiting to guide and assist them in Africa – knew he was on what is now termed "A deniable mission". Tom Winter says: "We had all signed a paper to that effect. If anything went wrong, we knew that we would be disowned." The *Maid*'s Swedish cover held good, however, against the casual scrutiny of boatmen and officials in the harbour. Lassen himself provided the authentic Scandinavian air assisted by the boyish blondness of Buzz Perkins whose full name is inside the log's cover: Frank Colbourn Perkins. He was only 16, a sturdy lad from Wokingham in Berkshire and stuck for life with a childhood nickname – "Buzz" because his baby sister, unable to say "Brother", always referred to him as "Buzzer".

His mother saw the war throw Buzz out of his stride: "Once it started, he couldn't settle at school or home. He was madly keen to do something." He was too young, though, for normal active service but someone knew someone who knew March-Phillipps well enough to ask a favour; so Perkins, like Lassen and the others, was issued with battledress and sent to Poole Harbour by way of 98, Horse Guards.

Jan Nasmyth regarded this enlistment of a schoolboy in an undercover unit as: "A typical high-handed piece of Gus recruitment. It wasn't good for Buzz who spent too many nights out drinking with men." The *Maid* herself also proved harmful to Perkins who received serious head injuries from a swinging boom but not before seeing the adventure completed and being presented with the log as a souvenir.

Fresh trade winds whisked the *Maid* along at a spanking pace from Madeira. She logged seven knots on the second full day out of Funchal and topped it on the following day. The entry: "Logged eight knots for half an hour" is worth comparing with the eight knots averaged on one day in 1986 by five America Cup yachts in qualifying races off Fremantle in Western Australia.

The *Maid* had not finished, there was still more speed in her. "Logged 10 knots in big seas" is a later entry on the same day, August 28, but the thrill was short-lived and bad news was right behind: "Took in topsail. Ship labouring. Wind strong. Ship making water badly. Discovered leak in exhaust gland, took up deck planking to get at it." The repair was unsuccessful at first: "Still making water despite stoppage of leak. Discovered real leak in store gland. Stopped in five minutes." March-Phillipps, satisfied with a job properly done at last, then entered: "8.00 p.m. Had my first meal of flying fish."

The *Maid*, despite the difficulties, averaged 146 miles a day in the five days after leaving Madeira and totalled 2,000 miles for her first twenty days at sea, but the trade winds were failing and her skipper began to prepare for the worst: "Altered course to westward to pass Cape Verde islands to westward fearing to be becalmed on edge of trade belt east of islands and opposite Dakar." The Vichy-French forces controlling Dakar naval base were bitterly anti-British, a legacy of the Royal Navy's unexpected shelling and sinking of French warships in the Mediterranean after the surrender to Hitler. Dakar was suspected of carrying these feelings to the point of being actively pro-German, so March-Phillipps knew there would be no escape from interception if the *Maid* was detected from French West Africa.

This danger was on his mind the following afternoon. The *Maid* was becalmed in a medium swell and still some 300 miles north of the islands when a look-out's cry electrified the skipper. A battle-cruiser and a merchantman had been sighted. "Man the guns," cried March-Phillipps, ready to go down with his two-pounder blazing against a hail of 11-inch shells.

The log is a hardback *Log Book for Yachts*, printed and published by Thomas Reed and sold in hundreds to weekend sailors. Several different hands are detectable in the entries but there cannot be the slightest doubt that March-Phillipps himself wrote this note, which can hardly be bettered for clipped relief: "4.30 p.m. Hove to. Boarded and questioned. English. D.G."

HMS *Dorchester* has been mentioned as the cruiser. This is not supported by the log which reveals no name and, after thanking God in Latin, turns once more to the tedium of by-passing Cape Verde in a windless ocean. The *Maid* had eight inner berths but the crew, once into the tropics, felt more comfortable sleeping in makeshift hammocks under a deck awning. They worked watch-and-watch – a hard job, as Lassen said. Six hours on, six hours off without dog watches, but with March-Phillipps using himself as the fifth hand to provide a rotation of duty times.

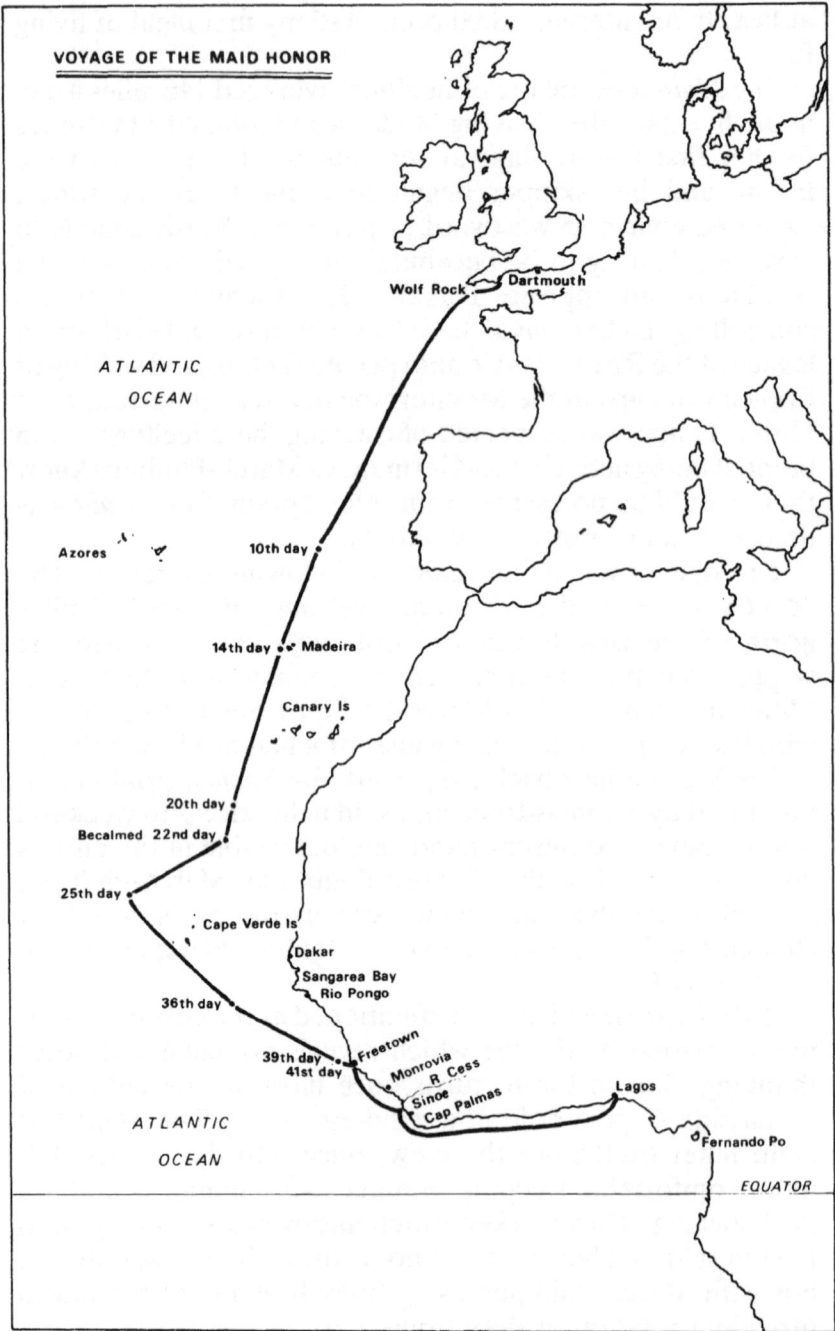

VOYAGE OF THE MAID HONOR

ATLANTIC
OCEAN

Azores

Wolf Rock · Dartmouth

10th day

14th day · · Madeira

Canary Is

20th day

Becalmed 22nd day

25th day

· Cape Verde Is

Dakar
Sangarea Bay
Rio Pongo

36th day

39th day
41st day
Freetown
Monrovia
R Cess
Sinoe
Cap Palmas
Lagos

Fernando Po

ATLANTIC

OCEAN

EQUATOR

Becalmed days provided the opportunity to rig a bosun's chair over the side while Lassen, Tottenham and Perkins tossed coins to escape a smelly task. The loser had to rod out the heads on each side of the fo'c'sle, which were often blocked. Each day of little mileage heightened March-Phillipps' concern about eking out the drinking water; throughout the voyage he allowed only sea water to be used for washing clothes, crockery and the crew. Lassen in these motionless hours demonstrated a trick from his tanker days. "Watch! Fish steaks," he said, placing a piece of carbide from the lamps into a pierced tin. Shoals, often of barracuda, never failed to gather as the tin sank slowly – before the carbide exploded and sent its inquisitive victims to the galley.

On Saturday, September 6, four days after her encounter with the cruiser, the *Maid* began at last to make some headway in her turn to the south. Easterly winds sprang up. "Wind dead aft. Hoisted spinnaker" is the entry, but the spurt was brief and followed by mechanical problems: "Engine failed to start. Discovered that water had got at it. After draining the water and failing again to start, have decided to take off the leads and do the job thoroughly."

Night fell on the *Maid* becalmed, her engine still out of action and the weather threatening. March-Phillipps noted: "Appearances of a tropical storm at sunset" and repeated this impression in the morning: "Every appearance of a tropical storm. Glass steady but low." Yet an hour later, he wrote: "Weather completely cleared. Wind steady from south. I do not understand it."

Lassen, the best man aloft, was possibly the look-out responsible for this entry two days later: "Sighted smoke from the masthead which gradually faded. Dead ahead." That same evening March-Phillipps marvelled at the sunset: "Amazing. Great banks of cumulus, pink and gold when the sun touches them. Red, green and crimson in the higher clouds." Multi-coloured skies were no compensation for the *Maid*'s lack of headway over two days and the log records starkly: "Becalmed, many difficulties on engine. No wind at all." March-Phillipps is remembered later as particularly praising Perkins' labours on the engine, although everyone

65

on board lent a hand or advice at the many breakdowns – and, on September 13, they were all temporarily defeated. The engines jammed at five in the morning. The log records: "So far can find no way of turning it."

Eleven hours of tinkering and head-scratching then produced only another despairing entry: "4.00 p.m. Discovered that the piston of the engine had rusted solid in the block after disconnecting the big end." Graham Hayes found the cure next day. "Engine turning over. GH unjammed it with a leverage on the flywheel."

March-Phillipps, confident of being soon under way once more, delighted again in nature: "A magnificent shoal of porpoises came up on our port bow in separating streams of phosphorescence and leapt, with anxious snorting noises, all about us." A further day dragged by, though, before the entry: "8.00 p.m. Engine miraculously started and pulled the *Maid* away at four and a half knots."

This combination of an unreliable engine and failing winds had reduced the average daily mileage by a third – from the 100 of August down to only 62, as can be calculated from the entry of September 16: "Longitude 21.50W. Latitude 10. *Maid Honor* logged the 3,000 mark. Turned to the eastward for Freetown." After her crawl of only 1,000 miles in sixteen days, the *Maid* revelled immediately in the voyage's highest sustained speed: "Sept. 18. The monsoon at last, *Maid Honor* covered 20 miles in two hours."

An Allied convoy was sighted on the port quarter next morning and one of the escorting destroyers peeled off to give March-Phillipps his position by loud-hailer: "Latitude 9.33. Longitude 10.45". A Sunderland flying-boat on RAF coastal patrol dipped down in the afternoon to investigate the *Maid* whose look-out also reported ships approaching on the starboard bow.

One of the crew, possibly Lassen, speared but failed to boat a porpoise from the bows on the final full day's run. "Got away, believed dead", says the log. Next morning – Sunday, September 21, 1941 – March-Phillipps logged the conclusion of 41 consecutive days at sea: "Pilot aboard at 11.00 a.m. 3,185 miles – total distance, Wolf to Pilot Freetown."

Appleyard, bubbling as always, wrote this enthusiastic verdict on the voyage: "I don't think it will be exaggerating to say it is one of the finest efforts of its kind in recent years." The temperature in the *Maid*'s galley had soared once to 135° Fahrenheit, only one degree below the world shade record, but March-Phillipps did not log that fact or refer to it in describing the voyage as: "A magnificent trip with no particular excitements." He probably felt, and quite rightly, that the *Maid*'s safe and punctual arrival said everything without the need of embellishment.

Lassen, on his birthday next morning, surveyed his surroundings and wondered if the destination justified the journey. Freetown, in war or peace, would rank low on any list of places in which to celebrate a twenty-first. Appleyard, who had been waiting there for a fortnight with Tom Winter and some two dozen men, caught the port's drawbacks in a sentence: "When it isn't raining, a dense cloud of steam arises from the earth, roofs and roads."

The presence of Appleyard and the reuniting of the complete force meant that March-Phillipps had to leave the *Maid* to take command ashore. Quarters were found for the unit at Lumley Beach, an anti-aircraft site whose guns had never fired at enemy planes although they occasionally loosed off warning rounds at Glenn Martin bombers on reconnaissance from the Vichy-French airfields to the north. March-Phillipps settled in here under the care of his Scottish batman, Jock Taylor known as "Haggis", Hayes recruited a native manservant answering to "Liverpool Black-out", and the *Maid* was left swinging round a buoy for three weeks while the authorities considered how to employ the unit in the months of waiting to raid Fernando Po, 1,500 miles to the south-east.

Time was filled partly by re-stocking. Perkins was sent to the naval stores for a gallon of gun oil, a drum of putty, a tin of Stockholm tar, two rolls of cleaning flannelette, two packets of sandpaper and a dozen tins of cleaning powder. Lassen, Tottenham and Perkins then scrubbed and chamfered the *Maid*, helped by working parties sent over the sides to scrape, paint and hold at bay the ravaging sea worms. As ever on a boat, the work was endless.

Copper tacks, thick dusters, 30 gallons of kerosene, tarred hemp, a coil of small twine and 30 fathoms of 1½-inch wire rope came aboard, but not the two dozen drinking glasses requested to replace the breakages on the voyage. "Not available", said the stores, making it plain that the soldiers of the *Maid* were expected to drink like sailors from enamel mugs.

The supply assistants in the stores, sleek Jack Dustys with few war aims beyond returning home unscathed and not being disbarred from their daily tot of rum and water, saw the *Maid* through matter-of-fact eyes as a comic warship, not as a symbol of piratical enterprise. A vessel with russet sails and only a two-pounder cannon under the captaincy of an Army gunner could not help but look out of place among the great, swivelling turrets and battleship grey of a harbour bustling with cruisers, destroyers and high-speed launches. No uninformed naval person could have guessed that her commander, this peppery pongo with a stutter, hoped to sink a U-boat before stealing an enemy liner, or that the crumpled paper balls thrown angrily into the rainbow-slicked trails of fuel oil around the *Maid*'s mooring were spurts of poetry pencilled on the back of naval message pads.

The opening of "Ebb Tide", a poem of four verses written while moored at Freetown, crackles with March-Phillipps' pent-up energy:

> The ebb tide dashing out to sea
> Sighs and surges under me
> Sets the captive vessel dancing
> Like a restless pony prancing
> Fretting to be free;
> Sidling, edging, plunging, shearing
> Like a maddened pony rearing
> Frantic to be free.

Lassen was edgy, too. The sudden, cold rage which hid behind his quiet affability was aroused by the trivial death of a pet monkey. Lassen collected pets; in the Aegean days yet to come they would usually be incontinent mongrel dogs but at

Lumley Beach he had adopted Chico, a creature hardly larger than a kitten and defenceless against the attack of a camp-following dog called Loopy. The lazy, hazy life of Lumley, where discipline was minimal and working uniform no more than shorts and plimsolls, was interrupted by the quite frightening sight of Lassen, pale eyes afire, armed with a knife in his left hand and a Colt .45 in his right as he hunted Loopy vainly through the lines of tents and criss-cross of guy-ropes.

Lumley, except that the climate provided frequent reminders of why West Africa had been called "The White Man's Grave", was the cushy number for which millions of conscripts yearned, but tropical idleness was unsuited to warriors like Lassen and his commander. March-Phillipps directed his own resentment at a song.

He seethed and boiled each time he heard the florid lyric sighing of reveries, garden walls, lost love and especially the lushly sentimental opening where the purple dusk of twilight time steals across the meadows of the singer's heart. Hoagy Carmichael's "Stardust" was the smash-hit of wartime nostalgia. It enchanted whole armies, but not Major March-Phillipps who searched the officers' mess looking for the record to smash. He threatened a junior officer, Lieutenant Ian Warren who not only sang but whistled "Stardust", "If I hear that damned song once more, I'll break it over your head, you bloody little man."

Warren, a small, twinkling Yorkshireman, did not seek a quarrel. On the contrary, he yearned to serve under March-Phillipps. He came from Knaresborough, just a few miles from the homes of Appleyard and Hayes – and he envied both of them in the way they bore themselves as fighting soldiers and not as holidaymakers, which was how a prolonged posting at Lumley Beach tended to affect many of the gunners.

Warren explains: "I wanted action. Firing at, but never hitting French planes was not the war for me." Appleyard wrote home: "Warren lost no chance of entreating Gus to let him join", but March-Phillipps brushed him away as a pest and derided him so openly as a bloody little man that the phrase became Warren's nickname: "The man." Warren

69

sought permission from his own commanding officer to go on the *Maid Honor* raid, but was turned down. Lumley Beach looked even more like an unwanted permanency for him, but then "Stardust" provided the lucky break. Warren says:

"Unconsciously, I whistled it in the mess again. Once too often for Gus, who said: 'I'll Stardust you. Didn't I tell you that I'd throw you out the next time I heard it?' I replied: 'Let's see you try, mate.' Gus wasn't a big man, but bigger than me, an inch or two taller. He grabbed hold of me, trying to shove me through the mess window. He lost. I chucked him out, instead. He was sporting about it, though, and said: 'You bloody little man. You had better join us.'"

Many months passed however before Warren got his wish. He was left behind when March-Phillipps sailed the *Maid* to her first African adventures. On October 10, 1941, armed with four depth charges, she chugged out of Freetown in late afternoon and then sailed north on "Submarine patrol".

6

Fernando Po

No feat of arms, perhaps not even his dream of sending the Tirpitz to the bottom single-handed, would have thrilled March-Phillipps more than sinking a U-boat from a fishing smack. Throughout the *Maid*'s five-day cruise along the coasts of Sierra Leone and Portuguese Guinea, his eyes lingered expectantly on the four explosive drums at the stern but his hopes were raised only once – as the log records on Sunday, October 12: "Sighted shape like a submarine which disappeared suddenly. Reported by wireless. Engine failed."

The *Maid*'s next mission sent her south, still hoping to surprise a submarine while searching the inlets, lagoons and deltas of neutral Liberia for secret Axis bases and supply dumps. A sighting of Cape Mesurado was logged on the third day but March-Phillipps steered clear of the adjoining capital, Monrovia. His destinations lay further south at the mouth of the River Cess and, a day's sail further on, at the small estuary port of Sinoe, now Greenville. Landing parties, led by March-Phillipps and including Lassen, went ashore at both places but found nothing, and the *Maid* continued its course south, along the Ivory Coast towards Lagos.

This first month in West Africa revealed that the *Maid*'s thick wooden skins were no defence against sea worms. They riddled her. Time between patrols became increasingly occupied by careening the *Maid* and then scraping her bottom; this work was done by native gangs, often under the supervision of Lassen when he was not shooting game fowl and pigeons for the mess.

Lassen had inherited a contempt of non-whites from his ancestor, the East Indies planter. "Niggers" and "Black devils" he called them in his diary, although also recording a proposed deal with an African father "to buy his exceedingly pretty daughter for £10 and two bottles of gin".

March-Phillipps himself was infected by attitudes that would outrage today's Race Relations Board; for instance, his view on Commando raiders blackening their faces: "If I am to die on one of those parties, I'll die looking like an Englishman and not like a damned nigger."

Tom Winter, well aware of Lassen's racism, asked in public one day: "How are you getting on with all those blackies, Andy?" Appleyard fielded the question by interjecting: "He's training them", only for Lassen to correct him grimly: "No. Taming them!" On Friday, November 7, the *Maid* passed through the Freetown anti-submarine boom and, hoisting sail, set out on her last solo mission which is logged in pencilled capitals as: "Pongo River Reconnaissance." This was a two-man search by March-Phillipps and Appleyard in a Folbot, a collapsible sea-going canoe that was able, when empty, to float in two inches of water and whose halves of plywood ribs and canvas could be assembled in fifteen minutes.

Buoyancy tanks of tennis balls provided later models with extra lift for loads that could total up to a quarter of a ton when counting two men, their kit, weapons and 60 lb of explosive. Folbots were easier to handle than to enter; the canoeists had to master the trick of sliding straight into the cockpit because any attempted entrance from the side would capsize the craft.

March-Phillipps lowered himself into the rear cockpit, the No.1's place, when the Folbot cast off some 10 miles from land. He and Appleyard paddled into the fading light and towards the Pongo River, more correctly the Rio Pongo, an estuary some 40 miles north-west of Conakry, a deep-sea port held by the Vichy French. Their comrades on the *Maid* reflected once again that the Folbot seemed a frail craft for a coast that was struck almost daily by tornadoes accompanied by torrential rain; they then went below for reviving tots of their latest acquisition from the naval stores, 10 gallons of lime juice and a gallon cask of the treacly, dark pursers' rum.

March-Phillipps and Appleyard moved stealthily all night along the Pongo's matted shores and tangled creeks;

their eyes straining for a shape or a light that might betray a U-boat or an installation that could be attacked. Progress was impeded only once. Appleyard, although paddling at his usual tempo, found himself unable to make headway. March-Phillipps hissed: "Come on, Apple. Do your bit." For answer, Appleyard whacked the obstacle with his paddle. The resulting splash indicated the departure of a crocodile that had begun clambering upon the Folbot's bow.

Maid Honor waited at 10.30 next morning out of sight of Boffa, the small port at the head of the Pongo. The rendezvous was punctual and smooth, the log recording: "Picked up Gus and Apple. Latitude 9.55N. Longitude 14.10W. Log 39", but March-Phillipps' parting orders had allowed for a less trouble-free outcome. They were:

1: From position when boat is launched approximately two miles due south of bar buoy, steer N 85W for 16 miles to position shaded in chart.

2: Anchor with kedge and warp in 10 fathoms – 30–40 fathoms of warp.

3: Keep mast-head look-out during daylight hours. If any large craft is sighted, get under way and steer NW as if for Bathurst.

4: If boarded, hoist red ensign and inform boarding party that M.H. carries mails to Bathurst from Freetown.

5: Avoid a fight if humanly possible, but resist capture to the last.

6: If still anchored on Monday, November 10, weigh anchor at 2.30 a.m. and steer due East . . . [the rest of the sheet is torn and indecipherable]

Three weeks later the *Maid* left Freetown for the last time. It meant goodbye to the fantastic fireflies, the daily spear-fishing, the sun-bathing within sight of coconut palms. Lassen and the rest did not mind; pleasure was not what they had come for, but they still enjoyed the farewell party and the Royal Artillery officers' presentation of a silver tankard to March-Phillipps, their fellow gunner. "A jolly good send-off," says the log.

March-Phillipps, still hankering for a crack at any unsuspecting U-boat, seized the first chance to get the *Maid*'s augmented crew into readiness. He logged on the third day of the voyage to Lagos: "4.0. p.m. Flat calm. Gun practice. VG. Dennis [Tottenham] and Apple – gun. André [Desgranges, a Free French petty officer] and G. H. [Hayes] – spigot."

Tom Winter believes that: "Gus's nightly prayers surely included one for a U-boat to surface and ask the *Maid Honor* for some fish. If one did, he was prepared to sink her with the hidden depth charges or to blow a hole in her with the spigot mortar which had a range of 100 yards." But no U-boats were sighted and so the fortnight's sail to Lagos proceeded uneventfully and, judging from the log, in ignorance of the war reaching a turning-point on their eighth day at sea – Sunday, December 7, 1941, when the Japanese bombed the American Pacific Fleet at Pearl Harbor and catapulted the United States into the conflict.

On that historic day, the *Maid* logged only: "Sighted large 4-engined bomber. Sharp wing-tips – JU 89 or Liberator." Sightings were logged at other times of the tanker *Caernarvon Castle* and of the "Corner of Africa", presumably Cap Palmos, near Liberia's frontier with the Ivory Coast. It seems probable that March-Phillipps knew nothing of America joining the war until December 14, a week later, when the *Maid* was towed into Lagos.

No-one aboard could have received the news more keenly than Lassen but, as he would do throughout the war, he kept quiet about his American ties and remained a man apart who received little mail and few tidings and whose longings for his own land and language were revealed only by an eagerness to seek out Danish ships in port. The Lagos schedule allowed nearly a month for such socialising between training for what could be construed equally as a daring raid or as flagrant piracy in a neutral harbour.

SOE needed extra, unpaid men for the operation that had been code-named POSTMASTER. The fighting part of the raid, as represented by March-Phillipps, Appleyard, Hayes, Winter and Lassen, needed non-combatant supplementaries to crew two tugs, the *Nuneaton* and the larger, steam-driven *Vulcan*. Volunteers were found easily, rallying from all over Nigeria to March-Phillipps' invitation: "Would you like to come to a party?"

These enthusiasts were mainly civil servants who downed pens and formed fours with *Maid Honor* Force only to be immediately impressed by the difference between themselves and the professionals. "They all struck one as being of the warrior type, somewhat contrasting to ourselves," said Leonard Guise, an SOE agent who had planned the details of what he called: "A cut-out operation. In other words, simple theft."

Simple, maybe. But Guise's preparations for the raid were cunning and thorough. A reconnaissance plane had twice invaded Spanish air space and photographed the *Duchessa* and the *Likomba* – at first, when they were alongside the dock offices and short jetty of Santa Isabel and then when anchored further out in the deep, cove-like harbour which is actually a volcanic crater breached by the sea.

The pilot was ready with plausible apologies for his "Navigational error", but they were not needed. A straying Allied plane aroused no alarm in Santa Isabel, largely because the intrusions had been so cleverly timed. Both sets of pictures show the little port wearing a dawn-on-Sunday look. Nothing moves on land or water. The crews of the Axis ships were also unobservant or they would have wondered why oarsmen sculling around the harbour paid such close attention to the dimensions of the *Duchessa*'s and *Likomba*'s anchor-chains.

Fernando Po, an island about twice the size of Anglesey, thought the war had passed it by and got on with planting coffee and cocoa; no-one there could have imagined that élite invaders were training 400 miles away in Lagos and that January 15, 1942, had been chosen for this first raid of Lassen's career.

Maid Honor Force moved at first light. The log states: "To F.P. [Fernando Po]. ST *Vulcan*, Tug *Nuneaton*. 5.30 a.m., left harbour. At 3.00 p.m., *Nuneaton* alongside to transfer men." March-Phillipps split them into five teams: cable party, engine-room party, boarding party, back-up boarding party and towing party.

Night practice on the *Nuneaton*'s fo'c'sle was staged for the cable party, whose charges were calculated to blow their quarries' chains without damaging the hulls. Vicious coshes were distributed among the boarding-party; these were foot-long metal bolts sheathed in rubber. Lassen flexed his wrist as March-Phillipps spoke: "When possible, intimidate. If not, use force. Speed is essential."

Bren gunners on both tugs were instructed: "Deal with any boats. Shoot across bows. No useless slaughter", and Foreign Office misgivings about the entire enterprise were reflected in this general reminder: "Women are Spaniards. Remember!"

Lassen was the automatic choice to climb swiftly and silently aboard and toss a line from the bows to the *Vulcan*. Once, in Cape Town, he had escaped an irate husband by shinning up a hawser with all the fearlessness and natural balance of an old before-the-mast seaman. March-Phillipps, therefore, had no qualms about his one-man advance party. The odds favoured Lassen. The watch would be lackadaisical after a stagnant year at moorings. The officers of both vessels, including the *Duchessa*'s German captain, were dining ashore at the home of a Spanish doctor. Power-starved Santa Isabel was blacked out every midnight, the hour that signalled the end of most social functions. But the doctor turned on a set of Tilley lights and kept his party going; he didn't want the ships' officers leaving so early – for he was a British agent and his dinner was a decoy.

SOE had foreseen everything except the illogical time difference. Fernando Po, being 400 miles east of Lagos, ought to have been on Nigerian time or even an hour ahead; instead, it kept Madrid time and was an hour behind. March-Phillipps and the tugs arrived at midnight to find the lights on.

Their gleam showed Lassen his prey for the first time – a single yellow funnel and the hull painted black instead of the Triestino line's peace-time white. The *Duchessa* was long, indeed, at 150 yards enormous, when compared with the

Maid or the tugs; she was also ugly, with a quartet of four-strutted steel masts sprouting from her deck like miniature oil rigs. Cabins for the officers and permitted quota of 58 passengers were compressed into two short decks amidships. A shelter deck at the stern offered the only outdoor refuge from the sun.

Appleyard was kept busy calming March-Phillipps who was fretting and shouting: "I'm going in – and to hell with it!" Leonard Guise was aboard and heard the argument clearly, remembering it as: "A sticky little scene. Gus struck me as completely intrepid, almost to the point of overdoing it. This was a burglar's operation and burglars don't go in shooting, but Gus gave the impression that he much preferred to do a job when he did go in shooting."

The darkness seemed unnaturally black when the power-switch was thrown. The tugs began to creep forward. The order to move followed what Tom Winter called: "That most ancient of spy signals, a blind raised and lowered at a lighted window by the docks."

Hayes directed the *Nuneaton* towards the *Likomba*. The *Vulcan* slid towards the *Duchessa* until it was close enough for Lassen – "lithe as a cat" in his mother's phrase – to jump for the rope ladder hanging from her side by the cabin decks. The cosh hung from his waist; he also carried a line attached to a rope and coiled to throw.

Robin Duff was on the *Vulcan*'s bridge where often, in the scorching Lagos sun, he had stood in jacket, tie and peaked cap – a picture of formality except that he had stripped for coolness to his underpants. Lassen and Duff had got on well together – and the first words of the raid were shouted to him by Lassen as the line, looped round a bollard on the *Duchessa*, flew back through the dark and dropped on the *Vulcan*'s deck. "Pull," he called. "Pull, Robin. Pull like fuck!"

On the reply "All fast", March-Phillipps and his men swarmed aboard the liner, bounding along a plank attached to the rope ladder scaled by Lassen. One of the boarders, Desmond Longe, fell on his face after tripping over what he thought was a "panicking Italian" but which turned out to be one of three porkers kept on deck for fattening. There was no combat. The lone watch-keeper leapt over the far side at his first glimpse of raiders brandishing – as in Longe's case – pistols in one hand and knives in the other.

Leslie Prout found the greatest resistance where it had been least expected; that was in the depths of the *Vulcan's* boiler room where the African stokers came close to panic when the tug shook and echoed with the explosions that snapped the *Duchessa's* chains. Prout steadied them with the Army's infallible mixture of threats and inducements. Sparks soon flew as they shovelled with renewed vigour and built up steam for the *Vulcan* to take the strain of what SOE claimed as "The richest prize of the war so far."

Hayes on *Nuneaton* found himself with two prizes; not only the tanker *Likomba* but also a pleasure craft, the motor yacht *Bemuivoi*, that had been moored alongside. His first inclination was to cut the yacht adrift but Tom Winter, who had blown the *Likomba's* chains, urged: "Take her, Graham, because of these" – and shone his torch over snapshots found in the cabin. They showed a woman, thought by Winter to be the owner's wife, posing against a swastika flying from the *Bemuivoi's* jackstaff.

The action was over in thirty-five minutes. The five vessels left to the crack of Spanish anti-aircraft guns firing at imaginary bombers. The cable explosions had been mistaken for an air-raid and the confusion of the Spanish defenders deepened at daylight when Free French caps were found floating in the harbour. This SOE ploy failed to deceive the *Duchessa's* captain who guessed the truth immediately on finding his ship gone. He then hurried from the harbour and broke down the door of the British consulate where police arrested him before he could attack the consul. March-Phillipps was told later: "The captain has been jailed for three weeks."

The few captured Italian crewmen, supervised and reinforced by the raiders, were put to work on keeping the *Duchessa* under way while March-Phillipps turned about in *Vulcan* to search for Hayes who was falling ever further behind with his two prizes. March-Phillipps set off on this errand aglow with patriotism and saying to Longe, "This is a wonderful thing for the old country, you know," but he returned in a fury on seeing a Jolly Roger flying from the *Duchessa*'s masthead.

Leonard Guise said, "We painted it on some sheets while he was away. He gave us all a rocket." Les Wright remembered: "He shouted that we were British forces, not pirates or brigands. None of us had seen him so angry before. He ordered the Jolly Roger to be thrown in the boilers, but I believe that someone tucked it away as a souvenir."

March-Phillipps' tempers were summer storms that soon abated. His good humour returned quickly on approving the log's triumphant entry: "Boarded and captured and towed out *D'Aosta, Likomba* and *Bemuivoi*. No casualties. Cutting out went according to plan." Buzz Perkins pocketed two postcards from the *Duchessa* that were intended for passengers and stamped "Distribuzione gratuita". His comrades pounced on tastier loot by killing, roasting and devouring the liner's pigs before a midday rendezvous on Sunday, January 18, with HMS *Violet*, a corvette which escorted the little fleet back to Lagos.

The final entry on Wednesday, January 21, 1942 – "Sighted Casarina Trees. Pilot boarded" – logged the end of *Maid Honor* Force. The members scattered as the Spanish and Axis press and radio denounced "A gross breach of neutrality".

Desmond Longe told Henrietta March-Phillipps: "We had a tremendous reception in Lagos. The old General, who had been against us, came down and looked upon us as his chaps who had pulled off a successful operation. We got all sorts of congratulatory telegrams from the Cabinet, from the Foreign Office and so forth; then, of course, the jitters set in on the part of authority who thought: 'My God, what have we done in a neutral harbour?' So we were all dispersed to the four corners of the earth."

Appleyard, Prout, Winter, Evison the cook, and others were sent to Northern Nigeria at first. Tom Winter recollected: "We also did a job in the Belgian Congo and, before

79

going to Cape Town for two weeks, stopped in what I think was French Equatorial Africa. There were Germans in the same hotel dressed, like us, as civilians. One day I happened to ask at the desk: 'Where's Graham Hayes?' and a German answered, 'Your brother officer has gone to Angola'."

Les Wright, posing first for a souvenir snapshot against the stern of *Maid Honor*, was in another group that went directly to Cape Town. Lassen fell in with the hunting set at some unnamed location: "We used to drive along the roads by car and shoot birds when they flew up. Fine sport. I think I bagged several hundreds in a short stay."

The *Duchessa* was sailed to Scotland and a new life in Allied transport as the *Empire Yukon*. The *Maid*, her glory days over, was put up for sale on the Nigerian marine slipway at Lagos, although not before Buzz Perkins, still trophy hunting, removed a painted panel from the main cabin. A simple fishing smack once more, the *Maid Honor* ended her days as a "civilian" working out of Freetown, Sierra Leone.

The year brought March-Phillipps a bride, the Distinguished Service Order, the *Duchessa* and death in a crowded hour. For Lassen, 1942 was the year that he became an officer. "Put your pips up, Andy," said March-Phillipps on the way home from Africa, confident of squaring the commission with SOE who were accustomed to creating instant officers of scientists and technical experts who had never set foot on a barrack square.

An emergency appointment as a second lieutenant on the General List was confirmed in May. Lassen was astonished. He had by-passed Officer Cadet Training Units, selection boards and even basic Army training; these omissions go a long way to explain the occasional resistance and resentment that he met later in the war from non-commissioned officers who had been schooled in traditional regiments.

"They just gave the pips to me, I did nothing," he said later that year when talking to a Danish volunteer, Peder Hansen. To Tom Winter, he confided: "The biggest promotion I've had until this was being made up to able seaman." To old comrades from the other ranks, Lassen said: "When I was like you, I did what I was told. Now I'm a boss. So you do as I tell you."

Anders Lassen, Second Lieutenant "specially employed", returned to Poole Harbour ready at last to step out from among the extras and towards centre stage.

7

ANDERSON MANOR: COMMANDO CAMELOT

Service numbers are seared into the memories of British forces from the day of enlistment, branded so deeply that veterans on their death-beds might still bark a response to: "Name, rank and number?" No man has ever longed for escape from these regimented masses without dreaming wistfully of finding a unit whose members could say: "Numbers? We don't have numbers. We all know each other!"

March-Phillipps began forming exactly that kind of loosely reined group on reporting to SOE headquarters, clad theatrically in bush-hat, breeches and riding boots. His new force became known as the "Poole Commandos" at their old base, the Antelope. SOE gave them a cover-name with a more official ring, No. 62 Commando. Their real name was the Small Scale Raiding Force.

In the view of one Admiral, March-Phillipps was incapable of writing a sound operational order; also he could be impetuous, sulky and short-tempered but the men who had served with him didn't mind. The Old Guard rallied round again – Appleyard, Hayes, Prout, Lassen and Winter while Ian Warren, that "bloody little man from Lumley Beach", fretted on the parade ground at Woolwich in fear that his troopship back to Freetown might sail before March-Phillipps could claim him. Warren, who won an MC later in Burma, remembers: "There was leave every 15 months from Freetown because of the weather and Gus promised that I'd hear while at home. Nothing happened. I rang SOE and got nowhere. I wrote to Gus, 'I'm getting desperate, mate'. There was no reply.

"I had actually packed to catch the boat when the Regimental Sergeant-Major came up and said: 'Mr Warren, sir. You are to report to Room 98, Horse Guards.' I was off like a shot. It was one more instance of Gus wanting a man and getting the man."

March-Phillipps had now been given the free hand that he usually took without asking. His stock had never been higher and a cascade of decorations followed operation POSTMASTER – a DSO for March-Phillipps, a bar to the Military Cross for Appleyard, a Military Cross for Hayes.

The Ministry of Defence, writing in 1986, regretted: "That no citations exist in respect of those awards. The only information available is that all three awards were made in recognition of services whilst employed on secret operations." The official files on POSTMASTER are locked away under the 75-year rule but Henrietta March-Phillipps found this unsigned letter from someone who had been close to Churchill:

> I think this incident above all others gave an insight into what an old buccaneer the Old Man is at heart. There was considerable dudgeon, as you must know, from all the reputable authorities over so disreputable an incident – and they left Winston absolutely profoundly unmoved.

The Foreign Office papers, when released in 2017, may do no more than confirm that General Franco decided against reprisals for the most realistic reasons. Spain, still torn and weak in the aftermath of a bitter Civil War, was in no shape to fight over a faraway island where neither Spanish citizens nor Spanish property had been harmed.

The drastic reprisal to hand would have been approval of Hitler's requests for free passage through Spain for a German land attack on Gibraltar; this step, though, would inevitably have dragged Franco into a war that he didn't want and that, since the entry of America, he probably felt the Axis could not win. Action was filed under Mañana.

Political repercussions were the last thing on March-Phillipps' mind at the London party to celebrate the success of *Maid Honor*. He was in love, smitten and spliced as swiftly as his fictional huntsman, Victor Greenwood. Greenwood meets Joanna Croft-Hartigan, daughter of a coal-owner, at a hunt ball – "The idea of an introduction never entered his head" – and, at five in the morning, he announces their engagement.

Marjorie, Lady Marling, the widow of March-Phillipps, remembers:

We met in February 1942. I told him that I worked the lift at 74, Baker Street, the SOE headquarters, and he swallowed it. I remember saying to him rather pompously: "Perhaps all you want is to go to bed with me," and he said: "Not at all, not at all. Shouldn't dream of it. Shan't until I'm married to you." And we were married on April 18 and Gus was killed on September 12. So we had a very short time but of such intensity.

He was just taller than I was when wearing high heels and, although his ears stuck out, frightfully conventionally good-looking if you got him at the right quarter – and very beaky if you got him at the wrong one. And there was the marvellous scarred, beautiful mouth. Gus March-Phillipps was a very remarkable man, older and more complicated than Andy Lassen. An ardent Catholic, while I doubt if Andy had fastened on to any religion very much. Yet there was an affinity between Gus and Andy; I think the combination of dash, pride, disdain and immensely serious purpose attracted Andy to him.

I worked for SOE and, when Henrietta was 18 months old, I went back and worked for the Special Air Service, the British regiments of SAS as well as the French and Belgian SAS, also the Special Boat Squadron and the PPA, Popski's Private Army. The English have a genius, haven't they, for small private armies which arouse great resentment among the PBI.

I found all the men in these private armies remarkably adventurous, and, in most cases, intelligent and very idealistic. The SSRF was numerically small but very high in quality and its justification was the necessity, at that time in the war, to make any gesture of vitality or kick left in the United Kingdom. But there was such a high percentage of officer class in the Small Scale Raiding Force that the casualty rate was very expensive when anything went wrong.

Appleyard touched on the same point in writing of the Jacobean manor that March-Phillipps had chosen for SSRF headquarters: "Initially, there'll be about thirty of us living here – nearly all officers."

Anderson Manor, completed in 1622, is in Dorset on the banks of the narrow Winterborne River, aptly named because it dries up in summer. Anderson is square and red-bricked with an octagonal chimney for each of the seven large rooms and huge kitchen. Its history of changes in occupancy and steady decline could be duplicated by hundreds of similar country houses – two centuries of residence by the Tregonwell family from the Dorset village of Milton Abbas were followed by demotion to a tenanted farmhouse and then neglect, almost to the point of dereliction, until a restoration before the First World War.

The repairs had not extended to installing modern amenities. Anderson, in 1942, had neither electricty nor mains water, and drainage was by cess-pit. Its owners, the Cholmondeleys, concerned themselves, instead, with fine furnishings and panelled walls. They worried what damage soldiers might wreak.

The stately homes of England were often dumps for the "debris" of Dunkirk. Country houses not required for British Forces were pressed to find a roof, or tent space in their grounds, for the fighting jetsam of Hitler's conquests, the separate and sizeable groups of Czech, Polish, Dutch, Belgian, French and Norwegian volunteers. Several dozen other grand homes and manors, the more secluded the better, were commandeered by the alert and acquisitive controllers of the Special Operations Executive; thus did Anderson Manor become home to the Small Scale Raiding Force.

March-Phillipps knew the Cholmondeleys. He had lived only a few miles away in Bere Regis when writing *Sporting Print*. Assurances of respect for the property were given; the furniture went into store and light, protective boarding was tacked over the panelling. The SSRF then moved in. A generator provided power for lighting and to pump water from the manor's well; then, satisfied with the arrangements, March-Phillipps wrote home, a house in Central London lent to the newly-weds by Marjorie's cousin:

I wish you were here. It's really a marvellous place and the weather is perfect. Every morning I ride out through woods full of primroses and bluebells and violets with the dew still on them, and the sun shining through the early morning mist. I think when the war is over we must settle down here, perhaps in this house if we're very great people then, and spend a lot of time in the garden. It's one of the most perfect gardens I've ever seen.

The bride travelled to Anderson to see for herself:

I was there two or three times. It was a beautiful house and the weather was always lovely. I can still see Andy Lassen by the balustrades of lawn alongside the river. Straight yellow hair, a high complexion that was also sunburned, and a rather gappy grin because a lot of front teeth had been bashed out.

Andy behaved impeccably while I was there but you could see he was wild. One of the wildest of the lot, I'd say. Gus was pretty wild himself but not like Andy – and it's said, although I don't know this at first-hand, that Andy became very tough as the war advanced. They were undoubtedly very brave men. Peter Kemp, for instance, so incredibly gallant. And I remember John Gwynne, a scholarly-looking man but with a fanatical gleam in his eye.

Major Gwynne, the SSRF planner, was known among the men as "Killer". He was a vegetarian, a teetotaller and he shaved only in cold water. Peter Kemp was a war-seeker, a man so determined on testing himself in action that he rose from being "unfit for military service" to eventual command of the Small Scale Raiding Force; he had failed the British medical in 1939 as a result of severe wounds received a year earlier while fighting in the Spanish Foreign Legion on the side of Franco: a mortar bomb had shattered his jaw.

Tony Hall, who was a close friend of Lassen, told Henrietta March-Phillipps: "This charming, small manor with its mulberry tree, the nuts, the kitchen garden made you feel that it was the England we were fighting for. Gus at Anderson created a world of people who loved doing things honourably. With him as leader, you knew that nothing would ever be done that was of evil intent."

Entertainment immediately around the manor was scanty. This corner of Dorset was unknown to the travelling troupes of ENSA, but there were weekly whist drives at the village hall in Winterborne Kingston; also daily flirting with the bronzed and brawny Land Army girls on the surrounding farms, as well as regular evenings at the World's End. It became the practice for uniformed customers to autograph the ceiling of this thatched inn. Ian Warren said: "All of us signed at some time – Gus, Apple and Andy included, although Andy didn't go there often. I believe that even General Montgomery put up his signature one day. So that ceiling could have been worth a fortune today. Unfortunately, it was wiped clean after the war."

Neither isolation nor the certainty of hard training for a dangerous, and probably short, life deterred volunteers from beating a path to March-Phillipps' door. The word had spread that this fire-eating major was, as Peter Kemp observed, "Really a very reasonable man with a complete contempt for small regulations that sometimes make life in the Army tiresome and uncomfortable." Room was found somehow for everyone who might be suitable and Tom Winter counted: "From nine men at the creation of *Maid Honor* Force, we grew to 55 officers and other ranks at Anderson." The newcomers included Baron Howard of Penrith, Lord Francis Howard as he was then and, because of his height, known to the men as "Long John". He remembers:

I didn't have much to do in SOE's Belgian section and I thought that I would rather go to an active unit. Appleyard was doing the interviewing and decided to take me on, despite my age being rather above the average. I was given the rank of captain which I'd had in SOE.

It was, more or less, the beginning of the Anderson Manor period. There were rather more officers than men and our training was probably fairly standard. We built an assault course and, I think, did the same thing as the

Commandos at Achnacarry – crawling under wire, climbing walls, running, and crossing ropes slung between the trees in the drive.

We trained with plastic explosives, gelignite and so on. We did grenade throwing, pistol shooting. There were ranges all round the manor. We did some exercises with live detonators stuck in potatoes which we threw at each other; one had to duck out of the way or risk being hurt. It was a very pleasant unit in which everyone got on extremely well, and there didn't seem to be much difference between the ranks.

We did a lot of exercises in small groups or with just one or two partners. We also did a lot of practice at sea because the whole of Poole Harbour was at our disposal as well as most of the coast. The beaches were supposed to be mined but we got through the wire and used all those wonderful beaches and sandbanks. We had a large rowing boat for hard, difficult work against the tides; we also had canoes in which we went up the rivers and round the harbour as far as Bournemouth.

Nothing was overlooked that might be useful for training. For instance, when German bombs in an air-raid exploded on a patch of clay, Gus used the clay to make a model of Les Casquets lighthouse. We got hold of a Dutch sailing-ship, the kind without a rudder but with steering boards on either side. Is that a schouw? The others spent three days running about the decks, but I opted to do the cooking.

Training was designed to accustom us to the sea, particularly to rough seas. Sometimes they were too rough; I once made a canoe party pull under the cliffs at Bournemouth because we were getting swamped. We then dried off in an empty house. We tended to do that. If there was an empty house, we'd use it.

We did a lot of night work. Maps of the Wareham area would be given to us to memorise and then, after they had been taken away, we were expected to find our way back on foot and in twos from unknown destinations where we had been dropped by lorry. Roads were not signposted, but we had to try and identify every road that we came across. It was a great help if there were stars. There was also a secret headquarters that we were supposed to penetrate without being caught. We spent quite a lot of time round it at night and I think somebody got through the perimeter, but not much further.

Lassen did all this SSRF training. He was also sent later on the parachuting course that became part of the curriculum; this meant staying for a time at Dunham Massey, a country house near Knutsford in Cheshire, and jumping at Ringway airport south of Manchester. Lassen was dubious about the project and inquired of Kemp: "Tell me, Peter. Is Dunham a much bullshit place?"

Kemp interpreted Lassen's misgivings as a simple loathing of all forms of instruction and regimentation, but they sprang more probably from the instinctive knowledge that leaping from aircraft and tethered balloons was not his game. Old comrades of the SAS testify: "He hated parachutes."

The qualms of pupils were never soothed, either, by the gallows patter of the instructors:

"Sergeant, what happens if my parachute fails to open?"

"That, sir, is known technically as jumping to a conclusion."

"Sergeant, if it doesn't open will there be a lot of blood?"

"No blood, sir. You spread on the ground like jelly, all your bones broken – but never any blood."

Lassen, although he qualified for parachutist wings, remained happier on water – or on land, as in a long night march remembered by Lord Howard:

We were paired off together and, after being set down somewhere between Anderson Manor and Lyme Regis, told to walk to Lynmouth in North Devon about 60 miles away. We had sleeping bags on our backs and hard rations, with a little tea and some chocolate, in our pockets. We slept out on Exmoor under the stars and arrived in Lynmouth so very hungry that we went down to the sea and began eating winkles and molluscs that we prised off the rocks with our knives.

Andy was a very pleasant companion to have on that sort of a walk. Not only as a nice person to be with, but as one of those physically extraordinary people who are completely tireless. He never told me much about himself and I learned hardly anything about his family. He gave me the impression of being an adventurer, and I feel that being in the same unit as Andy Lassen was rather like serving with Achilles. For Andy did easily what nearly everyone else found difficult.

Other people were very good on the assault course. They were all so fit but Andy, without seeming to take any trouble, was much the best. He just floated everywhere, up the ropes and then along them. He was like a wonderful rock climber, someone like Chris Bonington with the gift of being able to do everything he wanted on heights. And if there was considerable risk, Andy enjoyed it all the more. It was wonderful to see him. When everyone else was straining and making an effort or pulling themselves together, he'd just enjoy himself and do the assault course better than anybody.

We went climbing in the Lake District, a group of us that included Graham Hayes, André Desgranges and Andy. We did Pillar Rock on Great Gable which is an international climb, and we did Great End Gullies, not a listed climb but rather a bad rock on which you have to be very careful. Our gear was on a trolley, or handcart, which we pulled from the station to spend the first night at Dacre Castle, a small castle more like a Peel tower. At that time, it was a shell without furniture and with nothing but those little stone alcoves where they slept in medieval times – and where we slept, too.

Next day we took the trolley up the old Keswick road, which isn't a tarmac road, and then went up Borrowdale and set up camp under canvas at Seathwaite. A bull was in the next field and Andy, the moment he saw it, jumped the fence and stood in front of the bull, saying: "Does he push?" The bull didn't charge but it was typical of Andy to challenge the beast as soon as he saw it. But he'd have got away if the bull had gone for him.

Lassen, like a matador, banked on nimble footwork for escape. He was also armed, should the worst have come to the worst. A pistol was holstered on his left hip with its butt forward, the cross-draw position favoured by British forces. A photograph of SSRF in the Lakes shows Lassen with the pistol clipped to a lanyard, but there is no sign of the knife that, as Fairbairn advocated, he carried sometimes at the back of his left hip in addition to the F-S knife nearly always worn on his right side.

Les Wright remembers a speed exercise from the knife-fighting lessons: "A knife would be dropped between two of us. We would grab for it and then the man failing to pick it up would have to defend himself against his armed opponent. I still bear marks on my body from doing this drill with Lassen because it was difficult – indeed, almost impossible – to disarm him when he had a knife."

Knives interested Lassen as a means of silent killing; he was keener, though, on the bow and arrow as a raiding weapon. Reviving the bow was not an idea gleaned from kids' comics and adventures for boys. Lone archers had raided successfully in the Spanish Civil War – as Lassen may have heard from his father or from Kemp who had served at first in Spain with the Carlists, a royalist faction responsible for the bow's re-introduction. Carlist raiders, all in black and armed with short black bows and arrows, infiltrated Republican trenches on night-raids and killed sentries silently on challenge.

Lassen put his case to the War Office: "I have considerable experience in hunting with bow and arrow. I have shot everything from sparrows to stags, and although I have never attempted to shoot a man yet it is my opinion that the result would turn out just as well as with stags."

The War Office considered his claim that a trained archer could fire up to 15 virtually soundless shots a minute, each capable of killing "without shock or pain". The War Office then arrived at a typical compromise by sending him two hunting bows with arrows – but not the permission to use them against the enemy. The bow and arrow in 1942 was classed as "an inhuman weapon", a ruling that drew a scathing paragraph from Appleyard: "Such is the anomaly of modern warfare that the traditional weapon of Crécy and Agincourt should be prohibited while recourse is permitted to such horrors as rockets and atomic bombs."

Lassen's disappointment at not being allowed to kill Germans with a bow probably lasted no longer than the time required to unpack the War Office consignment. Soon he was proving his skill against pop-up targets on the Manor's rifle range. Next he was ranging all over the Dorset countryside, along the Roman road and past the ancient burial mounds, through the coppices and across the heaths of Bloxworth and Morden. He crept through Great Coll Wood and Bere Wood, bow in hand and alert for any prey. Villagers talked of him as "The Robin Hood Commando".

The routine at Anderson Manor lent itself to freelance roaming. Lord Howard said: "Gus told us to get out at six o'clock every morning and not come back until breakfast. As long as we exercised ourselves, he didn't mind what we did. We could take a gun. We ran or we walked. We could shoot rabbits or do anything else we liked. And the countryside was absolutely beautiful and there was nobody else about along the beaches."

Lassen, in his early morning archery, may have imagined every slaughtered pigeon or hare as a German guard. Lord Howard noted, as did everyone who served with Lassen, "He had a real hatred of Germans, much more than most of us had. He wanted to get at them somehow, rather in the same way that Sir Francis Drake felt against the Spaniards. Drake couldn't bear them, and I've never been able to discover the reason in history. I've always wondered about Andy's hostility towards the Germans; was it simply that they had invaded Denmark? Andy was very nice, not a frightening man – but when he said that he'd like to kill Germans, I believed that he meant it."

Hatred of such intensity is satisfied best by a personal dispatch of the foe with a knife, a bow or bare hands, not with a bomb or a spray of rapid fire. In readiness for a man-to-man squaring of accounts, Lassen sharpened his aim by unleashing arrows dangerously close to his good-tempered room-mate Ian Warren: "Seven or eight of us shared a big dormitory at Anderson and you could be greeted, as I have been, by an arrow from Andy thudding into the wall and quivering by your ear as you opened the door. He could hit a running rabbit with that long bow and was always throwing knives. This was part of his continual experiments in silent killing."

Lassen the archer attained the accuracy to back himself with the bow against SSRF men firing pistols. Les Wright said: "Once, he hit and ignited a 12-bore cartridge lodged in the fork of a tree. The distance was about 25 yards." Anything and everything, anywhere at Anderson sometimes seemed fair game for target practice. The log-shed and the old cart-shed had been joined together and converted into an indoor range, but the navels of two bronze cherubs on the lawn continued to be riddled by pot-shots from the upper windows.

March-Phillipps and Appleyard turned the butler's pantry into their armoury; the air-raid shelter became the explosives store and a Nissen hut was erected for close-combat training. The walled garden was unusually large; it enclosed an exact acre and had been laid perfectly flat as a playing surface for croquet, bowls and tennis. But the posters of the time exhorted: "Dig for victory", so the lovely turf was turned over and planted with vegetables.

Reginald Mullins, the head gardener, stayed on to work for March-Phillipps, telling Henrietta: "Always called him Gus, you know. There was no Army at Anderson. No Army regulations. We were just a happy little band." This informality extended to the many evenings at the World's End where officers and rankers, leaving their green berets and often their uniforms at Anderson on instructions, drank together on first-name terms.

They washed away the taste of water from ditches and duck-ponds which, after the addition of a chlorine tablet, was the only liquid allowed to them on exercises. Sporadic beer shortages might hit the rest of Britain and in two years' time, as the Allied invasion forces concealed themselves in the woods of Dorset and Hampshire, a uniformed man might easily be turned away drinkless unless he had remembered to come with his own glass, perhaps a jam or pickle jar. But in 1942 no-one left thirsty from the World's End. There was always Tanglefoot on tap.

"Tanglefoot was very strong cider. People were supposed to reel home after drinking it," says Lord Howard. One of these convivial exits is remembered by Ian Warren for annoying a brass-hat from the Royal Tank Corps at nearby Bovingdon: "He complained to Gus that his staff car had been held up by a crowd of us, men and officers, spread across the road on bicycles and holding each other's arms as we rode away from the pub. Gus lectured us, saying: 'This has to stop. Here, ranks don't matter. Outside, you comply with military discipline.'"

Lassen was not among the cyclists. His social interests were further afield in Bournemouth and Poole, sometimes accompanied by Appleyard. Warren said: "Apple and Andy were both good-looking, and Andy's broken English charmed the girls. Whenever they turned up at a dance, as I remember them doing at the Antelope, the rest of us knew we'd probably be going home by bus because Apple and Andy would walk off with the best girls.

"Round about the July of 1942, when Appleyard got the bar to his MC, Andy was occasionally missing at nights. He was always a great favourite with the ladies and this time he'd met a young widow in Bournemouth. Young widows were becoming plentiful after nearly three years of war but it had been this lady's misfortune to lose two husbands. Andy – and he was so proud of thinking of it – dubbed her: 'My viddo and bar'."

The widow, in doing her bit for the war effort, helped while away a summer in which Lassen and the rest wondered when the SSRF would fire a shot in earnest. The summer sped by in training, or in haymaking for Farmer Stephenson next door and in going on leave, dressed as a civilian, at every opportunity. March-Phillipps, using his hot-water bottle cover as an overnight bag, slipped off to London to see Marjorie before she went on an SOE parachute course. He had written to her: "Please send me lots of Sanatogen, it makes me feel very brave." She thought to herself: "But he is very brave. A very brave, nervous person."

Combined Operations kept March-Phillipps straining for the starter's pistol until the onset of darker nights in mid-August. The SSRF were then allowed to make their début in OPERATION BARRICADE. They began by shooting up German guards, killing three, near a gun-site on the east side of the Cotentin peninsula and followed that by a clean sweep of Les Casquets lighthouse, a raid which handsomely anticipated Churchill's words: "There comes out of the sea from time to time a hand of steel which plucks the German sentries from their posts with growing efficiency."

March-Phillipps had done far better than snatch sentries in the raid. He had abducted the entire crew of Les Casquets lighthouse and radio station, eight miles north-west of Alderney in the Channel Islands. Tom Winter remembers OPERATION DRYAD as: "One of our most successful raids. Seven prisoners, not a shot fired and complete surprise achieved despite seven previous attempts – as well as the difficulties of landing in the tide-race." Five of the prisoners were in hair-nets, an accessory unknown to the average British male. This led to March-Phillipps, as admitted in his report, to mistaking the sex of one of them and interrupting Lord Howard with the cry: "Fr-Francis. You can't take that! It's a w-w-woman!" The captured seven, all Germans, were reported as: "Very docile".

In thirty-five minutes, the same time that had been required in Fernando Po, the SSRF climbed an 80-foot cliff, netted every enemy on the rock, wrecked the radio station with axes and began re-embarking with prisoners, papers, code-books, rifles and a rapid-firing Oerlikon cannon. Interrogation by Adam Orr, a Pole who had been born Abraham Opoczynzki, showed the prisoners to be three sailors, three soldiers and a marine NCO; this mixture ensured an argument between the Kriegsmarine and the Wehrmacht when blame and future measures were considered. In the end, the Germans stationed a garrison of thirty men under a Wehrmacht officer on the bleak and waterless outpost. Opoczynzki, as well as receiving an anglicised name had been briefed in a British scholastic and family background as a precaution against falling prisoners to Nazis eager to make short work of a Continental Jew. In much the same way Jan Ludvik Hoch became Robert Maxwell – later a captain and recipient of the Military Cross.*

Orr's special task, as for other fluent German speakers on raids, was to shout confusing orders and question prisoners instantly. He had no need to hurry, though, after Les Casquets; there were a good two hours to spare as MTB 344 battled through a rising sea back to Portland Bill.

MTB 344 – "The Little Pisser" in reference to her hotted-up performance and sub-standard size – cruised at 33 knots and had been stripped for speed of all armaments apart from a pair of Vickers machine-guns. Tom Winter recalls:

> She had been fitted with a silent-running engine with its exhaust in the water. As we approached the shore, the main engine was switched off and we crept forward on the silent engine until close enough to paddle the rest of the way in our canvas-sided Goatley float which, at a pinch, could carry 18 or 19 men – as it did at Les Casquets.

Winter, pursued by March-Phillipps' comment: "You look like a bloody Hun", landed at Portland wearing a German helmet. Maybe seven prisoners and a helmet was not much to show for five months of waiting and training while March-Phillipps whipped the SSRF into shape but no-one, not even Lassen, had minded the delay at the time. Indeed, as their testimony has shown, survivors look back on Anderson Manor in the summer of 1942 as a Commando Camelot.

Lassen, four nights after returning from the lighthouse, went raiding again on the first weekend of September. He was in a six-man party that landed on the Channel island of Burhou, actually a deserted rock some 700 yards long and deemed by the Germans as fit only for gunnery practice.

This reconnaissance earned Lassen a weekend pass for September 12, the Saturday night when March-Phillipps led the SSRF to the Normandy mainland in a second attempt to carry out a raid code-named AQUATINT. Lassen rode off to Bournemouth. His commander went quietly to the chapel in the Manor's grounds; he was seen there by Tony Hall who said: "I was there praying – as usual, not to be afraid. I saw Gus hidden away in the corner. That helped me." March-Phillipps would never again kneel in church. He was going to his death. AQUATINT was a disaster.

---

* Subsequently a publisher, MP and newspaper magnate, Maxwell died in 1991 after falling from his yacht.

8

OPERATION AQUATINT

The Small Scale Raiding Force knew how to strip and load a submachine-gun, Allied or enemy, in total darkness. They had been taught pistol-shooting in the Shanghai method by which even a novice, through pressing the butt-hand against his navel, can fire almost like a marksman; they had learned the "double-tap" trick of firing successive shots in the belief that at least one would hit the target.

They bristled with weapons; for instance, Peter Kemp listed his raiding equipment as: "A tommy-gun, seven magazines each with twenty rounds, wire cutters, two Mills bombs, a fighting knife and two half-pound explosive charges."

They were bravely led and thoroughly trained volunteers who had taught themselves how to suppress the awful knowledge that, no matter how soundless their paddling to shore, they were dead ducks if spotted in the water by German defenders. AQUATINT was spotted. March-Phillipps was the victim of a double foul-up; he landed on the wrong beach on a night when luck sided with the Germans.

The aim of OPERATION AQUATINT was, like many missions, simply to test German defences, take prisoners and generally shake up the enemy. The destination was the village of Sainte-Honorine-des-Pertes on the eastern boundary of the beach destined to become immortalised two years later as "Omaha". The "Little Pisser", though, set down the raiders off St Laurent-sur-Mer, a couple of miles to the west. Survivors still seem unaware of the mistake and believe they landed at the right place but French civilians, although unable to witness the action because of a curfew, say the shooting came from the direction of St Laurent.

A blithe, cavalier bravery inspired the raiders as they closed again with the Normandy coast, and a recollection by Tony Hall suggests the SSRF that night hardly cared where they landed as long as it was enemy-held. Hall, a tommy-gunner and one of the first into the Goatley float, said: "We were meant to climb up a little kink in a certain cliff, but we couldn't find the ruddy kink. We went the second night and we still couldn't find it. Then Gus said: 'What do you think, chaps? Shall we have a bash?'"

Lord Howard says: "The plan was to land under a cliff but it was a pitch-black night and we landed in the middle of a very large, open beach." Contact with the enemy was then established rather too quickly, as Hall explained: "As we landed a German patrol came along. Our job on that occasion was to get prisoners, so I grabbed hold of one chap and began dragging him to the float. He was saying the whole time: 'Nicht Deutsch, nicht Deutsch. Czechish, Czechish.' Then someone came up and clobbered me from behind." Hall was knocked unconscious by a German stick-grenade, the so-called potato-masher, used as a blackjack on the side of his head. Then the shooting started. Lord Howard was guarding the float:

In the scrap, I got shot in the leg and could hear the patrol saying in German, "Look, there's a boat". We got into the float, which was canvas-bottomed and not very suitable for going against the waves in a sea running a bit high. But we got a certain way out – and then everything went up. Flares and more shooting. The Goatley sank. I don't know if it capsized or was hit by a shell. I could still swim despite my wounded leg, though not very much. Luckily, I bumped into the overturned boat which saved me. André Desgranges was on it, too. I don't know what happened to the others."

Appleyard was unable to land in AQUATINT. He had broken an ankle in slipping on the wet, weed-covered rocks of Les Casquets, so his role at St Laurent was confined to staying on the MTB as an observer and spare navigator. The flares showed him the landing-party trapped by machine-guns on the beach; he was close enough to hear shouts that he thought came from March-Phillipps and Hayes, but Tom Winter says

Appleyard was mistaken: "Graham Hayes didn't yell. I'm definite about that. That was me calling out. Graham was already swimming down the coast; he was wiser than the rest of us – although less fortunate in the finish."

March-Phillipps rallied a group of raiders and tried to swim with them to the torpedo boat but Lord Howard remembers: "Only one person got anywhere near the MTB – and then, in the dark, it didn't see him. The MTB stuck it out rather beyond their orders, which were not to risk a naval vessel. When they got a shell near their rigging and a bullet in their starboard engine, they thought it was time to go."

Eleven of the Small Scale Raiders landed, none returned. Three were dead: Major March-Phillipps, aged thirty-four; Sergeant Alan Williams, aged twenty-two, and Richard Lehniger, a 42-year-old German Jew from the Sudetenland area of Czechoslovakia, serving as Private Richard Leonard. Two were badly injured. Lord Howard's leg wound turned to osteomyelitis and led to his repatriation from a German hospital in 1943; Tony Hall had been so savagely battered down his right side – his face, arm and leg – that he needed an operation and a further six months of rehabilitation. Four escaped, although three of them were re-taken within a couple of days. Only two were captured unhurt, Winter and Desgranges. Tom Winter says:

Next morning only André Desgranges and myself were fit enough for the sad job of dragging Gus's body up the beach. It's been said that he drowned, but I don't think so. I am sure that he died of wounds. Also because Leonard's gravestone is dated a day later than the others – September 13, instead of the 12th – there has been speculation that he might have been executed. That isn't so. He was killed. I saw his body, and that of Alan Williams.

The Germans made André and I drag all three bodies above the high-water mark. They filmed us doing it and included the sequence in a propaganda film, *Midnight at Cherbourg*, I believe. The Germans then took me to see Francis Howard and Tony Hall in hospital but, knowing the room must be bugged, we talked of nothing important.

100

Capture for me meant two months of knocks and kicks under interrogation. At first, until they sorted out the ranks, I shared a cell with Captain John Burton and then they began questioning me about the company sergeant-major badge on my sleeve. They ripped off the badge and found the Scotch plaid with which I'd padded it to make the badge stand out on my sleeve.

An SS officer asked me what the padding was. I said, "Scotch plaid" – and got a wallop for it. They found the maps hidden in my epaulettes but missed my secret fly buttons. One held above the other formed a compass. The Germans also didn't grasp the codes we had learned for messages home.

I sent coded information for years through my wife in Cockfosters, and John Burton sent an early message about the sinking of the Goatley float, which he believed was caused by a single bullet striking the spring-loaded wooden upright. I cannot remember the exact wording, but it was something like, "The razor is no good. It folds at the first knock."

Appleyard hobbled ashore before dawn at Portland. His mood matched the blue, feeble bulbs on the milk-train that he boarded to see Sir Colin Gubbins in London. The SSRF was ravaged, its commander had gone, everyone was missing – and relatives and friends needed to be informed more personally than by the postman's tread and a War Office telegram. Marjorie March-Phillipps heard the news at Dunham Massey where she had started a parachute course unaware of being two months pregnant.

Her mind flashed back to the phone call that she had missed only three days earlier: "The very nice girl who worked for me told me that Gus had rung up while I was out; that he had rung to say goodbye. I had a most astonishing physical sensation, my heart dropping like a stone."

The French civilians on the spot soon learned that the raiders had been undone by the patrol's dog, the raiser of the alarm and often seen afterwards trotting through the thickly hedged lanes of St Laurent with an Iron Cross on his collar.

The dog angle – a gift to Fleet Street in different circumstances – was ignored in the German communiqué which reported baldly: "The capture of a Gaullist naval officer, some British officers and others. Several dead, among them a major. A wooden boat, rubber dinghy and three tommy-guns taken as booty."

The Germans, judging from their communiqué, seemed unaware that four raiders remained at large – Hayes on his own, and a group of three led by Burton, a powerful and determined red-head from the Lincolnshire Regiment. His companions were the Pole, Adam Orr and a Dutchman, Jan Helling. Burton's widow Anne, writing from her home in Cape Town, gave this account:

The Germans had the beach very well defended and the raid was a disaster. John, with a Dutchman and a Pole, managed to get off the beach and swim for the MTB, but that was under such heavy gunfire that it had to leave before they could reach it. They swam down the coast for some way and then went ashore.

In the daytime they hid and were given clothes and food by the French, and at night they walked. One night they walked right into a German patrol, so that was the end of that. They had been trying to get to the Spanish border, but found out that they had been going round in circles. They were handed over to the SS who put them against a wall and said they were going to shoot them and then, for some unknown reason, changed their minds. John was sent to a prisoner of war camp in Germany. He didn't know what happened to the other two.

The fate of Jan Helling is a mystery. The Commonwealth War Graves Commission found only two servicemen named Helling in its records and four named Hellings – but none was Dutch. There is a known grave for Orr, but it's at Durnbach in Southern Bavaria some 600 miles from the scene of his capture. The date is imprecise: "On or shortly after April 12, 1945" and so is the cause: "Presumed killed in action."

Firing squads, as the SS threatened at the outset, may have

been the end for both the Dutchman and the Pole. Nobody knows for certain, but there is no longer any doubt about how Captain Graham Hayes, MC, of the Border Regiment, became the man with two gravestones after swimming two miles west from St Laurent to an unguarded beach near the village of Asnières-en-Bessin.

The Norman coast in 1942 abounded in hiding-places ranging from bushy ravines through deserted holiday homes to those banked, bocage hedges that, as the British Liberation Army learned two years later, grow with a solidity that can stop a tank. Hayes hid himself. He was sopping wet, hungry and defenceless – but not despairing; temperamentally, as a close, controlled character always happy to work alone, he was as well equipped as anybody in the SSRF to succeed in a solo escape.

But his French was poor and he needed help; as dusk approached, he stepped out and threw himself on the mercy of a farmer, Marcel Lemasson. Arrangements were made immediately to move Hayes 150 yards to the Château d'Asnières, the home of Paul de Brunville, whose daughter Isabelle writes:

> The Germans came along the road with a police dog as my father, my brother Olivier and I were bringing the Englishman to our home – but they didn't see him. After some refreshment and a wash, he discarded his uniform and asked if he could leave the house and hide in a hayloft. I kept some souvenirs before destroying his uniform as requested. These were a shoulder-strap, some buttons and tissue maps that had been concealed in the hem of his jacket.

Hayes remained in the loft while the Germans buried March-Phillipps, Williams and Lehniger side-by-side in the tucked-away churchyard at St Laurent where the stone walls, hedges and elms might have been transposed from a Dorset village. News of the funerals was brought to Hayes and a few days later – wary, but unsuspected – he left the château to walk the twelve miles to Bayeux railway station.

He was shadowed along the road by a cyclist; this was Olivier de Brunville, later to win the Croix de Guerre in France when serving with General Leclerc's armoured Second Division. Hayes met a Resistance agent at the station and boarded a local train to Lisieux, whereupon de Brunville turned and rode away, satisfied that everything had gone smoothly.

Hayes and the agent, Septime Humann, walked six miles from Lisieux to Le Pin, a village screened by woods and known only for its stud farm; here, Hayes was installed in the safe house of a Madame Septavaux. Everything had gone smoothly, but not secretly; the presence of an English officer became known quickly to many villagers, including the postman. Soon it was known in Paris to Hugo Bleicher, of German counter-espionage, and to his mistress, Marie-Suzanne Laurent from the Café Pelican in Caen.

A traitor had been planted in the Lisieux Resistance. Robert Kiffer, arrested in 1941 while directing a Resistance network near Cherbourg, had been turned by the Gestapo version of: "An offer you cannot refuse". Bleicher wrote after the war: "Nobody who has not had one foot in the grave and looked a firing party in the eye should be hasty in condemning these fellows as traitors." France's eventual understanding of this terrible duress on young men may account for the many reprieves from execution of double-agents. For instance, Kiffer himself was freed without explanation after appealing against being sentenced to death in 1949 by a war-crimes court; yet he wrought havoc on behalf of the Gestapo. In the words of his trial report: "By November 1943, Kiffer and three companions had decapitated the Norman Resistance organisation. They left behind them tears and mourning. The departed ones and the shot ones would be difficult to count." That kind of sad counting began swiftly in Lisieux once Hayes had left Le Pin on October 20, 1942, some five weeks after AQUATINT.

Two members of the network were found in the woods, riddled with bullets. Dr Paul Hautechaud, head of the Lisieux Resistance, was sent to his death in Buchenwald; his wife was deported and never heard of again. House searches were suddenly resumed along the AQUATINT coast and, prudently, Isabelle de Brunville burned her souvenirs; meanwhile, the Resistance passed Hayes along from Le Pin to Paris and never suspected that the Germans followed his every step.

Hayes was entrusted to a Parisian agent called Orkl as a letter from Lilian Hayes, Graham's mother, explains:

An English woman, Mrs Davidson, told us that Orkl who lived near and whom she knew very slightly, brought Graham to see her. She said Orkl passed Graham off as a deaf and dumb relative and took him about Paris, even to the pictures and a football match. Graham did not care much for this, but Orkl assured him it was the safest way. They left together for Spain about the 28th of October. Orkl came back and told Mrs Davidson that he had seen Graham over the border and he would soon be back in England.

The Spanish frontier in 1942 was a particularly risky crossing for Allied escapees because of General Franco's stance as a "non-belligerent", not a pure neutral. Spain's Blue Division fought alongside the Germans in Russia, Franco's sympathies were aligned with what he saw as an Axis crusade against Communism and, fatally for Hayes, his ministers had agreed that any runaways caught within 12 miles of their border would be handed back to the Germans who were ready and waiting after occupying Vichy France in November 1942, as a defensive response to the British and American landings in Tunisia. The return of Hayes, once his route had been monitored by the Gestapo, might well have been pre-arranged and the Spanish, if reminded by German intelligence, would have derived a keener pleasure from knowing that a *Maid Honor* raider was at their mercy. The capture, though, was kept secret while Kiffer continued his deception of the Norman Resistance; his trial judges were told he showed round a letter purporting to come from Hayes in Spain and that he claimed to have heard on the BBC: "Le capitaine est arrivé à bon port."

Arrests began as soon as Hayes was flung into Fresnes, the

fortress prison south of Paris. Madame Septavaux and Monsieur Humann were seized, then released when Hayes convinced the Germans of their innocence. Hayes betrayed no-one throughout a captivity that, in view of the German passion for working from the book, was doubtless identical to that endured at Fresnes a year later by the SOE agent, Wing Commander F. F. E. Yeo-Thomas; in other words, brutal warders, a diet of turnip soup, coffee fabricated from roasted acorns, and bread from the coarsest grain and so uncooked as to be barely distinguishable from dough. Nothing to read apart from two tiny squares of newspaper issued daily as a substitute for toilet roll.

The only break from solitary confinement in the large, bare, cold cell was the regular trip – fettered in a prison van – for interrogation in the Rue des Saussaies, the Gestapo headquarters by the Elysée Palace, where questions were punctuated by beatings, head-first immersion in freezing baths and lashes from an ox-gut whip into which a flexible steel rod had been inserted. Hayes withstood everything, he was uncrackable. Years later, Isabelle de Brunville wondered, "How was it that we never had a search of our place at Asnières?"

The Germans, baffled, sent the obdurate Hayes back to Fresnes. They promised that he could go to a prisoner of war camp. They broke their word. He was left alone in his cell, cut off from all news. He never knew that his young brother Malcolm, a Flying Officer in RAF Bomber Command, had been shot down and killed in February 1943, while raiding the Loire valley.

His mother writes:

It was from a young Flying Officer who was also in Fresnes that we finally heard what the next step had been. He was in a cell under our son who used to shout good morning and good night and then signal in Morse; he said Graham seemed to be in very high spirits and did much to cheer him up. A few weeks later he got no response to the usual greeting and so he concluded that Graham had at last been taken to a PoW camp.

106

On investigation by the British authorities it was found that he was taken out and shot on July 13, 1943, and was buried in the special section of the cemetery at Ivry set aside for those assassinated by the Germans.

The headstone remains to this day at Ivry bearing the name "Gream Hayes"; an acute accent over the "e" would produce a near-perfect pronunciation of Graham. The body, though, was moved in 1951 to Viroflay near Versailles, where it rests under a standard War Graves stone.

The Paris Resistance wasted no time in wreaking vengeance albeit on the wrong man. They killed Orkl in September. The French authorities sent for Mrs Davidson's son to identify the body. He feared that asking about the fate of Hayes might reveal guilty knowledge, so he kept quiet. Hayes' mother, in a letter dated 1946, comments on a grim coincidence arising from the execution date: "I wonder if Graham spoke to you of Apple who fought with him and lived in this village [Linton-on-Wharfe]. He did not land on that September day as he had hurt his ankle, but lived to win more battles and frustrate the enemy until the day that Graham was shot – and on that day, he also died."

Appleyard disappeared in a flight over Sicily when attached to the 2nd SAS Regiment. His plane, on a mission to seize a bridge in the path of the invading British Army, was lost without trace or explanation. Some old comrades suspect a cover-up; they believe he was shot down by Allied guns.

But, as Lilian Hayes observed, Appleyard won some battles before his mysterious exit. The first of them was a raid on Sark only three weeks after AQUATINT. Appleyard led it, accompanied by Lassen among others, and the notorious consequences contributed to German feelings of justification in their execution of Hayes as "an unpardonable Commando prisoner".

9

SARK

The Channel Islands surrendered on June 30, 1940, two days after a raid by Heinkel bombers had killed forty-four people, including an ambulance crew, on Jersey and Guernsey. All the islands were unprotected because British troops had been evacuated from what their commanders saw as a lost cause, an open target for gun batteries on the captured Norman coast.

Hitler's advance guard cut the telephone lines to England, ordered an immediate curfew, called for the handing-in of fire-arms and ammunition, and installed censors in the newspaper offices. Occupiers and occupied then settled down to a life undisturbed by armed resistance of the type fomented by SOE throughout the Continent. "Set Europe ablaze" was a cry unheard in the only part of the United Kingdom on which the Germans set foot. Their detachment on Sark, usually a dozen soldiers under a lieutenant, found themselves with an unusually cordial posting. They were billeted cosily in the Dixcart Hotel, welcomed to suppers in civilian homes, invited to whist drives at the Mermaid Tavern and, the mark of greatest favour, provided with a reserved enclosure at the annual cricket match against Guernsey.

The Wehrmacht responded by making toys for the Sark children as well as giving them a Christmas party. This idyll lasted only until OPERATION BASALT, the code-name for a visit by Appleyard, Lassen and an SSRF team supplemented, after the losses of AQUATINT, by five members of No.12 Commando. Dusk closed over a tranquil sea as they left Portland, on the evening of October 4th, hoping for a crossing without the usual discomforts of MTB 344 which Bombardier Redborn, one of the dozen raiders, summed up memorably: "An MTB doesn't bob up and down. It ploughs steadily ahead until hitting a wave, when it shakes, seems to stop and then surge forward again in a series of jerks and ear-splitting noise from the engine."

The torpedo boat bluffed the look-out on Little Sark that it was a German vessel seeking overnight shelter in Dixcart Bay. It was then navigated faultlessly to the beach beneath the jutting cliffs of the Hog's Back. The raiders rowed ashore by dory. Dennis Tottenham, from the original *Maid Honor* crew, was left to guard the boat; a second man, Skinner Flint, was posted on the cliff-top to watch for German patrols, and strips of luminous cloth were tacked into the brambles as a guide for rapid descent of the steep path.

Appleyard had spent school holidays on Sark. He knew his whereabouts at the top and, as the island's population was only 400, it is probable that he also knew the lady of the house that received the raiders' first call. Frances Pittard was erroneously described after the war as, "An elderly English lady, an old woman"; in fact, she was only forty-one and in a nothing-to-lose mood since the death four months earlier of her husband, Sark's retired medical officer.

La Jaspellerie, a square, stone house with extensive sea views from its verandah, lay halfway along Appleyard's route to the German quarters. Les "Red" Wright, who was on the raid, believes: "It was no accident that we stopped there." Mrs Pittard was the daughter of a Royal Navy commander and, according to Wright, "had family connections with military intelligence".

Appleyard talked to her alone upstairs while his men broke a window at the back, a sign of forcible entry intended to mislead the Geheime Feldpolizei. Mrs Pittard produced a map of Sark's defences which were stronger than expected; they included anti-tank guns, flame-throwers, mortars, heavy machine-guns and scattered fields of S-mines – the anti-personnel device known to Americans as "Bouncing Bettys" and which leap knee-high to spray intruders with a maiming hail of ball-bearings.

Mrs Pittard had also handed over that day's copy of the *Guernsey Evening Star* containing an order for the deportation to Germany of 2,000 able-bodied workers. Appleyard urged her to return with him, saying: "You're in danger here – and you've no cause to remain now that you're on your own." She refused. "This is my home," she said. "I've lived here for fifteen years and I don't want to leave it. Besides, if I go the Germans will punish the Sarkees. I think it's best to stay and brave it out."

There was no time to argue or reason; Appleyard had to march on. He was immune to normal stress, his low, deep voice accurately indicating personal steadiness and will-power – but BASALT was no ordinary raid for him. It was his first since the death of March-Phillipps, his first as commander and, as had happened with AQUATINT, it was under the ill-omen of having been called off once.

Appleyard needed a success on Sark because the SSRF might not survive a second calamity, yet he now knew from Mrs Prittard that his force might be outnumbered by two to one. Twenty Germans, including a small unit of field engineers quartered in the hotel annexe, were on Sark that night under an Oberleutnant Herdt.

Appleyard intended to capture some of them – silently, if possible, and, as at Les Casquets, without shooting. He signalled Lassen forward near the hotel grounds; like most of the others, Lassen was armed with a Colt .45 automatic but showed greater interest in blooding his F-S knife. Wright says: "This was my only raid with Andy Lassen and Apple had already stopped him from doing in a sentry who passed us as we lay doggo for a few minutes after climbing the Hog's Back."

The leash was slipped, though, when – as Redborn told Lassen's mother – "Andy said he could manage the one sentry on his own. We listened to the German's footsteps and calculated how long it would take him to go back and forth. Andy crept forward alone. The sinister silence was broken by a muffled groan. We looked at each other and guessed what had happened. Then Andy came back and we could see everything was all right."

The German engineers, sent to build a boom defence at Creux harbour, were asleep in single rooms when the raiders entered at 2.30 in the morning. Redborn's intended prisoner was heavily asleep and snoring. His capture was farcical. Redborn whipped off the sheet and blankets but the German, drowsily, dragged them back again. Again, Redborn tore away the bedding. The German then awoke and, before being able to voice any shock at the sight of his interruptor's blackened face, was returned to sleep by a knuckle-duster.

All five engineers were in the bag. Appleyard gave the order to tie them up; this was SSRF practice and the raiders had been issued with strong, grey cord for the purpose. Wright says: "We tied their thumbs together and, after cutting their pyjama cords, made them hold their trousers up.

"We were just snatching prisoners for interrogation. We didn't sail with handcuffs and manacles and, even after all these years, I'm still angry about suggestions that we silenced the Germans on Sark by stuffing their mouths with mud. It's like saying that we were animals." Lassen himself the following year, in conversation with Colonel David Sutherland, mocked the accusations of gagging the prisoners, saying: "It's not true we stuffed their mouths with mud. We used grass."

Wright cannot recall any gagging and Appleyard's report supports him: "The prisoners were assembled under cover of trees near the house. In the darkness, one of them suddenly attacked his guard and then, shouting for help and trying to raise an alarm, ran off towards buildings containing a number of Germans. He was caught almost immediately but, after a scuffle, again escaped, still shouting, and was shot. Two of the other prisoners broke away and both were shot immediately. The fourth, although still held, was accidentally shot in an attempt to silence him by striking him with the butt of a revolver. The fifth prisoner remained quiet and did not struggle."

Redborn's memoir ran:

Major Appleyard shouted: "Shut the prisoners up!" and this began a regular fight. My prisoner had freed his hands, I bowled him over with a Rugby tackle but he got free again. He was much bigger than me; I couldn't manage him, so I had to shoot him. Andy was still holding on to two prisoners, then lights came on in the hotel. Andy wanted to throw grenades through the windows but Major Appleyard said: "No, we might need them later." The

111

Germans had started to come tearing out of the hotel, so we preferred to run for it. We still had one prisoner, and he was petrified.

Wright's Bren gun covered the confused retreat to the waiting dory and the raiders clambered back aboard the MTB just before four in the morning. Wright asks: "How many prisoners were killed? Two, maybe three. Who hit who? Nobody knows." On Appleyard's count, four prisoners had been shot, one accidentally. On Redborn's account, supported by an entry in Lassen's diary, a sentry had been knifed to death by Lassen.

Ian Warren, not on the raid but relying on his memory of conversations at Anderson Manor on the following day, says: "The accidental killing was by Captain Dudgeon, a bloody big bloke – 'Toomai, the Elephant Boy', we called him. He hit his prisoner with the barrel of the pistol, not the butt – and, forgetting his finger was on the trigger, blew the top of the German's head off."

The Germans, though, announced only two dead, a third man slightly wounded and a fourth, a bespectacled corporal called Weinrich, taken prisoner. Their casualties were light but their anger was great. It filled a page of the *Guernsey Evening Star* two days later with a proclamation from the Führer's Headquarters under these headlines: "British Attack and Bind German Troops in Sark. Immediate reprisals for Disgraceful Episode." Hitler linked the Sark raid with the tying (the German word "fesselung" carries a meaning closer to "fettering") of seven soldiers and five civilians in the British and Canadian raid on Dieppe some six weeks earlier in August 1942. Under German orders, the *Star* printed this part of the proclamation in black capitals:

A similar incident occurred on the Channel Island, Sark, on October 4th. In the early morning hours, sixteen British soldiers attacked a German working party consisting of an NCO and four men. The German men, clad only in their shirts, were bound with strong cord, prevented from putting on any further garments and taken to the shore.

When the German soldiers offered resistance against this unheard-of treatment, the NCO and one man were killed by rifle shots and bayonet thrusts, while a further man was wounded. This fact is confirmed by the statements of a German sapper who succeeded in escaping in the scuffle. The cross-examination has brought to light that the binding had been planned by the British beforehand.

The concluding paragraphs broke the news of counter-measures ordered by the German Supreme Command:

1: From noon on October 8th all British officers and men taken prisoner at Dieppe will be bound. This order will remain in force until the British War Office can prove that in future only truthful declarations regarding the binding of German prisoners of war will be issued and can further prove that its orders [not to tie prisoners' hands] will be carried out by the British troops.

2: In future, all territorial and sabotage parties of the British and their confederates, who do not act like soldiers but like bandits, will be treated by the German troops as such and wherever they are encountered they will be ruthlessly wiped out in action.

Generalleutnant Erich Mueller, the Channel Islands commander, had moved fast already on Sark, relieving Oberleutnant Herdt of command and sending him for court-martial on a charge of allowing men to sleep in undefended quarters. A horse-van owned by the Dame of Sark (Mrs Sybil Hathaway) was requisitioned to carry two swastika-draped coffins to the harbour en route to burial on Guernsey. Sark's junior school was seized and fortified. The Misses Duckett and Page, co-owners of the Dixcart Hotel, were questioned at length by military police and Mrs Pittard was taken to Guernsey for weeks of interrogation. The *Guernsey Star* soon announced the sowing of 13,000 extra mines on Sark and the closing of cliffs and beaches to residents. The curfew was brought forward an hour to 9.00 p.m. and dog-owners were ordered to keep their pets leashed. "Any dog running loose will be shot by the military patrols or guards," said the Germans, not out of cruelty but through awareness of the danger threatened by animals straying into trip-wired minefields. Islanders were heard to grumble, "That beastly raid spoilt everything."

Bitterness deepened in 1943 when 25 Sarkees, including Mrs Pittard, were deported as "unreliable elements capable of giving information to British Commandos" and sent to work on farms in Germany. In fact, Commandos never again penetrated Sark's defences although a four-man team, three of them French, tried at Christmas 1943. They scaled a sheer 200-foot cliff in the dark only to walk into a minefield on the Hog's Back where two of them were killed. Their leader, Ambrose McGonigal (later Sir Ambrose, a High Court judge in Northern Ireland) suffered wounds that left him with a permanent limp but which did not prevent him from joining the SAS later in Italy and becoming a double MC.

McGonigal's raid was over and forgotten in half an hour, except by the unfortunate participants and their next of kin, but the raid by Appleyard and Lassen was brooded upon by the Nazis throughout the war and used to justify the murder of selected prisoners under an order known as "Sonderbe-handlung" – Special Treatment, a euphemism for execution.

Every paragraph of propaganda value was extracted from the two bound and dead engineers. Headlines in the *Guernsey Star* highlighted the story circulated by the Germans throughout Europe: "British Government admits truth of Sark barbarity. German prisoners not only Bound but Shot on the Spot". Combined Operations Headquarters, caught on the wrong foot, tried at first to dismiss the charges as: "Inaccurate details announced from ulterior motives."

COH eventually issued a statement: "The main purpose of the raid was to obtain first-hand information about suspected ill-treatment of British residents in the island . . . Deportation [of civilian workers to Germany] took place last week at the shortest notice. Eleven men of Sark were warned to go, but two committed suicide and only nine left. One prisoner was brought back to this country. He has confirmed these deportations and has stated that they were for forced labour.

The repercussions of Sark were felt immediately by prisoners on both sides through months of international tit for tat.

Canada shackled 1,376 German prisoners in Canadian camps in retaliation for Germany's chaining of 1,376 officers and men captured at Dieppe. The Swiss offered their services as mediators and the British put this case to Geneva: "The circumstances on Sark amounted to a battle and there is a wide difference between what is appropriate to a prisoner in safe custody and to prisoners in the course of a battle."

This interpretation did not mollify the Germans who announced that the chaining would continue until the British "forbid the binding or shackling of prisoners in any circumstances whatsoever." Tom Winter was chained although taken at St Laurent, not Dieppe. He says:

It probably saved my life for I was still under interrogation by an SS unit. Their officer, and I can still see his delighted expression, said: 'You tie our prisoners up. We have something for you now.' With that, he sent me away to a camp to be chained because that was the order from Berlin. He was as pleased as Punch – yet this was an outfit that thought nothing of rubbing people out.

At first, they had no chains so they used the string from our Red Cross parcels. The string was worse than chains because the guards tightened the knots round our wrists. The chains, when they came, at least allowed us to slip one hand into our pockets at a time which helped to ward off or, rather, defer the terrible chilblains that came from wearing them. The chains were wide and we soon learned how to slip out of them, although at the risk of being made to stand facing a wall for two hours at attention, mostly, and under the supervision of two guards. The slightest unpermitted movement was penalised by a blow in the back from a rifle butt. The Canadians called this punishment "The Wall-flower". Sometimes half a dozen men would be undergoing it together.

Winter, even chained or against a wall, was luckier than he knew. His captors had licence to shoot him. Only a fortnight after Sark, Hitler authorised the extermination of captured raiders and accused the Commandos of "brutal, underhand behaviour", of "recruiting animals" and of being instructed "not only to tie up prisoners but also to kill unarmed captives". This secret order – marked "In no circumstances to fall into enemy hands" – amplified Hitler's threat after the Sark raid to "ruthlessly wipe out soldiers who act like bandits". The details allowed no leniency. German forces could either annihilate Commandos to the last man or hand them over, along with individual agents and saboteurs, to the merciless SD, the Securitheit Dienst.

Graham Hayes faced his firing squad under this order, so did five SAS soldiers captured north of Paris in 1944. That same year six men from the Special Boat Squadron (with which Lassen was raiding by then) were executed in Greece after being captured in the Aegean. There were many more. And the justification – if murder of prisoners can ever be excused – was not only obedience to Hitler's orders but also the widespread German delusion that British special service troops were mainly hooligans and blackguards.

It is true that units such as the Long Range Desert Group, the Commandos, the SAS, the SBS and the Small Scale Raiding Force tended to attract rumbustious other ranks as well as ultra-patriots like Lassen – "With us it was on parade and off parade, but Andy was always serious about the war," said Tom Winter.

Audacious, independent natures were common among the men and often made them disciplinary handfuls in regimented formations which, in consequence, gladly expedited requests for transfer. Unruliness, though, is a far cry from criminality and Brigadier John Durnford-Slater, DSO and bar, made exactly that point when discussing the selection of men for No.3 Commando: "We never enlisted anyone who looked like the tough guy, criminal type as I considered this sort would be cowards in battle."

Yet the German belief that British raiding forces were the sweepings of Dartmoor, Strangeways and Wormwood Scrubs persisted throughout the war and beyond it to the Nuremberg trials in 1946 when General Alfred Jodl, the Wehrmacht's Chief of Operations, told the court: "The fact that many previously convicted persons and criminals were included in the Commandos, who were of course reckless people, was proved by the testimony of prisoners; and the fact that the prisoners were shackled was obvious from captured orders and witnesses."

Jodl admitted to "grave misgivings about the legality of the Führer Order" but said:

Photographs [from the Dieppe Raid] definitely convinced me that unarmed men of the Todt Organisation had been shackled in such a way that they had strangled themselves. Some time later a Commando troop made an attack on the island of Sark. Again we received official reports that German prisoners had been shackled.

Finally, the last straw for the Führer was the capture of the British close-combat instructions which showed by pictures how men could be shackled in such a way that they would strangle themselves, and it was stated exactly when death would occur.

Jodl was referring to a technique that Captain Fairbairn had dubbed "The Grapevine" by which a prisoner could be fastened without ropes to a slender tree or pole purely through a forced contortion of his knees and ankles. Fairbairn's note to his instructional diagrams reads: "The average man placed in this position would get cramp in one or both legs within 10 or 15 minutes when it is not at all unlikely that he would throw himself backwards. This would kill him."

Hitler's anger and its consequences were unimagined by Appleyard's men as they landed at Weymouth, climbed over the tailboard of their waiting lorry and rolled through the lanes towards the bacon and eggs sizzling for them at Anderson Manor. Captain Bruce Ogden-Smith probably spoke for all of them in saying years later, "We never thought about the significance of what we had done until the Press took it up."

Lassen, who always intended that his diary should go to his mother in the event of his death, wrote: "The hardest and most difficult job I have ever done – used my knife for the first

117

time." The quiet satisfaction of the entry conceals the true exultation of Lassen's return from Sark as experienced by Ian Warren: "I hadn't been on the raid and was still asleep when they got back. Andy woke me. He held his unwiped knife under my nose and said, 'Look, blood.'"

10

The Schau Strain

The knifing to death of a German soldier – whether a fully armed sentry attacked silently as Redborn averred, or a roped and struggling prisoner as the enemy claimed – can be seen as marking the start of Lassen's headlong rush into a style of warfare that brought decorations and renown but also, in the judgment of his friend Porter Jarrell, "consumed and, finally, devoured him".

Lassen could not foresee the end. His future in the last quarter of 1942 seemed to be set unwaveringly fair. The action on Sark had been approved on high and Churchill, after congratulating Appleyard in his private room at the House of Commons, taunted Hitler: "The British Commando raids along the enormous coast, although so far only the forerunner of what is to come, inspire the author of so many crimes and miseries with a lively anxiety."

Life was good that autumn for Anders Lassen. He looked forward to a reunion with Frants who had escaped to Sweden as the first step to joining his brother in British uniform – "Delighted and proud . . . Expecting you soon," ran Anders' telegram to Gothenburg. Anders had his own news. He had been cited for his first Military Cross although the award, signed by Lord Louis Mountbatten, Chief of Combined Operations, was marked "On no account to be published". The decoration was a compendium of recognition for Lassen's part in POSTMASTER, BARRICADE, and on Sark, as well as a landing on the "dangerous and rocky island" of Burhou in the Channel. The citation called him: "An inspiring leader . . . and brilliant seaman possessed of sound judgment and quick decision".

Anders also had been selected by SOE to ginger up their recruitment of Danish agents and was sent to Achnacarry where sixteen fresh volunteers were training.

His face was still bruised and marked from the fight on Sark and the Danes imagined that his missing front teeth must have been knocked out in the same struggle; in fact, the teeth were lost some months previously when mistiming his jump aboard an MTB and colliding face-first with the rail. Peder Hansen, one of the sixteen, recalls:

He talked to us informally in a Nissen hut after being introduced by the Commandant, Colonel Charles Vaughan – an old Buffs man and so, because of the regiment's long association with our royal family, friendly and interested in us Danes.

Until then, Anders Lassen had been only a rumour. The seamen in our group – and many of them were seamen – had heard of him but even they thought he had come over by fishing boat. Then there he was, talking about the killing of two Germans and in British uniform with two pips on his shoulder. When we asked what tests he had passed for his commission, he said, "Oh, they just gave it to me."

I was an agricultural student marooned in England by the war and, I suppose, a docile character by the standards of my comrades who were mostly rough-and-ready, seafaring lads, all of them a bit hot-headed. Lassen was not like any of us, he sounded well-educated and had that upper-class assurance. I guessed he would have a lot of initials to his name.

Times were hard in my boyhood and I used to help my father with the haulage on estates where families like the Lassens lived. People of the big house, we called them. Some of them, although not blue-blooded exactly, had titles. They were all rich. By ordinary Danish standards, they lived in luxury. The bond between us, though, was resentment of the Germans being in our country.

We didn't know that the Germans were jibing at Denmark as "The whipped cream front". At least, we'd not heard those exact words but we knew their soldiers regarded it as a comfortable posting at that time, although it wasn't later – not by a long way. We knew that Nazism had spread before the war among the young unemployed and the poorer farmers, but we didn't know much of what was happening there during the war. My family received not one word from me in the war, nor I from them. Even Red Cross letters never got through.

Lassen understood the volunteers' predicament more clearly than any recruiter the SOE could have sent. He shared it with them – the homesickness and anxieties arising from lack of news; he had contacts at a level denied to most of the others – through the Reventlows at the Danish Embassy, through an aunt and friends in London able to drop hints of news in letters to Sweden, and through Danish businessmen who might tuck a little basic information into a phone call – and yet in six years he was able to communicate only twice with his parents. Firstly, in a telegram that had to be passed on verbally from Sweden – "Perfectly all right, Anders", later, in May 1942, through a letter which reached his mother, as she wrote, from "a very special source that could not be used again", in fact, a former Danish diplomat from Sweden. He didn't need a platform to put over his message that Danes should do their own fighting. He stood on the concrete floor and let his emotions pour out. The volunteers were convinced to a man, as Hansen recalls:

He proposed that all sixteen of us should join his unit, No.62 Commando. He didn't hide the dangers; instead, he stressed them. He said: "I'll make it quite clear that you have only a 50 per cent chance of coming out alive." In spite of that, and in spite of Colonel Vaughan also warning us of the great risks, all of us decided to apply for a posting to Anderson Manor.

Hansen and the volunteers envied Lassen's luck in getting into action while they trained and waited for a chance that might never come – as Lassen had done the previous year at Gumley Hall under Captain Iversen. Hansen says:

Iversen was only a nominal captain with no real authority or influence. A lot of volunteers thought they had been

121

tricked. One of my friends took his uniform to the Danish embassy, saying: "Here, you have this, I'm off", whereupon he walked out and found a job on a farm in Norfolk. Others threw their uniforms at Iversen and one, at least, struck him.

So I think the offer of places at the Commando Training Centre at Achnacarry was bait to keep us happy with the extra danger-money and lodging allowance. In practice, we would share a double bed with another Commando and split the saved six shillings and eightpence between us.

Hansen, in the end, had to go to Burma with No.1 Commando for a sight of the enemy. His time with the Small Scale Raiding Force, by then more generally known as 62 Commando, was spent mainly in trailing round country houses – Anderson Manor for a month, then Luton House near Torbay with a revolver range in its cellar, finally Wraxall Manor near Crewkerne in Somerset.

The Danes liked to go from Wraxall to Yeovil for a night out, but the town was often banned to them because of fights with British troops. "We spoke another language among ourselves – and that didn't go down well," says Hansen who experienced, even earlier then Lassen, the wartime distrust of foreigners:

An element of the general public hated us. For instance, there was the day when I was moving sows and pigs on a lorry before joining the Army. One of the sows became so bad-tempered that it was dangerous to go near her. The boy with me said: "I'll call her Mrs Hitler" and, unknown to me, painted a swastika on the side of her drum.

This was seen by the Home Guard and the police came round when an incendiary raid on the farm followed. They searched the premises and asked if I had a radio. My relationships with the police had always been excellent but they worried because I was an alien. After the raid, I was stopped from driving the farm's car. My bike was confiscated – and no-one wanted to talk to me. I moved to another farm.

While the English police wondered if Hansen might be a German spy, the Danish police – in that same year of 1941 – convinced themselves that he was a British parachutist and searched his parents' farm at Haslev in Zealand. Long, pointed rods like spears were poked into the haystacks and the thatched roof, but nothing was found. There was a parachutist, though. Hansen says: "His name was Boelskov. We came from the same town."

Mogens Hammer, the ship's officer who had persuaded Lassen to join the original volunteers, was killed after parachuting into Denmark and Doctor Carl Johan Bruhn, a signatory with Lassen of the Free Danes' oath, died in SOE's first drop. They had both been commissioned as captains in Special Forces.

But the Danes who had been promised danger and action by Lassen were left fretting as 1943 approached and the minds of the Allied commanders turned away from small raids and towards the mighty enterprise of the Normandy invasion. One last throw, though, was planned for Hansen and his comrades:

> It was a raid by speedboat carried out by a dozen Danes under English officers – but I don't know on what! The briefing was done from huge maps without place-names and the crossing was like being bumped around in a farm-cart before we changed to silent running and climbed into the floats. We had just begun paddling ashore when the searchlights picked us out – and the MTB signalled us to return. They said: "Jerry's waiting for you."

Lassen called once at Wraxall to ask about his protégés' progress but, instead of inspiring the Danes, shocked them by his indiscriminate use of weapons. Indoors or out, Lassen in his earlier years was always likely to be doing something hair-raising. Knives thrown round the boys' rooms at home, arrows fired inside the dormitory at Anderson Manor. There were many other instances.

The last time Suzanne Lassen saw her elder son had been in Hamburg – he was stripped to his waist and hiding behind the curtains of a hotel window from where he fired a catapult at pedestrians – "His first, though not his last, attempt at shooting Germans," she wrote.

And at a stately home beside the Thames Lassen's occasional heedlessness with fire-arms had almost led to tragedy. This was Greenlands, the home of Lord Hambleden where Lassen had always been made welcome and allowed to shoot the pheasants with his pistol. He was walking in the grounds with Esther Hambleden, his host's mother, one summer day when a squirrel scampered along the top of a hedge. Lassen fired instantly. A moment later, a small child stepped unharmed from behind the hedge. Lady Hambleden, horrified by the thought of what might have been, returned to the house. From that day, she refused to accompany anyone with a gun.

This escape kept Lassen in check only until the next time. The Danish Commandos discovered this at Wraxall where, Hansen said:

We were walking along a grassy path through the village when Anders suddenly cried "Look!" and, pulling the gun from his hip, fired twice one way and then, shooting on the turn, put two bullets into the clock on the church tower.

An old lady had been walking the other way along the path. He hadn't aimed at her and she was unhurt, but she was badly frightened. She screamed and stumbled, then ran away as fast as she could. Afterwards, talking among ourselves in our quarters, we agreed: "That was out of order. It was quite wrong to terrify an old woman." This incident affected our opinions of Anders Lassen, the young adventurer. We realised that he was courageous, very likeable personally and full of drive – but we had now seen the overgrown schoolboy in him. Not the playful boy, but the bad one. The boy who'll do anything for a dare or a lark.

Trigger-happy tendencies were never likely to be quelled at Anderson Manor where every front window served as firing-points for .22 rifles that riddled the cherubs on the fountain. Frants Lassen joined Anders at Anderson early in 1943 shortly before the break-up of the Small Scale Raiding Force. The journey from Copenhagen to Britain, including one false start, had taken the younger brother from May to Christmas:

The Danish Army continued to exist in a very minor way under the occupation while the Life Guards, by agreement with the Germans, remained at full strength and in full training. I managed to get myself called up early by the Life Guards and served until May 1942 – six months as a recruit, six months in an Officer Cadet Training Unit and six months having my own platoon.

After that, I was absolutely determined to escape to Sweden and signed on as a mess-boy with the DFDS shipping line on a route via Copenhagen, Gothenburg, Oslo, Copenhagen and Stettin, the German Baltic port. My idea, after acquiring some Swedish money, was to jump ship in Gothenburg and make my way to the British Embassy in Stockholm from where I would be sent immediately as a great gift to the Allied cause. I was nineteen at the time.

Anyway, the ship received mail in Gothenburg including a postcard from my family telling me to come home immediately. This was a pre-arranged code; I obeyed it and went back, knowing that I could always do the trip another month. Apparently, the Danish and Swedish authorities had agreed that anyone jumping ship would not receive political protection as a refugee and, therefore, I ran a great risk of being sent back. This was a few months before Montgomery's victory at El Alamein and at a time when the Swedes were still quite sure that the Germans would win the war.

I thought: "What do I do now?" For a start, I decided to obtain a passport – which I hadn't had on the first trip – and then to stow away on my old ship which I knew inside out, having worked on her serving food and washing up for thirty-two people. She was a nasty little ship, the *I. C. Jacobsen*, but a steady run – and the next time she was going north I went down at night to Copenhagen harbour and hid aboard with a little bag of Marie biscuits.

But there was an air-raid that night in which the harbour was mined, delaying departure for two days – and then she sailed straight to Oslo, instead of Gothenburg. So I was left sitting in a hold with my biscuits for eight days before we proceeded to Gothenburg. In the last couple of days I had to contact the cook. He gave me some food.

Swedish customs at Gothenburg let no-one through without seeing their passport and a card that they issued to crew members. I had arranged that one of the crew, after being issued with his card, would leave it and his passport in the galley where I could steal them; then I should walk ashore, showing his passport and keeping mine in my pocket.

Another member of the crew was going to follow me and go through on his own proper papers. As soon as we were clear of customs, he would overtake me and I would give the other chap's passport back. I had expected the whole business to take no more than two days when I stowed away; in fact, it took nine. But when I finally got ashore – why, that was beautiful! All the delay was worth it.

I bought a ticket to a public bath-house and went next morning to Stockholm where the British Embassy said: "My God, you should have gone to the Swedes first. You'd better go to the Swedes immediately – and don't tell them you've been here." So I went to the Swedes and they put me in jail.

Frants and two other escapees, both Danish airmen, cooled their heels in Sweden for several months after being released from custody and permitted to stay. They had little money and no priority on the courier flights from Stockholm to Edinburgh. Frants says:

There would always be some very important person to go in our place on our plane even though we got as far as sitting in the aircraft a few times, dressed up in Mae West lifejackets with whistles and electric torches. If a German night fighter shot our Hudson down in the North Sea, we could light our little lamps and blow the whistles.

Eventually, we were flown to Scotland and taken to the Royal Patriotic School in London where most foreigners were screened, then Anders got me in with his crowd at 98, Horse Guards and I was sent to Achnacarry with something called the 3rd Police Intake. I'll never forget it – 300 bobbies who had been reserved in previous call-ups and who had been soldiers for only two or three months. I then went to Anderson Manor and saw Anders again.

The first reunion of the Lassen brothers had been over lunch at the Danish Embassy on Christmas Eve, 1942. Frants remembers: "It was great fun to see Anders again after three years. He hadn't changed, except for looking a bit older and a little more mature." They talked of family and friends and of the cousins, the von dem Bussche brothers, ranged against them in the war. The Lassens understood exactly a point made by Axel von dem Bussche many years later: "Strange as it may seem to the British it is not unusual on the Continent for cousins to stand against cousins in a war." That is why Frants can say of that lunchtime discussion:

When Anders and I talked of our German cousins and their faith in victory, we did so without hatred.

I cannot agree with the British belief that Anders hated Germans individually. I don't think it's true. What he hated was Germany's presence in Denmark. He hated Nazi lies and their concept of world domination; I felt the same cold anger and fury myself every time I head Doktor Goebbels yelling on the radio. Anders fought because the Germans were in his country – and he would have fought any other occupier just as fiercely.

This ferocity, except at Sark, had not then fallen fully on the enemy and the name of Anders Lassen, although soon to

127

have a price on his head as "that damned Dane", was as yet unknown to German forces.

In March 1944, there was an award that ensured the Lassens of being the only family in World War II whose branches encompassed both a Knight's Cross and a Victoria Cross. Axel, Freiherr von dem Bussche-Streithorst – his full title – won his Ritterkreuz for heroism on the Russian front as a captain in the 9th Grenadiers. He tends to dismiss the decoration as: "That thing you wear round the neck; there were 7,200 of them. The British VC is certainly rarer than the Knight's Cross. The Oakleaves to the Knight's Cross might correspond to the VC, but that's a guess." It may have been in von dem Bussche's mind, too, that the Knight's Cross along with the various extra classifications of oakleaves, swords, diamonds and golden oakleaves, was instituted by Hitler, the leader he had volunteered to kill.

The 9th Grenadiers with twenty-year-old von dem Bussche marching tall in their ranks, swept through the Polish Corridor in the vanguard of the onslaught that began World War II in September 1939. They marched in the blitzkrieg of 1940 through Luxembourg, Belgium and into France where a Vietnamese sniper from a French colonial regiment shot away von dem Bussche's right thumb.

The 9th, however, did not march into Denmark where his divorced mother lived, but he behaved as circumspectly as if they had. He always travelled to Copenhagen in civilian clothes and says: "I restricted my yearly visits to three days so as not to irritate my Danish family. There were always one or two telephone calls between Aunt Suzanne and myself, but no other communications with the Lassens. We never met during the war – and after it, I didn't go back to Denmark for five years."

Potsdam, the military heart of Prussia, was alive in 1939 with fine young officers like von dem Bussche. Regulars whose pride in their élite regiments and determination to fight with dedicated professionalism and, as far as possible, classic chivalry overrode their reservations about the Third Reich and bound them to the war far more tightly than the mandatory oath of loyalty to Hitler. Uppermost in their

Major Geoffrey Appleyard, DSO, MC and bar, MA

Gus March-Phillipps as novelist and [inset] as soldier in the passport photograph "taken to frighten the Germans"

The Deerslayer... Anders Lassen and prey near his boyhood home

The *Maid Honor* photographed from the bowsprit by Graham Hayes and showing [foreground] Appleyard in swimming trunks and "Marco", a Yugoslav, by the gunwale and [background] March-Phillipps stooping, Perkins akimbo and sailing instructor Blake Granville in a trilby

The harbour at Fernando Po showing
the *Duchessa* and the *Likomba*

Anders Lassen and Bren gun aboard
the *Maid Honor*

Anderson Manor… "a Commando Camelot"

Major Grant Taylor instructing a general in handling a submachine-gun, in Palestine

SAS training at Kabrit ... men sometimes collapsed in the fumes

Jellicoe [left] at breakfast on the *Tewfik*. Note the giant tea-pot and tin of Golden Syrup

Pipo ... about to take Anders Lassen
for a walk in Beirut

"Is THIS the British Army?" the
inspecting brass-hat inquired icily.
"My fighting men," replied Anders
Lassen ... and here are two of them,
both Military Medallists: Dick
Holmes [left] and Duggie Pomford

Two of the Alimnia Six (executed by a German firing squad in 1944) are in this group:
Gunner Ray Jones, MM [third from left with his back to the palm tree] and "Digger" Leo
Rice [bottom right]. The others are: [back row, left to right] Duggie Pomford, Jack
Nicholson, Hank Hancock and [front row, left] Patsy Henderson.

Visiting day at the hospital after Comacchio: [back row, left to right] not known, Hank Hancock, Mick Conby, MM, not known [centre row] Corporal Pollock, Sergeant Waite, DCM, Sean O'Reilly, MM, Sergeant Patsy Henderson, MM, [front row] not known

The last picture: Anders Lassen talking to a war correspondent just before Comacchio

The bust of Lassen at his brother's home: another was erected outside Denmark's Museum of Freedom in Copenhagen in 1987

Argenta Gap...Anders Lassen's grave in Italy

minds was the wish, as von dem Bussche puts it, "to prove ourselves as good as the boys between 1914 and 1918" and so they closed their eyes and ears to the crudities and cruelties of the Nazis, to the anti-semitism and to such sights as Jews being herded out of their homes and forced to run with their luggage – as von dem Bussche saw for himself in Poland.

This standpoint of lofty detachment or deliberate blindness ceased to be tenable for von dem Bussche in October 1942. In the month when Anders Lassen raided Sark and Frants Lassen kicked his heels in Stockholm, first cousin Axel saw the SS execute 2,000 Jews – men, women, children, babies – on a disused airfield near the Ukranian town of Dubno.

The massacre went on through two sunny autumn days until the mile-long queue of Jews waiting helplessly to be shot had disappeared into the great, deep graves that they themselves had been forced to dig. The 9th Grenadiers training regiment, with von dem Bussche as its adjutant, were ordered to cordon off the airfield while the SS went about their bloody business. Calls for action by von dem Bussche were met by the objection from his commanding officer that Hitler would then send tanks and shoot them all for mutiny; yet the CO knew, as did his officers, many of whom were in shock for days, that Hitler had stained the honour of the Grenadiers. The Führer, von dem Bussche decided, had forfeited any claim to allegiance and should be eliminated; after a year of delicate contacts with Wehrmacht officers opposed to Hitler, von dem Bussche was offered a way to do it by sacrificing his own life. He accepted.

Anders Lassen, if he had lived into his sixties, might have looked very similar to his cousin when interviewed by the author in 1985. A large, impressive man with a commanding, sometimes booming, voice and quite unbowed by the disabilities of an artificial right leg, severely damaged left leg, missing thumb and the scar of a Russian bullet through the lungs; he could, even then, have stepped confidently on a parade ground – and it was this military bearing that held the key to a plot hatched by the leaders of the conspiracy and drew him to the attention of a general staff officer, Lieutenant-Colonel Count Claus Schenk von Stauffenberg.

Blue eyes, blond hair and a long, straight back were striking advantages in a society obsessed by wild dreams of Aryan racial purity; von dem Bussche was aware of looking like an SS officer or, as he put it, "like they wanted to look", and von Stauffenberg, visualising this young idealist erect in valeted field-grey and embellished with his wound stripes and row of medals, hit on the daring notion of spiriting the assassin into Hilter's presence as a front-line mannequin.

The Führer had agreed to inspect a new range of Russian-front uniforms and combat dress in November 1943, at Rastenburg, his East Prussian headquarters known as the "Wolf's Lair". Who more perfect to model them than von dem Bussche? The nomination was approved, then the conspirators began to plan.

Fire-arms were ruled out. If the first shot wasn't fatal, the attacker in the usual ring of SS bodyguards wouldn't live to fire a second. The reliable British hand grenade was considered, but only in films can they be activated with a tug of the teeth; their stiff ring required a two-handed pull – and von dem Bussche had no right thumb. A bomb was required because of the plan's gory simplicity. Instead of turning this way and that for closer scrutiny by Hitler, von dem Bussche would jerk a short fuse in his pocket when stepping forward to seize and whirl Adolf (the conspirators always referred to "Adolf") into a pirouette of death, blowing both of them into eternity inside four seconds. A standard German grenade, but sawn down and packed with two pounds of explosive, was chosen in the end – and von dem Bussche, untroubled by doubts and fearful only of losing his nerve, smuggled it aboard his train to Rastenburg.

He waited there for a week in vain. The train with the uniforms had been left bombed and burning in Berlin by the RAF. A fresh date was set and von dem Bussche, still game, volunteered again. This time he was refused leave. There was no second chance. In the New Year, he lost his leg in Russia.

He was still in hospital when Frants Lassen, at last, found an active role in the war. Frants says:

130

My only operation with the 62 Commando was directed at Herm in the Channel Islands but we couldn't land because the tide was wrong. So we sailed back again. Then I joined the Danish section of SOE and was sent to a place next to the Victoria and Albert Museum where they dyed my hair. I didn't think it was a very good idea but they kept re-dying it, blue-black. I would stick out a mile in Denmark.

Frants was dropped into Jutland in February 1944, as part of the SOE networks that had helped and encouraged the violent riots, sabotage and general strikes that plagued the Germans in Denmark from 1943. He said: "I discussed this with Anders many times. I felt it was terribly important for Danish status that something should happen in Denmark. It wasn't enough that some Danes were fighting with the Allies. A lot of people in Denmark wanted to fight but didn't know how to use their potential."

The Nazis had over-run Denmark, murdering three border guards at Krusaa en route, with intentions of setting up a "Model Protectorate" controlled with courtesy and consideration by troops who had been instructed: "The Dane has no idea of military discipline. Therefore give few orders and don't shout. It arouses opposition and is useless." German amiability, such as it was, had been long exhausted by 1944 and Danish doctors everywhere stocked up with a multi-vaccine against cholera, typhus and the main diseases of the concentration camps to which more and more of their patients were being consigned.

A concentration camp awaited Frants Lassen after six months at large. A revolver was found in his luggage at a railway station. He was taken to Gestapo headquarters at the Shell House in Copenhagen. Frants had been organising radio links, teaching the preparation of explosives and planning limpet-mine raids on the harbour. The Gestapo knew! Frants recalls:

The first thing said to me was "Gefarbes Haar" (dyed hair). They had arrested my father before I was picked up, but let him go because they couldn't prove anything. They knew all about him, though. They knew where he lived and went there to browbeat him, without actually pulling him in. I was chained to a bed in the Shell House and later a German prison. I was taken out only for interrogation and to be beaten up.

They knew so much about me. They had a thick file on me. They knew about Hatherup Castle near Cirencester where we trained and they knew who we had trained with. They knew almost to the day when I had arrived in Denmark and what I had been doing in Jutland. They knew, more or less, what I was doing in Copenhagen. It's very nasty when the Gestapo says: "We know you have been there, and therefore you must know so-and-so" . . . and when they say: "We must know in twelve hours because in twenty-four hours it's no good to us."

Underground war is nasty. They cannot get information by shooting captives, so they beat it out. They work on your family, they work on your friends. They put on every pressure for the first two days of imprisonment. I was treated badly by the Germans. They told our group that we would be condemned to death. There was no trial. They didn't even use the death sentence as a threat, they just said we would have to expect it. One morning, they announced: "We have decided to shoot you." Then they changed their minds and decided to keep us.

They used the word "Schutzhäftling" which means someone taken into protective custody, but the protection was for their benefit, not for ours. We were a form of hostage, prisoners who could be used later in bargaining. I was in Dreibergen prison near Rostock in what is now East Germany. It was very unpleasant. We were three to a cell. There was no heating, we were cold and became very thin – but we still lived far better than people in the concentration camps.

Frants Lassen, with other Scandinavian prisoners, was transferred eventually to Neuengamme concentration camp in northern Germany. Early in the spring of 1945, negotiations between the Germans and Count Folke Bernadotte of the Swedish Red Cross led to the release of all Norwegians and Danes a few weeks before the war ended. Frants returned to Denmark by train but, with four other parachutists, jumped off outside Copenhagen for fear of being seized again and used as a hostage.

The tread of torturers and executioners echoed through the Third Reich when von Stauffenberg's bomb failed to kill Hitler at Rastenburg on July 20, 1944. The explosion was "heard" instantly in the mind of Axel von dem Bussche lying in an SS hospital with his leg off and with the name of a von Stauffenberg associate in the orderly book as his most recent visitor. The bomb that Axel had designed for Hitler was out of reach of the investigators at last. A trusted friend had removed it from the bedside locker where it had lain since being forwarded with his effects in that meticulous, unquestioning Army way. The bomb was at the bottom of a lake. But there was still the address book.

On the night of July 20, as a shaken Hitler affirmed his survival in a nationwide broadcast and as von Stauffenberg was shot out of hand in Berlin, Axel von dem Bussche huddled beneath the sheets out of sight of the suspicious, fanatically Nazi chief nurse. There, through the night and into the small hours, he completed a desperate task. Scrap by scrap, he ate his address book.

Nearly 5,000 suspects were barbarically tortured or executed in the Nazi revenge. Some, on Hitler's orders, were hung by piano wire from meat-hooks. None implicated von dem Bussche and the SS interrogators treated him gently, their mistrust allayed by the unbreakable alibi of six months in their very own hospital. Forty years later, von dem Bussche – after careers as a military attaché, as headmaster of a German boarding school and as secretary of the World Council of Churches – remains anxious not to be seen in any way as the forerunner of an age where nonentities achieve a brief fame by shooting Popes, presidents and pop-singers. "Give the motivation," he urges, "that it was based on the Jews. That I witnessed mass executions."

And the parallel between himself and Anders Lassen, both winning the highest honours in battle and both so ready to sacrifice their lives? "A strange coincidence that has something to do with genetics," he replies.

The war effectively ended in 1944 for both him and Frants Lassen but those genes – "the Schau strain", as von dem Bussche terms them – were kept in spectacular employment almost to the end by Anders Lassen. In February 1943, the SSRF virtually wound up, and he flew to Cairo for the founding of the Special Boat Squadron.

11

CRETE AND BEIRUT

Anders Lassen won his second Military Cross after nearly three weeks behind enemy lines on Crete where he led one prong of a triple raid in the first independent operation by the Special Boat Squadron. The SBS had been formed under Lord Jellicoe a few months earlier in the spring of 1943 by the division into two of 1st SAS – a title, incidentally, lifted by the regiment's originator, David Stirling, from the name for Britain's first batch of paratroops: "Special Air Service Battalion." The other half of the 1st SAS, some 250 officers and men, became Special Raiding Squadron under Robert Blair Mayne, who finished the war as a Lieutenant-Colonel with three bars to his DSO. "Paddy" Mayne, a red-haired Ulster giant, had been both an Ireland international Rugby forward and the heavyweight boxing champion of the Irish Universities.

Mayne never ceased to be quick with his fists, a characteristic that led him into the SAS. He was under close arrest in Egypt in 1941 when invited to become one of Stirling's six founding officers and his acceptance sidestepped the prospect of a court-martial for knocking out his commanding officer. This was Lieutenant Colonel Geoffrey Keyes who was killed in Libya later that year when winning the VC for attacking a house that had been wrongly identified as the headquarters of Field Marshal Erwin Rommel. Lassen, like Mayne, could be too ready with his fists but was not arrested when he also knocked out his commanding officer. Lord Jellicoe remembers: "It was in a bar in Tel Aviv. I had said something to rouse his Danish ire and Andy could be very impatient and hot-tempered. I was struck absolutely without warning and was rather surprised, as his CO, at finding myself flat on my back so quickly."

Jellicoe let the matter drop. He had a soft spot for Lassen

and, confident there would be no repetition of the assault, probably felt that a court-martial would achieve nothing beyond costing him a valuable officer; in the same way, a French protest about Lassen's rough-and-ready methods was smoothed over by David Sutherland:

> We were on exercise in what is now the Lebanon and which was under French occupation. One of the tasks was to grab a vehicle and Lassen found himself rather behind schedule, so he put his chaps by the edge of a road and then stepped out with a sub-machine gun to flag down the first truck which came along. Two enormous Senegalese were in the driver's cab, whereupon Andy had a fist fight with them. I think he laid them both out, for he was physically very strong; then he seized the wheel, told his own chaps: "Pile in here, boys. Off we go." This was typical of him, but it attracted substantial comment from the French commandant who wanted to know what was going on. In the end, we were able to convince him that it was all in good fun as part of an exercise.

Jellicoe's SBS embraced not only the 250 officers and men from his share of 1st SAS but also the 55 members of the old Special Boat Section, plus remnants of the Small Scale Raiding Force in the shape, principally, of Lassen and Captain Philip Pinckney from the raid on Sark. According to Sergeant Jack Nicholson, the continuing German outrage about Sark was prominent in Sutherland's thoughts when preparing for the raid on Crete.

Nicholson, who was to win the Military Medal on Crete, recounts a conversation that catches an echo of Appleyard's advice to Sergeant-Major Winter when Lassen joined *Maid Honor* Force. He says:

> Major Sutherland called me in and told me that he was putting Lieutenant Lassen in charge of my section. I said, "Very good, sir" but there was more to come, perhaps because we knew each other from peace-time.
>
> "Lieutenant Lassen needs watching. He's been in trou-

ble, something about killing a prisoner in a raid on France. I want you to keep an eye on him. Restrain him!" Well, I was startled. I've never had such an introduction to an officer, and I never think of Lassen without remembering it. Also it wasn't an easy instruction to carry out; at least, not in the latter part of his career, although you could tell him things at first.

In June 1943, Lassen and Nicholson with five men, including two radio operators and an interpreter, landed with Sutherland and his main party on the south coast of Crete. The beach was a stretch of boulder-strewn shale beneath a jagged cleft that said everything about the terrain to come, 60 miles of marching through gorges, fords, mountains, thorn-bushes and clouds of insects. Baking by day, freezing by night. Lassen's destination was Kastelli Pediada airfield near Heraklion on the north of the island and his mission was to destroy enemy aircraft on the ground and keep the skies clear for the impending Allied invasion of Sicily, which led directly and quickly to the overthrow of Mussolini and then the surrender of Italy in September 1943.

They were accompanied at the outset by a party led by Lieutenant Ken Lamonby and including Dick Holmes who, like Nicholson, was destined to win a Military Medal on the raid. Holmes says:

Our destination was the airfield at Máleme but we marched with Lassen's group for three days. On the first night, I think, a little guy in my group called Eddie Sapsed sprained his ankle but was determined to go on. If he came with us, someone would have to carry his pack. I was lance-corporal so I carried it for most of the night. Nicholson was there, so I said to him, "How about you having a go?" I tossed the rucksack to him and he carried it for a couple of hours, then I carried it again. Lassen never offered a helping hand, he would never have dreamt of that. If a man couldn't make it, I felt he would leave him there. He would never carry anyone else's kit – and Lamonby was the same.

137

The raiders were passed from guide to guide through the apparently trackless mountains; they slept where they could – on makeshift stone beds under borrowed blankets in the mountains or hidden in the vineyards of the warmer valleys; their pouches bulged with iron rations of oatmeal, raisins and tea. Space was also reserved for tins of corned beef: "We hated it, but the Greeks loved it," says Holmes. Villagers brought hard-boiled eggs, bread and wine, sometimes cucumbers.

All the time, the Germans were searching. Their Cretan airfields had been raided by Jellicoe and Sutherland in 1942 and they remained alert to the possibility of a return visit as well as to the presence on the island of SOE agents and marauding Allied escapees like Les Stephenson who later became one of Lassen's first-choice men. This German vigilance enforced the utmost caution on Lassen. For two days he lived in a cave by the airfield, a cave with an entrance hardly wider than a sewer. He and his men wriggled inside and waited for July 4, the night set for the attack. They had been on the run for almost a fortnight and only four were left to carry out the mission.

Nicholson says:

The airfield was on a steep hill and was about half a mile across. Corporal Sidney Greaves and myself were to cut the fence on one side while Lassen and Corporal Ray Jones did the same on the far side, but a searchlight swept towards Greaves and myself as we climbed the hill. We hit the ground.

I wasn't frightened of anything in the war, not even when I was fighting in Crete in 1941 as one of only 16 survivors from No.7 Commando. I believe in mind over matter and in the powerful effects of repeating to yourself: "No pain, no pain" – as I've done even after an operation. But being nearly trapped by that searchlight was the closest I've come to being scared.

I collected my wits, though, and said to Greaves: "Start climbing again, but don't drop down. Stand still." We did, and the searchlight swept by without pausing. We did this repeatedly until reaching the fence. I'd realised that the operators were attracted only by movement. Anything stationary deceived them.

Eight Stuka dive-bombers and five Junkers 88s, twin-engined low-level bombers, stood on the airfield with a few fighters. Greaves and Nicholson slipped explosive time-pencils into three of the aircraft as well as leaving a timed bomb by a petrol tank; meanwhile, a small war broke out on Lassen's side of the field. Two Italian sentries had been killed ruthlessly by Lassen; the first silently in the approved Fairbairn-Sykes manner with a hooked grip round the jaw followed by a downward thrust of the fighting knife, and the second swiftly by Lassen firing without troubling to remove the pistol from his pocket. The knife would have suited Lassen better but he had no choice because the sentry, unlike three others he had bluffed in the cordon, was standing off and refusing to believe his claim to be German.

The shot brought the garrison scurrying from their bunkers, banishing the dark with flares and firing at every suspicious movement. Lassen and Jones ran for it. The citation for Lassen's second MC picks up the story.

Half an hour later this officer and other rank again entered the airfield, in spite of the fact that all guards had been trebled and the area was being patrolled and swept by searchlights.

Great difficulty was experienced in penetrating towards the target, in the process of which a second enemy sentry had to be shot. The enemy then rushed reinforcements from the eastern side of the aerodrome and, forming a semi-circle, drove the two attackers into the middle of an anti-aircraft battery where they were fired upon heavily from three sides. This danger was ignored and bombs were placed on a caterpillar tractor which was destroyed.

The increasing numbers of enemy in that area finally forced the party to withdraw. It was entirely due to this officer's diversion that planes and petrol were successfully destroyed on the eastern side of the airfield since he drew off all the guards from that area. Throughout this attack, and during the very arduous approach march, the keen-ness, determination and personal disregard of danger of this officer was of the highest order.

Nicholson, though, eyes the official version with scepticism. He says: "Andy Lassen was a brave man and a cool man. I would call him stupidly brave, except that he kept getting away with it – and sometimes I think he got credit for things he didn't do. Kastelli airport is an example. That was no diversion, it was a bungle, Lassen and Jones were meant to be as silent as me and Greaves."

The firing had been so intense on the far side of Kastelli that Nicholson and Greaves thought it impossible for Lassen and Jones to have escaped capture or death, so they made their own orderly return towards Sutherland's base camp by the beach. Sometimes, they disguised themselves as shepherds with cloaks and crooks; one night they slept on a hillside among villagers in flight from the hostage-taking Germans heading for their dwellings.

The Cretans' fears were well-founded; fifty-two hostages were shot in reprisal for the raids and a further fifty were threatened with death unless Sutherland's saboteurs were handed over. No-one came forward and, despite the risk, peasants sheltered Jones when he was separated from Lassen in their escape from the airfield. The same village took care of Lassen when he, at last, dared to show himself after two days of hiding in fields, living on raw onions and cabbage. They gave him water, reunited him with Jones and sent them with a guide along a route where other hamlets, places of desperate poverty, waited with wine, plates of roast kid and, best of all in Lassen's opinion, cigarettes.

Lamonby's patrol was also heading through those ankle-wrecking ravines with a tale of success for Sutherland, even though it had been achieved against a substitute target thanks to Holmes:

We were supposed to attack the airfield at Heraklion itself but there had been no planes for two days and nights so, instead, we attacked a petrol dump at Peza. I was the only one to get in but then, while the others waited outside, I was held up by a German dog patrol that was wandering around. The first delay was for twenty minutes and the second for a quarter of an hour.

So I was stuck amid rows of fuel barrels that I'd primed to explode on two-hour pencils. By the time I got out, an hour had been used up. Then we had to cross two roads to make our escape, so we couldn't stay to see the damage. The Greeks told us about it later. Two of the barrels that I'd blown had flown so high that they cleared the wire of the neighbouring dump and set that ablaze, too.

Lamonby and Holmes were safely into the hills at one in the morning when their first bomb exploded. The whole of Heraklion heard it and saw the pillars of flame followed by further explosions and, much too late, the bells of fire engines. Some 50,000 gallons went up in smoke. Holmes says: "Almost the whole place was destroyed and I was awarded the MM, which was sent to me after the war with £20." Lassen and Lamonby reached Sutherland's base camp separately with a couple of days to spare, but were not to be reunited for long. German patrols were sniffing round. The invasion of Sicily that day had put the Cretan garrison on full alert and the security of the SBS hide-out was then threatened by the noisy arrival of nearly two dozen Cretans clamouring for passage to Cairo and enrolment in the Allied cause. These irregulars, ragged in dress and discipline, looked as if they had been transported from the Khyber Pass with their assortment of ancient fire-arms, huge daggers and crossed bandoliers.

One German patrol, attracted by the noise, was captured. The next pair of Germans were cannier. They fought their way out of an engagement with the Cretans, firing against British orders, and they killed Lamonby when he led an SBS search for them. The body could not be found. Lassen and Sergeant Doug Pomford searched for it. They had heard the shot but the sound proved no guide. Dusk was gathering and the ground, a tangle of bushes and jumble of rocks, was impassable to anything except Crete's chamois, the Agrimi. Lamonby was left where he fell.

He was the only casualty of an operation that was saluted a few weeks later by a cascade of awards – bars to their Military Crosses for both Sutherland and Lassen, Military Medals for Ray Jones, Sidney Greaves, Dick Holmes and Jack Nicholson. The decorations recognised the tenacious bravery of raiders who had refused to be undone by the inaccurate intelligence that had targeted an unused airfield. Sutherland's men, although knowing they deserved better results, sailed away in good heart with a story of partial success, as well as a couple of prisoners and the Wehrmacht's new self-loading rifle. Sutherland said, "We were lucky to get hold of this weapon. It was way ahead of its time and provided valuable information for the powers in Cairo." The prisoner caught with the rifle was a graduate who spoke excellent English. It's said that he and his partner were taken by Sutherland and Lassen for ice-cream sodas at Groppi's, a teeming pavement café in Cairo, but Nicholson demolishes this legend:

> The officers knew nothing about it. They had told me and Corporal Greaves to place the Germans in custody at barracks but when we got there, the guard-room said, "We don't accept prisoners after six o'clock." I turned to my mate and said, "Greavesie, what should we do now? Because our night out is gone unless we take the Jerries with us." Then the boy with the good English said, "We won't try to escape. We give you our parole." On the strength of that, we took the pair of them, still in German uniform, to Groppi's for a meal, then we showed them Shepheard's Hotel before finding a bar where we drank Stella beer (I think it was Stella) until the four of us dossed down in barracks at midnight."

Groppi's in 1943 was such a kaleidoscope of uniforms, such a whirl of table-hoppers and bustling waiters that Nicholson's party dined unchallenged and left unaware that the field-grey of their guests had been spotted and reported. "Someone must have sneaked. There was a hell of a rocket," said Sutherland, who accepted full responsibility and still defends the hospitality: "These unfortunate chaps were going into prisoner-of-war camps. One day in sunny Crete basking on that idyllic shore, the next day impounded by the rather rough SBS and sent across the sea to Canada. Why not give them a good feed? It was 1943, so they had two years inside to come."

Sutherland, Lassen and the SBS also had almost two years to come. Two years of fighting without air cover because the Italian island of Rhodes remained in enemy hands. General von Klemann, with 10,000 German garrison troops, seized control before the 35,000 Italians on Rhodes could hand it over to the Allies as stipulated in the armistice. Churchill said, "The key to the strategic situation in the Aegean is: Storm Rhodes!" but the Germans were on the spot and the Allies had no assault force but only Jellicoe ready to take a daring gamble:

I was dining at the St Georges hotel in Beirut when I was tapped on the shoulder by a military policeman who said I was wanted back at Raiding Forces headquarters. I was asked there to report to GHQ, Middle East where I found a conference going on to decide what to do about the Italian surrender taking place that night.

The more I listened to the suggested plan, the more it struck me as impractical and outlandish. The idea was that a very fast RAF crash-boat would disembark a small force, six or eight men, on Rhodes to speak to the Italian commander-in-chief, Admiral Campioni, who would receive news of the mission from the resistance – such as it was on Rhodes at that time. It hinged on a Greek peasant receiving the necessary signal on a wireless transmitter that hadn't been working for a month and then crossing the German lines to inform the Italian C-in-C.

I said it didn't seem feasible. I said the sensible thing was to drop someone in. So I found myself with Count Dobrovsky, a Pole who went under the name of Dolbey, and a wireless operator called Sergeant Chesterton flying in a Halifax which had been sent down from Palestine unbriefed and without warning. The crew were told, "Find Rhodes and drop these three people." We never found Rhodes. We flew over Turkey all evening and all night looking for Rhodes and then, as the light dawned, the pilot said he would have to turn back. We tried to persuade him to go on, but he wouldn't. There were German fighters. So it wasn't until the next evening that we dropped in.

The three parachutes were spotted in the dusk and fired on by rifles, as well as being scattered by a brisk wind. The interpreter Dobrovsky, who had never jumped before and was rather old for it anyway, broke his leg; Chesterton crashed on a steep hill and Jellicoe came down more than three miles from the intended landing place. When they were eventually reunited and taken to Campioni, they found the Admiral sympathetic. It had been good public relations to send him Jellicoe, son of a famous First Sea Lord; nevertheless, the mission failed.

Campioni knew that his forces were superior to the Germans only numerically; von Klemann's troops were better armed, better equipped with transport and morally more militant. They could be turfed out only with the assistance of an Allied landing of far greater strength than Jellicoe could promise. After a day of stalling by both sides, Jellicoe left at night in an Italian torpedo boat before the Germans arrived and added the city of Rhodes to the three airfields they had commandeered from Campioni.

Jellicoe says of the attempt to gain Rhodes by negotiation:

It was all due to pressure by Winston, who always had a strong feeling for exploiting mobility. In First World War terms, he was an easterner, not a westerner as was shown by the campaign to force the Dardanelles. He certainly saw very clearly the advantage of opening a possible third front and bringing Turkey into the war. Rhodes was the key to that – and it was really Winston's driving force that impelled Middle East HQ to do something for which they were inadequately prepared.

144

Churchill succeeded, though, in bringing Turkey into the war. Not directly, but covertly. Secluded inlets and harbours at Deremen, Yedi Atala and Kiervasila on the supposedly neutral Turkish coast were put at the disposal of the SBS as raiding bases; none was further from Rhodes than 50 miles as the crow flies and each was within easy sailing distance of Jellicoe's prey, the twelve islands of the Dodecanese. Two of the islands, Simi and Cos, were captured within a week of Jellicoe's return from Rhodes. He himself took Cos while Lassen, under Ian Lapraik, landed on Simi under the noses of the Germans only a dozen miles away on Rhodes.

The seizure of Simi and Cos was the first fruit of inspired recruiting by Jellicoe, reorganised training by Lapraik and navigational wizardry by Commander Adrian Seligman.

"Two great tricks", in Seligman's phrase, enabled Lassen and all SBS raiders to move unsighted and remain undetected in enemy waters for two or three weeks at a time. The first was a foolproof method of navigating at night without lights of any kind; the second, thanks to the chance meeting of Seligman with another Old Harrovian, was a way of camouflaging Greek caiques so that not even a fighter pilot informed of their presence could distinguish the vessels from the rocks against which they moored.

Seligman bumped into Maurice Green, chief camouflage officer of Ninth Army, in Beirut and said to him: "Now look, Maurice. If only we had some really effective camouflage for our caiques, instead of just going to the nearest island and getting back in one night, we would be able to hide over the day and go on to further islands."

Major Green considered this interruption to what he called "A good drinking session on arak"; he then promised to help. He said: "It was completely *ad hoc*, a most informal arrangement. I just pinched the materials from the Ninth Army store, which I could do unquestioned, and let the SBS have what they wanted. The netting had to be re-designed with a different scrim, which is the cloth tied to the net. The old scrim reflected more light than the rocks, so we needed something dark grey. We went up and down the coast from Beirut working out average reflections, trying the camouflage

145

in both the light of the setting and rising sun. We tried to conceal MTBs as well, but the shape was too difficult."

Seligman had another useful chum up his sleeve for the day when Green at last pronounced himself satisfied with the netting, the scrim and the way of draping it to break up the outline of a caique. This was a Beaufighter pilot called Reid, and Seligman said: "We took one of the caiques up to Juniye, which was just a cove in those days, and laid it against the rocks. Next day our friend Reid came over in a Beaufighter with a camera, testing if he could see the boat or record it on film. But he couldn't see a thing and nothing appeared on the photographs, either. The caique looked like a continuation of the rocks. It meant we would be able to do much longer trips – and the further we went inside enemy territory, the safer we were because no-one expected us or were on the look-out for us."

Seligman, a round-the-world sailor before the war, organised and assembled some forty caiques into the Levant Schooner Flotilla under the motto, "Stand Boldly On". He said:

We lost only two of them while I was there. One was jumped, the crew taken prisoner and bumped off; the other one was intercepted and destroyed by an Italian submarine. Some of the caiques were fitted with Matilda tank engines, much too powerful but enabling us to make eight knots at quarter throttle – and that meant no noise at all as well as the range to go where we weren't expected.

Fundamentally, though, what started us off was devising navigation at night by silhouette. We needed a simple, foolproof method because our officers, very young and with only a few months' training, had to land soldiers at precise points on beaches in pitch darkness because we never operated by moonlight.

You started off on a course knowing that, at a certain point, you would see a rock or an island – and that was your point of departure. You would then alter course until seeing one mountain in a gap between another mountain when you would alter course again. We would tell our

146

chaps: "Go until you see an island on your port hand. The moment it's on your beam, alter course until a mountain appears – and then you alter course again." We could bring them closer and closer to the beach so that they would have a very short run-in. They couldn't have lights or a chart, but only a series of directions: See the rock, see a transit between the rock and an island – and, which was always a pretty good mark, see the cut-off between two islands overlapping. We invented this method of navigation and it worked very well. Mind you, it was used always in very good weather.

Seligman, an author and journalist, wrote a radio script on Lassen from which these excerpts are taken:

The background to a portrait of Andy will be filled with glimpses of the light-hearted (and sometimes deadly) piracy that went on for nearly two years in those waters of the Greek islands where, to quote the rather dispirited letter of a German garrison commander to his superior officer – a letter we captured – "the British come like cats and disappear like ghosts." The British were Andy and the men of his patrol.

In character, he was a fascinating mixture – quiet, sensitive, poetic at times and deeply sentimental, especially about children and dogs. On several occasions I have seen him with tears in his eyes over a family of starving Greek children, whom he was powerless to help because of enemy reprisals. He took with him everywhere a miserable little woolly-coated cur he had picked up in a back street of Beirut. It was mangy and bug-ridden and smelt abominably – by no means a pleasant shipmate in a 26-foot sailing boat, already crammed with men, stores and ammunition, on a ten-day voyage creeping from island to island under cover of night; hiding under camouflage nets among the rocks by day. But it had pathetic eyes, and Andy refused ever to be separated from it.

On the other hand, he was brave with a calm, deadly, almost horrifying courage, bred of a berserk hatred of the

Germans who had overrun his country. He was a killer, too, cold and ruthless – silently with a knife or at point-blank range with pistol or rifle. On such occasions, there was a froth of bubbles round his lips and his eyes went dead as stones . . . When not on operations, Andy was scatter-brained and harum-scarum, usually penniless and (owing to his really godlike beauty and quite devil-may-care manner) excessively attractive to women – though he didn't care much about them himself, except for his mother still in German-occupied Denmark.

One morning he turned up at our base in Beirut in a great state of nerves. He was trembling, his face was white and four front teeth (false) were missing. He couldn't remember where he had been – he and his woolly dog – the night before, but he was certain now that he had swallowed his teeth and would die. He insisted on being X-rayed; he was as terrified as a schoolgirl.

While Andy was up at the sick bay, a smartly turned-out and very deferential Arab servant arrived at the base with a small paper parcel. In it were Andy's teeth. They had been found under a pillow, quite the wrong pillow from a diplomatic point of view; there might have been international repercussions at a very high level throughout the Middle East if the wrong person had found Andy's teeth.

Seligman, in mentioning Lassen's magnetism for women, knew the "very sweet girl" with whom there was a long affair. Her name was Aleca, the diminutive of Alexandra. She was a showgirl and first met Lassen at her workplace, a Beirut cabaret. The SBS forward bases could never be on the itinerary of ENSA, the British forces entertainment organisation said to stand for "Every Night Something Awful"; neither could they listen to BBC Forces radio in their operational bases. Army newspapers arrived late, if at all, and mail might be collected only every two or three months.

The raiders, forbidden by censorship to describe their duties, told each other that their folks back home imagined them lolling about in the cushiest of numbers – SAS probably being the initials of non-combatant South African Supplies while Special Boat Squadron was obviously a fleet of pleasure craft for Desert Rats on leave. Public ignorance of their activities and the hardships of life behind the lines were compensated partly, though, by an abundance of showgirls. Jellicoe's men could return from operations and go on leave amid a variety of night-life unimagined in wartime Britain. "Sorry, no beer", the notice that shut every pub at home at least once, was unknown in the Eastern Mediterranean.

Officers on a night out at the Hotel St Georges in Beirut might find that Pierre Charitou, the establishment's suave and vaunted barman, had been supplanted by a Royal Navy lieutenant who had a way with rainbow cocktails. This was Gordon Hogg, a jolly captain from the Middlesex Yeomanry who had transferred to the Navy on becoming the signals' officer of the Levant Schooner Flotilla:

A dry martini at that time cost the equivalent of fourpence, so you could afford a rainbow cocktail. Now, I doubt if anyone could because the drink comprises seven liqueurs poured separately and carefully in the right order – cherry brandy, as the heaviest, at the bottom. Among my friends, and because the official dispenser handed out cards proclaiming him "Pierre Charitou, barman", I became known as "Le 'Ogg, barman" but, as my naval duties included collating weather reports from the Eastern Mediterranean and trying to forecast landing conditions on the beaches, I protested that it should be "Le 'Ogg, isobarman".

I mostly saw Andy Lassen ashore in Beirut with his girl, who was very pretty. Once, when going off somewhere for a spell, he asked me to look after Pipo, the little dog which loomed so large in his life; I agreed but he had forgotten about the arrangement when he came back and suggested that I'd tried to pinch the dog. I wouldn't have liked to be at the wrong end of Andy Lassen's anger although he was a great charmer and, in all his relationships with his confrères, showed a very considerable gentleness; I think it's often the case that people capable of great violence when conditions require it are not necessarily that way in more docile surroundings.

Aleca, Andy's girl, was a singer and dancer, one of many in Beirut's vigorous and demi-monde entertainment trade. From Istanbul to Cairo in the war years, night clubs flourished – and those of Beirut were places of considerable relaxation for troops coming back from action. Good food, no black-out, girls dancing, a piano. The influence was French and their colonial government had kept prices down although, by 1943, Beirut was becoming rather expensive. Hollywood had a shot at the night-life atmosphere by creating "Rick's", the club run by Humphrey Bogart in *Casablanca* – but it was only a shot.

The Eastern Mediterranean in those days swarmed with blackbeard organisations under various initials: SAS, SBS, LSF for Levant Schooner Flotilla until there was an objection that this stood for Landing Ship Flak to be used in the Normandy invasion and we had to change to AHS for Anglo-Hellenic Schooners. There was LRDG for Long Range Desert Group, OSS for the American Office of Strategic Services, ISLD for Inter-service Liaison Department, the SOE, as well as MO4 and MI9. I remember in this connection Beaumont "Beau" Pinney who kept cropping up in the Middle East, he was only a major but always travelled in a priority manner, usually by aircraft. He arrived once by destroyer in the Aegean. We were expecting him, we had received a signal that Major Pinney, CMI, was coming to visit us. I thought: "Now I know why we're always bumping into him, that crown on his shoulder is bogus and he's really only one below the Director of Military Intelligence. This would account for his commanding presence." I decided to ask him outright what the initials stood for. He said: "Don't tell anyone, but I'm the Chief Meat Inspector." He was a wholesale butcher in civilian life.

12

ATHLIT

Levant Schooner Flotilla was a deliberately low-key title as, indeed, was Special Boat Squadron. In such a prying, gossipy city as Beirut, inconspicuousness paid. Hostile eyes sweeping the LSF's remote corner of the harbour would be drawn to the submarine base alongside rather than to the scruffy range of 10-ton to 30-ton wooden caiques that, in Jellicoe's words, had been "cajoled, bribed, paid or chartered to come together".

The water stank, perhaps no worse than anywhere else in the port but enough to make medical officers keep a stomach pump handy; yet the coast beyond the city remained as entrancing as when described thirty years earlier by James Elroy Flecker: "It is towards evening that our cottage on the Lebanon is most beautiful. The sun pours down an intense gold through the garden and all the trees are hung with flowers like lamps." It is a verse from Flecker's "Hassan" that is engraved on the new SAS war memorial at Stirling Lines, their barracks at Hereford:

> We are the Pilgrims, master; we shall go
> Always a little further; it may be
> Beyond that last blue mountain barred with snow
> Across that angry or that glimmering sea.

The pilgrims of 1943 in their beige berets, crêpe-soled boots and blue shirts of fine Indian cotton did not go on with the poet to wonder "Why men were born" but only how to kill them. It was in this frame of mind that Lassen first found them that spring, some 90 miles south of Beirut. The place was Athlit.

John Verney, Jellicoe's adjutant at Athlit and a considerable writer, caught the feel of the place perfectly in describing:

A lovely spring, an ecstasy of fitness and sense of mission . . .
Days and nights spent tramping over thyme-scented
Mount Carmel – in swimming across the bay, in naked
races along the sands, in landing canoes and dinghies on the
rocks watched only by a few tattered Arabs living with
goats and chickens amid the ruins of the Crusader castle . . .
The latrines were buckets emptied by the people of the
Kibbutz. From a distance, and against the evening sky, the
buckets looked like truncated columns of a ruined Greek
temple for the contractor who supplied them had failed to
provide any kind of shelter or partition. Most of the pirates
didn't mind. The site alone, with its view across the
Mediterranean, was worth a visit.

At first, there was no adjutant, no blanco, no parades, no
drill, no bugler and not even a Union Jack on a flagpole. This
informality reflected the spirit of Jellicoe who was the
Commanding Officer, in Verney's opinion, by right of being:

> The most experienced raider and probably the most daring.
> His title was an undeniable advantage in wresting conces-
> sions from senior officers . . . He was a Lieutenant Colonel
> at twenty-four but lived in permanent disorder, with the
> camp littered by his socks, shirts, ties and handkerchiefs.
> His trousers never had buttons; he would turn up at grand
> parties in Haifa wearing sodden, muddy sandshoes or rush
> into the morning sea in the dancing pumps he'd worn all
> night . . . But in the things that really mattered, he was
> extremely efficient and we all loved him.

Jellicoe and his "legitimised pirates", as Verney dubbed
them, hardly constituted a hand-picked audience for the
Army's compulsory lecture on the Beveridge Report, a
thankless task handed one wet afternoon to a chaplain who
had to try interesting these tough, reckless men in a promised
Utopia of free milk and orange juice for expectant mothers.

Athlit, in setting and climate, was an improvement on the
first SBS base in the Suez Canal zone at Kabrit where a wind
like emery-paper scoured the Great Bitter Lake, but the

amenities were still a shock, wrote Verney, to new officers who "arrived expecting a well-ordered Officers' Mess with batmen and silver plate and copies of the *Times Educational Supplement* awaiting perusal over a glass of sherry".

Lassen could never be bracketed with such sybarites; he didn't mind at all that sand might blow down his neck while the mess drank Palestinian burgundy out of tin mugs. Philip Pinckney, his companion from the SSRF, was a young man of even more spartan tastes; he believed that his new comrades of the SBS should learn how to survive in hiding on a diet of wild plants, grasses and weeds. Pinckney therefore concocted "Palestine soup" which made its one and only appearance in British Army rations as the sole course served after an all-day march. The ingredients – various grasses, clovers, dandelions and snails – were boiled into a broth instantly pronounced uneatable despite Jellicoe quashing objections by wolfing down his own bowlful and declaring the dish a surprise test of endurance. Verney wrote drily: "It became a surprise test of bowels, too."

Lassen impressed the men in this unit immediately, as Sutherland recalls:

We were starting training to work up our raiding technique when he suddenly appeared and was dropped into the squadron that I was commanding, and I remember, very early on, a major exercise that George Jellicoe organised to try us all out. This involved marching more or less straight from our camp by the sea to the Lake of Tiberias (the Sea of Galilee) which isn't 50 miles as the crow flies, but was quite far enough. With lying up on the way, doing various manoeuvres and tactics as well as attacking simulated targets, it must have been the thick end of 100 miles. Lassen outmarched us all, he had a quite extraordinary capacity for marching. We thought that we could march a bit but he was far better than all of us. And it so happened that he was far better than all of us at all the martial arts – shooting, thinking tactically, physical endurance, bravery. He really outdid everyone. That's when I first met him and afterwards we were always very close.

153

Vanity was not one of Lassen's noticeable failings but there is no question that he relished a reputation as the master marcher – and his jealous guarding of it led to a personal clash with Dick Holmes:

> We went on a march in Trans-Jordan, three legs of 20 miles each. In my group I had two people from Motor Transport and they both became so badly blistered that we had to stop the night at a Palestine police post and send one man back. Next day another man, Alan Sanders, got sunstroke, so we had to cut corners, doing 50 miles instead of 60. Sutherland came up in a jeep, I explained it to him and he made no complaints; I said that I'd come in next morning.
>
> We were first in next day because we'd had the shorter distance to go. Lassen came in second as we were sitting there. As soon as I saw him, I knew he was furious with me for beating him home. He came over and asked, really nastily, "What happened to you?" So I explained about the blisters and the sunstroke forcing us to cut corners. Sean O'Reilly, senior NCO from the Irish patrol, was with him and Sean was in his forties; Lassen said, "If O'Reilly can do it, surely you can do it!"
>
> Now if there were two members of the SBS entitled to be classed as good marchers then they were me and Roger Wright of "S" detachment. I couldn't shoot worth a damn but, by God, I could march. I could carry a pack and keep on all day – and I was very proud of it. So I exploded at Lassen: "Listen, there's nothing anyone in this regiment can do that I can't do. And that includes you, SIR!" Whereupon I saluted him and walked away. That was my first meeting with Andy Lassen.

This confrontation had been forgotten or, at any rate, buried by the time that Lassen and Holmes, both cited for bravery, returned from raiding Crete to find that training at Athlit had passed into the hands of a Cameron Highlander with this creed: "You should never underwork a unit." His name was John Lapraik – familiarly "Ian" or "Jock" – and the evidence of his importance in SAS history is a hall-marked silver Folbot on a plinth. It bears this inscription: "Presented to Colonel J. N. Lapraik, DSO, OBE, MC, TD, DL on his retirement as Honorary Colonel by all ranks of 21st SAS Regiment, Artists Volunteers, after forty years of SAS service." This replica, so life-like that Lapraik recognised his own posture in the cockpit, commemorated the night when he paddled the 70 miles from Sicily to Malta with his No.2 wounded.

The opportunity for this exploit was owed in a large part to the chivalry of Field Marshal Rommel – as Lapraik related in an interview only a fortnight before his death from a stroke in 1985. He said:

After capture in North Africa, I had been engaging with others in slapping our driving gauntlets against our thighs. German officers still did this and sentries sprang to attention on hearing the sound; they were rather cross to find out that they had leapt to attention for a prisoner.

Rommel, showing what I deemed to be good common sense, came round to see what our morale was like and he said to me, in reasonable English, "I hear you've been annoying some of my young men." I admitted it and then Rommel, undoubtedly a fine man, noticed the bullet wound in my arm and said, "You are wounded. You must go to hospital." This was an excellent move for me because the Germans were going to fly me back that night for the benefit of the Gestapo which I don't think would have been very healthy.

It was even more excellent to find that the doctor at the hospital was a man I had run against pre-war. I ran everything from the mile to a marathon but was most comfortable between three and six miles; I took it up to strengthen my leg after being crippled as a boy by tuberculosis of the knee. My leg was in plaster then for six years. Anyway, it was through running that I met the German doctor and he really was a very good fellow; he gave me the most whacking bandage and I escaped that night with the other walking wounded. We walked across the desert for about 100 miles before commandeering some jeeps back to British lines.

Lapraik fought in Abyssinia with Middle East Commando as something of a rarity, a Commando officer who had never attended Achnacarry; so he started from scratch in designing the assault course for his Commando school on Malta and soldiers who sampled both mostly agreed that Lapraik's course, featuring hurdles of flaming oil drums as well as the usual death-slide and the ground-hugging crawl under machine-gun fire, was tougher than the Scottish original. Lapraik said:

Sometimes the SAS in those days were a little casual towards training, but I believed that training saved lives. I believed in heavy marching. Marching at night on the compass; ultimately, we could land within 600 yards of the target over 20 trackless miles, which was not bad. The maximum training march would be about 70 miles and back-packs as high as 90 lb could be carried because of the demands for weapons and ammunition when on patrol for long periods, also the Mark II wireless was a wicked burden of between 60 and 70 lb. It wasn't so much the set that was weighty but the battery because we rarely had the advantage of plugging in. A 90 lb back-pack was a bit excessive in my opinion – and yet I've seen Stuart Macbeth, a lean man who was my second-in-command of "M" detachment, go out with 95 lb, which is shattering.

Earlier when I was with 51 Commando, an Arab and Jew Commando in Palestine, we set a British Army marching record of 52 miles in fourteen and three-quarter hours – and of that distance rather more than 20 miles was over desert. I tried to give these exercises names that would catch the humour of the troops – "Weary Willie", for instance, involved 40 miles of movement and an attack over trackless country working solely off the compass.

I also had my people out swimming two or three times a week, testing them for endurance and speed – and I used to swim five or six miles myself. But I didn't build an assault course at Athlit, the site wasn't suitable unlike Malta which even drew a visit from the Red Army. General Scobie saw me beforehand and said: "You're living in some style here and I don't want the Russians to see that. There's a general and half a dozen others and it's all when-we-were-in-Stalingrad, which isn't going down too well. So I want things here to be fairly rugged." Well, we stripped the messes and entertained them with beer and hard tack in a room with no chairs. Then we took them on the course and, rather incredibly, organised a little blood-letting when firing with live ammunition down fixed lines.

Lapraik saw immediately that an essential difference between his old Commandos and the SBS was the weaponry:

Commandos had heavier weapons than us. We were lightly but plentifully armed with a mixture of rifles, particularly sniper rifles, the American M1 carbine, and captured German Schmeissers which were superior to the Sten gun in being well-made and not having a safety catch. Perhaps that wasn't so safe, but it made for a better weapon. We also had the Bren gun but didn't carry a lot of them; I thought the Bren's great fault was in penalising inaccuracy quite abominably. It was very good for those who were accurate but, in action, you can't expect accuracy all the time.

This fairly wide choice of weapons wasn't always a good thing because it increased the amount of ammunition that we had to carry. At the same time, I was glad of being able to use such enemy weapons as the Italian grenade. I'd get as many of them as I could, I reckoned it was the best grenade of the war. A little tin grenade, you could carry thirty of them easily. It didn't create as many casualties as our Mills bomb but exploded with frightening loudness – yet, if pushed, you could follow right in behind one.

The Italian grenades, always painted by their manufacturers in a warning scarlet, were known to Lapraik's men as either

"Little Demons" or "Red Devils" after two of Britain's noisiest penny fireworks. Lapraik continued:

> Most of our troops also carried pistols. I had a Colt .45 automatic, a good and heavy weapon. Anyone hit by it was usually out of the game. He spun, at least. There was no possibility of a man who had been running at you being able to carry on running after you'd hit him with a .45. There's quite a kick on a .45 but you grew accustomed to that and you knew your weapon, yet it was very late in the war before the Colt .45 was being widely used by British forces. The Army never understood pistol shooting.

If the British didn't understand pistols, at least they had the sense to send for a man who did. His name was Grant Taylor, Major L. H. Grant Taylor. The only photograph of him in the Imperial War Museum shows a stereotype base officer with clipped moustache, Army glasses and the beginnings of a paunch restrained by his Sam Browne belt, but it also shows bright eyes that reveal how merrily he has entered into the spirit of a propaganda pose with a general pretending to be instructed in handling a tommy-gun. Down in the bottom corner, the camera has caught the clue that reveals Grant Taylor as rather more than he seems . . . An ivory-handled butt protrudes from his left-hand pocket.

Ivory handles are what Dick Holmes remembers from his first sight of Grant Taylor. Also that this thoroughly British officer from the Royal West Kents was American. According to Holmes:

> He was portly, nondescript and looked about 50. He wore a white shirt, khaki shorts and kept sipping from a glass of water but, when he left the lecture room for a moment, one of the lads nipped over to sniff it and said, "It's gin". Taylor, as he talked to us, kept spinning and twirling, cocking and uncocking these two long-barrelled .38s.
>
> There was a stage whisper behind me: "But can the fucker shoot?" One of our officers, deciding to find out, stood up and said: "Excuse me, sir, but I have an unusual

revolver of non-regulation calibre [I think he said it was .455]. I can't get ammunition for it and I'm having to make my own and I wonder if I'm doing it right. Could you advise me?"

Taylor said, "Let's go out the back" and led us through to a range formed from a wall of vertical, wooden railway sleepers. He fished in his pocket, found a small Palestine coin with a hole through it which he lodged behind a splinter on the sleepers. The range was about 10 yards. He said, "Let's have a look at the gun" and then, standing sideways on and firing instantly, he put a bullet straight through the coin's hole. Gravely he handed back the gun, saying, "That's all right". Yes, Grant Taylor could shoot. He was something else!

David Williams, another Military Medallist, was also spellbound by Taylor's wizardry:

He restored my belief in cowboys. I've seen him whip a pistol out of his shoulder holster and then, aiming from the crouch and firing from two yards at a five-of-hearts pinned to the wall, drill each of the four corner hearts and then the drawing pin through the centre. Five shots in a blur of speed. There was still a bullet left, so he turned the riddled card sideways on – and shot it in two when there was only the edge to aim at.

From 10 yards, Grant Taylor would put six bullets through the middle of an ace of hearts. And a playing card, remember, is only three-and-a-half-inches by two and a quarter. He used to tell us: "To shoot like me, you have to be born gifted – but you can get somewhere close with practice." His method was: Right foot forward, go into the crouch, point the gun as you would your finger, drop it about four inches and pull the trigger. The gun was cocked on the roll, pressing with the thumb and not the finger.

He taught us to fire left-handed as well as right, and with both hands together. He taught us to fire low, more points being awarded for shots in the body than in the head. It was said that he'd taught shooting to America's G-men. A few

159

of us, after being instructed by him, could hit an Ideal Milk tin at 50 yards firing a pistol from a crouch. But we never, ever came near to emulating his other speciality of flicking a 10-acker piece in the air, then drawing from his shoulder holster and hitting the coin before it fell.

Fairbairn and Sykes would have approved of Grant Taylor and his insistence on blinding speed and accuracy at ranges that might be despised by target-shooters but not by real gun-fighters. The Shanghai duo knew from experience that the setting for a shoot-out is never high noon in Main Street, nor is the prelude a slow walk and the courtesy of allowing the opponent the first move. Life bears no resemblance to a Western, as Fairbairn and Sykes wrote:

In the great majority of shooting affrays, the distance at which firing takes place is not more than four yards. Very frequently it is considerably less . . . The whole affair may take place in bad light or none at all . . . You may have to shoot from some awkward position, not necessarily while on your feet . . . And if you take much longer than a third of a second to fire your first shot, you will not be the one to tell the newspapers about it.

Britain's two inventors of Shanghai shooting differed from the American Taylor only in the amount of ammunition allocated to their pupils. Fairbairn and Sykes estimated for only twelve rounds a day but they probably never envisaged special service units who would be treated with such lavishness as the SAS and SBS. As Lapraik said:

On the Grant Taylor course, each of us fired 500 rounds and more. His method was based on ammunition. Fire and correct, fire and correct. You cannot train people unless they fire ammunition. Grant Taylor required at his passing-out parade that we hit a playing card at 25 yards. Nicking it was enough. And we were expected to do it five times out of six with the right hand; three times out of six with the left.

Anders Lassen was stamped with the Taylor seal of approval. "A very good weapons man," said Lapraik.

Marched well and was a natural in any scheme. Some people found him a little trying and insubordinate, but I got on with him very well. Most of the officers and pretty well all the sergeants would have followed him anywhere because he knew his job; I say "most officers" because not all of them appreciated his professionalism. They had the idea that Andy was a pirate, which was very far from the truth.

I've heard him compared with Stud Stellin, a New Zealander who came with me from Malta. I knew both of them well and Stellin was all right, but he wasn't in the same league as Andy who could have commanded a battalion. He had a natural eye for ground, for fire, for movement. He didn't need to be told – which I felt was a point too often forgotten about Andy.

He was what he was fortuitously. All the elements of a first-class soldier and very quick-thinking, which is one of the reasons that I felt his death was most uncharacteristic. I'd never known Andy hold fire. It could be said he was a killing-machine; you stayed alive if you became that. Andy and I went into Simi together on my birthday, September 13, in 1943 and it was non-stop for a month. I went back forty years later and my headquarters, which received a direct hit from a Stuka, was exactly as I'd left it, if a bit overgrown – and I wondered if my gear was still there, 30 foot down. Yes, Andy and I saw plenty of life on Simi. He'd been given command of the Irish patrol, an incredible collection of hoodlums – but it worked very well.

13

JELLICOE'S MEN

Jellicoe knew exactly what he wanted when scouring the Mediterranean to expand the SBS: "Volunteers with a certain capacity for physical endurance and the ordinary military skills of being able to shoot straight and quickly. We wanted self-reliant men with initiative and self-discipline, not the imposed discipline of the barrack square. Above anything else, I sought self-starters, men not dependent on an officer telling them what to do." They flocked to him from all over, a rich mixture of backgrounds and nicknames; for instance, the newcomer who insisted that Lapraik's assault course on Malta was severer than the training at Athlit was dubbed for ever "The Maltese Falcon". Christian names were swopped and switched without reason . . . Dick Holmes often found himself being called "Jeff"; Roy Trafford, Lassen's body-guard for a time, was known to all as "Sammy", and "Roger" Wright, MM, long ago abandoned hope of being addressed by his baptismal name of Douglas. The American Porter Jarrell answered to "Joe"; he says "For GI Joe". Unluckiest of all was the rock-fisted Scots Guardsman saddled with the name of his girlfriend. They called him "Myrtle".

Volunteers rallied to Jellicoe for many reasons. Ray Iggleden, an inside forward who played for Leeds United in the 1950s with the great Welsh international John Charles, joined the SBS to escape from football: "I was always being stuck in the C-in-C's staff to play football in Royal Marine bases. I wanted to be in the war and became determined to leave the Marines after what happened to me in Alexandria. I arrived on a damaged ship after being without any sleep for two nights – and was then put on a charge for having dirty boots!"

Alan Sanders, a wireless instructor from the Royal Tank Corps in Cairo, was ready when Jellicoe asked why he wanted to join: "To get away from bed-bugs, the barracks are overrun by them." Jellicoe laughed: "That's the first truthful answer I've heard today. You're in." David Williams was a Royal Marine gunner from X-turret, always the Marine turret, on the cruiser *Penelope* known as HMS *Pepperpot* because it had been hit so often. Jellicoe asked two questions: Could he speak a foreign language. "Schoolboy German, sir." Was he a first-class shot. "I have a marksman's badge, sir."

Paddy Webster was interviewed by Lassen and selected, he thinks, because: "Andy found out that, like him, I'd been in the merchant service and on tankers in the Gulf. He then started talking to me about small boats." Roger Wright says: "I was in the 6th Battalion of the Grenadier Guards near Baghdad, where the food was bad and we did nothing but training. Volunteering for the SAS meant an extra two shillings a day for parachuting, a lot in those days. You had to be an NCO or a former NCO to be accepted, and you had to have been in action – well, I'd been at Dunkirk. But the battalion only let six of us go – all the rum ones, not the goody-goodies. We'd all been in a bit of trouble, although nothing serious."

Sammy Trafford and his friend Tommy Kitchingman were Marine gunners from the cruisers *Orion* and *Euryalus* respectively. They volunteered while bored with guarding trains in Alexandria. Trafford recalls: "Jellicoe accepted thirty Marines at once. We were taken to a camp by Stuart Macbeth and told: 'If anyone wants to know who you are, you're SAS. You'll get a beret in the morning.'"

Dick Holmes says:

In the Grenadier Guards, I had no control over my destiny. It was just the opposite in the SBS where I felt that anything happening to me would be my own fault. I was cheesed off with the Guards and hated discipline; I'd done twenty-eight days in the field punishment centre for refusing to go on parade after coming off a 24-hour guard. They changed it to a bathing parade, but I still wouldn't go. If a Guards officer ordered, "Fix bayonets – and charge", I had to do it. That's what scared me because some officers were incompetent.

We did a night exercise in the Middle East to attack a Scots Guards transport depot and the officer in charge couldn't even take a compass bearing. The silly bugger rested the compass on his pistol and you couldn't explain to him that the metal would affect the reading; in the end, someone else had to do it for him. And that wasn't all . . . when we reached the depot we found it ringed by barbed wire but with an open gate through which lorries were entering slowly. I said to the officer, "We can get inside by jumping on the next lorry." He said: "No, that wouldn't be playing the game." I thought, "God, my life is in his hands. The further I am from him, the better."

Bob Bennett, the Regimental Sergeant-Major of the SAS, came into our camp recruiting. I knew Bob, we'd been prisoners together in the field punishment centre, and said, "Get me out of the Grenadiers" – which he did. I knew a transfer to the SAS meant parachuting, which frightened me, but it was also a move into democracy. For instance, myself and another SBS sergeant were assigned to instruct two South African officers, one of whom was a most objectionable man who wouldn't listen to advice and who kept getting his kit wet. We NCOs recommended that this officer be returned to his unit. Sutherland sent for him and asked if our complaints were true. He replied, "I suppose so," and Sutherland said, "In that case, you're on your way."

Few of Jellicoe's recruits could tell a stranger story than Porter Jarrell, a naturalised American who had been born in Canada and, like Lassen, had followed a long and winding road to the war. He was accepted, in the end, only by memorising the Army's eye-test chart:

In the autumn of 1941, I joined an ambulance unit attached to the Eighth Army. This was the American Field Service, often described as a Quaker organisation, which it isn't. And I'm not a Quaker, either.

I was at El Alamein with 10th Armoured Division and the lines were fluid for weeks with pockets of Italians and

164

Germans everywhere. These lines settled down at one of the wadis with the Germans on one side and our troops on the other side, shouting and cheering as the RAF came over. But the planes attacked us by mistake. The casualties were tremendous.

Medical orderlies don't strike back, you just pick up the bodies and the pieces. But I couldn't help thinking how the widows would have 10 shillings, or something like that, deducted by the War Office to pay for the blanket in which their man had been buried. Only the Japanese treat their soldiers worse than the British.

I didn't wish to continue with the Field Service and decided to volunteer for the American Army only to be told: "With your short sight and flat feet, you couldn't possibly serve in a combat theatre but maybe, if you went back to the States, you might get a job in a base." I said, "Thanks very much." I inquired about joining the Greek Army, the French Foreign Legion and the British Army, but learned from the US Consul in Cairo that I could lose my citizenship by serving in a foreign army under an act designed to prevent Germans and Italians going from the States to fight for the Axis.

Finally, I went into the British Army on condition that I could join the SBS having been given the impression that it was a new guise for the Long Range Desert Group, which I knew as an outfit. But you had to have a proper unit first so Eddie Wells, another American orderly, and myself were put into the Royal Army Service Corps. Then I saw Jellicoe for the first time and he said: "Private Jarrell, I've been looking into your file and am prepared to recommend you for a commission in my regiment, the Coldstream Guards. Would you be prepared to accept?" Well, I'd been next door to an officers' training school for some time, and they drilled longer than anyone else and then began blancoing equipment and polishing boots. So I said: "Thank you very much, sir, but I prefer to remain in the ranks." Jellicoe's offer gave me a strange situation in the SBS; I felt able to float between officers and other ranks although, as an American, I also found myself being held answerable for all the "Dear John" and "Tough shit" letters that arrived from the UK about American soldiers fiddling around with the wives of poor bastards stuck out in the Med.

Jarrell's glasses are like milk-bottle bottoms which, for ease of movement, he taped to his head on entering this unusual life of orderly-cum-combatant in his new unit. He had been in the desert with 10th Armoured, also with two armoured car regiments – the 10th Dragoons and 11th Hussars – and then in the mountains with remnants of the Foreign Legion, but he realised immediately that he had never come across anything like the SBS: "They were really tough people. They had a Cockney barrow boy very proud of literally splitting a man in half with a burst from a Bren. A Glaswegian told me about getting into an argument in Cairo with an American who he knocked down and kicked in the chin before breaking his jugular vein."

Everyone pointed out Duggie Pomford, boxing star of the SAS. Pomford, a Lancashire Fusilier, had already fought alongside one VC in Lieutenant-Colonel Keyes but his renown among the men rested on losing only by a split decision when conceding 10 lb to Bruce Woodcock, later the professional British heavyweight champion. Pomford won an all-England amateur middleweight title in 1938, fighting five times and knocking out the Irish Guards light-heavy champion in the first round. He won two Military Medals and returned from the war to run the Golden Gloves amateur boxing club in Liverpool where he perhaps sometimes remembered an incident recounted by David Williams:

An RAF sergeant climbed aboard an SAS lorry, wanting a lift without asking and obviously looking for trouble. He refused to leave and said so in a most truculent manner. Pomford, only a corporal, then stood up and said: "Sergeant, if you don't leave, I'll put you off." The sergeant sneered, "Who, you?" Pomford's punch knocked him clean over the tailboard.

Pomford was popular and pleasant and, except when wearing gloves, not normally violent but nobody tangled with him

166

willingly – not even Busty Aubrey, who is regarded to this day as possibly the strongest man ever enlisted by the SAS. As with Goliath, precise measurements of Busty's size are unobtainable but there is rough agreement on 6 feet 3 inches and 17 stones. He came from Stone in Staffordshire, according to Sammy Trafford. And according to David Williams: "He was neckless. His head sprang straight from that huge chest and shoulders. I punched him once when I was 14 stone and fit. The blow bounced off him." Trafford remembers Busty on the town, still quietly spoken even with his brain inflamed by drink: "He would try to pull telegraph poles out of the ground and to lift statues; I can still see that squat, massive face straining. He looked like Victor McLaglen, the old film star who'd been an Army heavyweight champion. I think Busty himself had been an Army boxer in India, but in fights outside the ring he would never strike anyone in the face, saying that he disliked spoiling their looks. So he always hit them on top of their heads, bringing down that great fist with the stunning effect of a drop-hammer."

A night out with such tumultuous characters led frequently, if not inevitably, to breaches of the peace. Assisted by some of Nick Benyon-Tinker's seamen from the caique flotilla, they wrecked a cabaret in Famagusta and were banned from shore leave in Cyprus for a month. Benyon-Tinker wrote:

Naval and SBS men found themselves embroiled in a first-class row. Naturally enough, they said, steps had to be taken to defend themselves . . . The cabaret was virtually gutted and the battle transferred itself to the street outside.

Most of our men came back looking as if they had been rolling in the gutter for a week. Gunner MacCormack returned with a chair which he was carrying in an absent-minded fashion. He explained that he must have picked it up to ward off some bottles that were being thrown at him. He had left after this as he thought the party was "Just a little too rough, sorr" (this from Mac, who would rather fight than eat) and went in such a hurry that he completely overlooked the fact that he still had the chair in his hand. And with this he brightened up considerably and put forward, in a wheedling and honeyed voice, that as the chair was on board by now it hardly seemed worthwhile taking it back. "It's just made for the wardroom, sorr!" What was one to do?

The King's Bar in Haifa made the mistake one night of rejecting an SBS request to play "God Save the King". David Williams was present: "So we threw their piano through the window, from three floors up". In Cairo, the favoured drinking spot was a bar called Sweet Melody; in Beirut, it was The Hole in the Wall which Williams called, "A sleazy den whose only attractions were English records and a woman who sang 'Smoke gets in Your Eyes'." The canteen of the 11th Battalion of the Parachute Regiment was also favoured with a visit after a disagreement between three of their members and Alan Sanders: "I was wearing a plaster cast when the three of them attacked me and I managed to gash the cheek of one with the plaster. So I was able to tell the lads, 'Not only did 11th Para do it, but I'll recognise one of them.' Duggie Pomford and eleven other mates then went round with me to the para's canteen. We wrecked it."

The SBS, as have troops from time immemorial, divided roughly into what A. E. Housman called in another context, "The lads for the girls and the lads for the liquor." Their new Danish officer was one of both at heart as Sutherland testifies:

Andy Lassen was very good on the drink when there was no action around, and he was a great womaniser. He let slip that he had been living for a time in London as a guest of Count Edward Reventlow, the Danish Ambassador . . . then wondered out loud: "What would he have said if he'd known that I'd slept with his parlour maids? Two out of three!" Typical Andy. No girl was safe. He was so very good-looking.

Slim, blond handsomeness, though, was no short cut to the hearts of Grenadiers, Coldstreams, Scots and Irish Guards, Royal Marines, Durham Light Infantry, Royal

Scots, Lancashire Fusiliers et cetera, among whose ranks were sundry veterans of detention quarters and glasshouses, as well as sergeants and corporals with histories of sudden demotion and equally rapid reinstatement. These men, schooled through the mill of square-bashing, spud-peeling, and boot-boning until the toe-caps gleamed like patent leather, comprised a quizzical, potentially hostile audience for a stranger with no regimental background and no grip on his Vs and Ws – never mind that he had one Military Cross and another in the pipeline.

Many men shared the first reaction of that down-to-earth Midlander David Williams: "I didn't want a foreigner telling me what to do!" Some of the SBS may have thought they detected a reciprocal hostility in Lassen, a suspicion voiced by Dick Holmes: "I felt he was contemptuous of the British; that he really didn't like us at all. He liked the Irish, though. He had a lot of time for the Micks." Ray Iggleden saw it another way: "He was a Dane in British forces and had to prove himself – which he did by becoming, like Paddy Mayne, the man talked about whenever raiding forces were discussed."

Lassen needed time to reach that status. Meanwhile, mocking stories circulated. There was one about taking morning parade as orderly officer and asking Sergeant Nicholson, "Do I say something?" Nicholson replied, "Yes, sir. Dismiss the men." To which a baffled Lassen is supposed to have responded, "But what do I say?" It was also claimed that Lassen, growing furiously impatient with his failures to spell "rendezvous" on a notice-board, crossed the word out and wrote an alternative: "meat".

Early doubts about Lassen were natural enough among working-class Britons of the time who, insular by geography and education, grew up believing that the only foreigners who were not either villains or comic fools were those with the good luck to live on the vast tracts of the globe that the school maps coloured Empire red. The SBS were also men who questioned everything, especially the unexplained arrival of an unusual officer. "We always asked 'Why?', something not encouraged among ordinary soldiers," said David Williams. "That's the wonderful thing about the SAS Regiment – they let you think. The only place for a bright lad in the Army is with the irregulars."

Nobody could have silenced scoffers and doubters faster than Lassen in the autumn of 1943. He won his first Military Cross partly in the seclusion of the Channel Isles and partly in the unpublicised raid on Fernando Po. His second Military Cross was gained before a British audience of only three on Crete, but his third was won on the Dodecanese island of Simi where everyone could see him . . . British, Germans, Italians and Greeks.

14

SIMI

The church bells of Simi rang out the joyful tidings within minutes of Lassen and Pomford stepping upon the town quay. Their Folbot reconnaissance of the blacked-out harbour turned instantly into a Greek liberation gala of kisses, handshakes, hastily fashioned garlands, proffered tots of ouzo – and such a bedlam of well-meant, contradictory information about the water's depth that Lassen settled the matter with, even for him, startling directness. He jumped in fully clothed and, on glugging back to the surface, told Pomford: "Call them in."

On this signal, Lapraik and some forty men in two motorboats entered the narrow bay beneath the steep little town where they would rule unchallenged for nearly a month. It was September 17, 1943, the Friday before Lassen's twenty-third birthday five days later. Similar raiding groups fanned throughout the Dodecanese in the wake of Italy's surrender after pressing into service almost anything that floated – Harbour Defence Motor Launches, the big, but slow, Fairmile launches, the RAF's high-speed rescue boat, two Free French sloops and, chugging along behind, Seligman's caiques sporting recognition signals (a splash of red paint on the deck, green trousers dangling from the rigging) for the benefit of any RAF planes that could be spared to cover a sweep combining brilliance and bluff in equal proportions.

Island after island – Leros, Cos and Samos among them – were seized with hardly a shot from the Italians and under the noses of the German generals in Athens, Crete and Rhodes. Lassen and Pomford on their own planted the Union Jack on three of the smaller islands next day, breakfasting on Piscopi, lunching on Alimnia and taking tea on Calchi. They returned with an Italian 20 mm gun removed by Lassen from Alimnia and needing only a small repair by Simi's blacksmith to make

171

THE AEGEAN

0 ——————— 100
Miles
0 ——————— 150
Km

BLACK
SEA

TURKEY

GREECE

Salonika

AEGEAN SEA

TURKEY

Chios

Athens

Samos

Patmos

Deremen

Leros

Paros

Kalimnos

Bodrum

Yedi
Atala

Naxos

Cos

Amorgos

Nisiros

Kiervasili

Santorini

Alimnia
Calchi

Rhodes

Kastelli
Pediada
airfield

Heraklion

CRETE

MEDITERRANEAN SEA

it workable. "No Jerries", they reported . . . but von Klemann on Rhodes was thinking already: "No, but there soon will be!"

German counter-attacks could not be repelled everywhere by troops spread as thinly as Raiding Forces, so the Allies concentrated on defending Cos, with its three landing strips, and Leros, with its seaplane base, submarine pens and floating dock. A squadron of Spitfires, some Bofors anti-aircraft guns and nearly 3,000 reinforcements were sent to these strongpoints while Lapraik was left on Simi to do the best he could. He thought of trying to hold Calchi, a nearby isle that was close to Rhodes but had been vacated by the Germans, and Lassen was sent to examine the possibilities. Lassen found the ground too rocky for digging-in and the best defensive position too susceptible to a mortar attack. His only hope lay in the resident Italian carabinieri, a dozen paramilitary police who he hustled through an improvised assault course and warned: "Resist the Germans if they return or I'll come back and have you all shot for cowardice."

The carabinieri didn't doubt him; he was the very figure of fervour and conviction, a warrior who sensed the struggle turning his way both in the Aegean and the Baltic. The news from Denmark heartened him: strikes in the shipyards, Resistance bombs in Copenhagen, the Government rejecting German demands to try Danish saboteurs in Nazi courts. Best of all, the population's provocation of the Germans to the point where General von Hanneken declared martial law, although too late to stop the scuttling of twenty-six Danish merchant ships earmarked for confiscation. Lassen, who had thought the Danes would never rise up, wrote promptly to Count Reventlow: "You never doubted for a moment that the day would come. It did come and I have never been so proud in all my life."

The Dodecanese, after three years of wartime privation, generally fitted Benyon-Tinker's description of Casteloriso, the first SBS conquest: "Poverty-stricken, reeking of decay and misery." All the islands simmered with hatred of their gorgeously uniformed, wasp-waisted oppressors as Porter Jarrell says:

The Fascists on Simi had been bastards, dyed-in-the-wool nationalists who beat up Greeks for not saluting the Italian flag. The Greeks, who had been ringing bells, jumping up and down and hailing us as liberators, wanted freedom for revenge. Then they found that we had to protect the Italians from them – and they just couldn't understand the niceties of the situation.

Lapraik was the last man who might unleash a local populace on his prisoners. He had a code and no qualms about enforcing it as he showed at the end of the war when Allied Military Governor on Chios, a large island near the approaches to the important Turkish port of Izmir:

I gave just one warning to a Petty Officer from Special Service who had been ill-treating German prisoners. I told him to stop the beatings, but he didn't. Some 4,000 Germans were under my control and I arranged that as many as possible saw my next step which was to draw my pistol and hit him across the face with it. The effect on the Germans was electrifying.

Lapraik's obvious integrity helped in aligning a proportion of the Italian garrison on the side of his defenders although he knew only limited reliance could be placed on soldiers whose own war was over. The days of trial, though, seemed far away that September as the SBS found Simi: "A place where we lay in the sun and jugged it up." Patrols hopped on and off Rhodes in classic SAS style although Stud (nobody called him Dion) Stellin was once forced to make an unclassical exit under the straw of a mule cart. They listened for von Klemann's starting pistol, but the Allies were still taken by surprise.

A seaborne assault on Cos was supported by paratroopers – "Toughest fighters in the German Army, tougher even than the Waffen SS," Hitler had once said – and it was followed by the landing of 120 Germans on Simi. Lapraik told me: "They came up by Pedi Bay, just south of the main port. I hadn't enough troops to control all the bays, so I had to rely

174

on information. By the time it was received, the Germans were well-established. Yet we defended successfully, killing and wounding about 40 of them and getting the Italians to put in a charge – because they had our guns behind them."

Hank Hancock, an SBS sniper and Bren gunner who had been in the Royal Armoured Corps, fleshes out his commander's account:

The 20 mm Breda that Lassen brought back was our heavy artillery. We mounted it on a hill dominating one side of the harbour and beside a school occupied by our patrol led by Lassen. We saw a large, unidentified caique sailing by the harbour mouth and opened fire with our gun, whereupon the boat zoomed into harbour and we found that the occupants were about twenty RAF men sailing merrily to Cos in broad daylight, not knowing it had fallen.

They were ground crew and maintenance men with a few spare pilots and a doctor from the squadron led by South African ace "Sailor" Malan, No.74 Squadron of Fighter Command. Hancock said:

They were allocated to our patrol so we began to split the duties between the RAF and ourselves. Lassen, in preparation for a reconnaissance on Rhodes, decided one evening on a good night's sleep and said: "The RAF can do the duty." In that time, the Germans came. The RAF let them come, they didn't think there was anything odd. The Germans literally landed at dawn, tied up their boat and walked ashore not knowing we were there.

They knew from a map what places to occupy, the strategic places that we'd already taken, and they were heading in those directions with their guns slung over their shoulders, unaware of anything. Lassen as soon as he looked down and saw the boats realised something was wrong. "Who the hell are they?" he asked. "Where have they come from?" The RAF said: "Well, they've just sort of landed." He sent two or three of our guys down a steep, narrow road. Our chaps were running down, the Germans were walking up and both parties passed each other in the rush but our chaps happened to be a bit quicker and captured them. They dragged the Germans up the hill where Lassen questioned them and said: "There's a landing going on." He then sent out the patrol while he stayed with me right on top of the hill where we had a machine-gun.

The 20 mm was a bit lower down and the RAF manned that. The Germans must have signalled that Simi was occupied because three Stukas flew over trying to bomb our position. The RAF guys shot one of them down with the Breda and they told us: "It's impossible for the Germans to hit this spot. Their bombs will always fall short because of the angle of approach needed to avoid the hills." We hoped they were right; in fact, it was true. The Germans couldn't bomb our 20 mm.

Lassen soon left his hill-top and sought action in the cobbled and higgledy-piggledy alleys of the old town. "He could actually smell Germans," said Sean O'Reilly who went with him. "He suddenly stopped by a wall and, sure enough, two Germans were sitting behind it. We fired over their heads and they surrendered." Simi was practically designed for someone with Lassen's zest for silent killing. He could hide in doorways and round corners, soundless in his crêpe soles while the Wehrmacht boots rang and echoed through the maze.

He ought to have been in hospital, not in action. Dysentery had weakened him and the backs of his legs were blistered and festering from nasty, but avoidable, burns. Hancock says: "We built a latrine on Simi surrounded by piles of uncemented stones like a dry-stone wall. To make it more hygienic, he poured in petrol and put a match to it. The latrine exploded and flames shot through the cracks in the walls, badly burning his bare legs. He then hit on the ingenious idea of hanging mosquito veil from the belt of his shorts and tucking it into his stocking tops to keep off the flies. But he should have had proper medical attention because he was in a rather rough state. Probably anyone else would have been shipped back."

Wonderment at Lassen's refusal to be unfit is noticeable in the citation for his third Military Cross, a document marked "Most Secret" and "Not to be gazetted" and which is signed by Colonel Douglas Turnbull, Commanding Raiding Forces, by Lieutenant-General Sir Desmond Anderson, Commanding 3rd Corps and by General H. Maitland Wilson, Commander-in-Chief, Middle East. It begins by stating: "This officer, most of the time a sick man, displayed outstanding leadership and gallantry" and goes on to record: "He, himself with a badly burned leg and internal trouble, stalked and killed three Germans at the closest range."

No range is closer than a knife thrust and that may be the implication. It fits Lassen as seen by Hancock:

Once he got going he'd kill anyone. He was frightening in that way – and his view of the Germans was more personal than ours because his country was occupied. I think he was driven by the occupation although it's difficult to assess if the killing instinct used the war as an excuse or whether it sprang from genuine hatred of the enemy. But I do know that if he had the opportunity he'd kill someone with a knife rather than shoot, which seemed a bit odd to me.

Dick Holmes was told by an eye-witness: "Lassen on Simi gave the impression of putting himself in a trance so that he saw no danger in anything." The citation strikes a similar note:

The heavy repulse of the Germans on October 7, 1943, was due in no small measure to his inspiration and leadership . . . At that time, the Italians were wavering and their recovery is attributed to the personal example and initiative of this officer . . . In the afternoon, he led the Italian counter-attack which finally drove the Germans back to their caiques with the loss of sixteen killed, thirty-five wounded and seven prisoners as against our loss of one killed and one wounded.

Lassen directed the Italians as well as leading them. His patrol, guns at the ready, marched behind their new, rather reluctant, allies in a demonstration of what the British Army means by "advice and backing" which is: "You may, only *may*, be shot by the enemy but if you run away you *will* be shot by us."

The Stukas returned next morning, wave after wave every two hours, to win in the air where the Germans had lost on the ground. Hancock said: "It was a shuttle service – take off from Athens, refuel in Rhodes, bomb Simi or Leros and fly back to Greece." Jarrell said:

> Until then I'd seen war only in the desert where it was a giant chess game for soldiers only. Simi was my first experience of civilian involvement, of seeing poor old people pawing in the rubble to recover their possessions from houses that disintegrated in the bomb blasts because they were built without mortar. Stukas were obsolete and slow but they could attack us with impunity because we had no air cover.

The Junkers 87 dive-bomber, the Stuka, was ungainly and unmistakable. A weapon of terror. Its fixed undercarriage housed a siren that froze the blood of refugees and retreating armies as well as sailors caught out of convoy in the North Sea and English Channel. The long, greenhouse cockpit sheltered a rear-gunner and, invariably, a mad pilot whose pride, as he screamed towards the prey at 70 degrees, lay in releasing the bomb at the last possible inch below the recommended minimum of 300 feet. Roger Wright said: "They would come down to about 100 feet with the siren blowing and we could see the pilot laughing at us. A terrible thing. Anyone who has been Stuka'd never forgets it." The Stuka's weakness was lack of speed, only slightly more than 230 mph. Fighters shot them down like grouse, but there were no fighters on Simi.

Forty civilians were killed in the first two raids and two servicemen, one RAF and one SBS, when Lapraik's headquarters fell in ruins after a direct hit in the lunchtime attack. Jarrell, yet to join Lassen's patrol, was the medical orderly at headquarters and his deeds that day and through a long night won him the George Medal. He still cannot bring himself to speak about performing an amputation by candlelight with a wood-saw while under air-attack, but a report and citation tell the story.

Corporal Sidney Greaves, MM, from the Royal Engineers, and Guardsman Tommy Bishop, from the Grenadiers, were trapped in the headquarters rubble. A rescue party led by Sergeant Whittle, a former miner, tunnelled towards the two SBS men and an RAF doctor, Flight Lieutenant Leslie Ferris, who had been injured and bombed out of his dispensary, came to help and later wrote this report:

Rescue work carried on ceaselessly in spite of continued air attacks. Because of the dangerous condition of the walls, it was not possible to free both men at once.

So, having made an airway to the one most deeply buried, we commenced to free the other. Towards dawn next morning it became obvious that amputation of a leg was imperative if either was to be saved. As my instruments and equipment had been lost in the building, others were procured from the civilian doctor. These consisted of a few artery forceps, dissecting forceps, tourniquets, scalpels, scissors and an ordinary small saw. Amputation was attempted just above the knee as the lower part of the leg was firmly trapped.

It was only with great difficulty that he could be reached and the position for working was a very awkward one. Tourniquets were applied and the operation was carried out under chloroform. The patient was then brought from among the debris. A few minutes after intravenous blood plasma was started, the patient died. It was only as a life-saving measure that the operation was attempted, and he had been suffering from shock and bomb blast, together with crushing injuries. It was now possible to start work to free the other man and, due to the valiant efforts of the working party and the SBS nursing orderly, this was accomplished. By way of the airway, morphia had been injected and water had been passed by means of a rubber tube. In spite of this, however, he died before he could be extricated.

179

Doctor Ferris, who was awarded the MC on Simi, looked back in 1987 and said:

> It was one of the most horrific operations I've seen. I couldn't perform it myself because I had a wrist injury through falling on the rocks, so I could only guide the SBS orderly [Jarrell], a fantastic bloke with his Red Cross on one shoulder and a machine-gun over the other. I was held upside down temporarily to see better what was required as we worked by candlelight. The men were terribly pinned down. They hadn't a hope in hell, but we thought that we had to try something – and operating was the only thing left.

The George Medal citation records that:

> Jarrell, acting with Sergeant Whittle, worked for 27 hours without rest to the point almost of collapse, exposing himself to extreme personal risk. He continued work throughout two further raids when a bomb falling any-where would have brought the remnants of the building upon him . . . He entirely disregarded personal risk, crawling along perilous tunnels through the debris to administer morphia, feed and cheer the trapped men. Owing to the RAF doctor having an injured wrist, under the doctor's supervision in appalling conditions, by candle-light, on his back, he did most of the leg amputation necessary to release one man.

Additional notes by Doctor Ferris reveal the primitive conditions on Simi. Water, obtainable only from deep wells, had to be sterilised or boiled for drinking. Medical supplies were restricted to the minimum and he commented: "It was only after protesting that I was allowed to take even this small amount along." Sanitary arrangements were "Very unsatisfactory. Each house had its own latrine which, as a rule, was foul smelling, dirty and of the squatting variety. The systems were always clogged."

His case list began with treating two SBS men for malaria,

two more for shrapnel wounds received on Rhodes and, when the street fighting began, SBS Captain Charles Bimrose who insisted on continuing patrols despite having two bullets lodged, side by side, in his right forearm. Lassen was also a stubborn patient: "I saw him on the island, he was patrolling with diarrhoea. I was running behind him trying to give him a dose of medicine but couldn't catch him."

Lapraik, twice ordered to withdraw from his hopeless position, yielded to the extent of evacuating prisoners and some wounded on the evening of the raid that wrecked his headquarters. Four days later he abandoned the island, but Lassen returned within a week to snatch eight Fascists and blow up a radio station before entering the serious fighting on Leros.

15

BOOTS FOR THE GREEKS

The first bombs on Leros landed by the brothel: "Whereupon the girls fled for the caves followed quickly by the Italian seaplane force." The witness – Hugh Stowell, Staff Officer (Operations) at the naval base – was seeing the start of 1,000 Luftwaffe sorties against an island too rocky for an airfield and too far away for defence by the RAF in Cyprus . . . "We had no long-range fighters available and the Americans wouldn't lend us any of theirs," said Stowell. "So the Aegean was just about the last place where the Germans had air superiority."

Dornier flying boats scouted for ships, naval or merchant, worthy of attack by their radio-controlled glider bombs. Two Allied destroyers were sunk. Mines were dropped in the shipping lanes and, as at Cos and Simi, the Stukas came in wailing waves, tiring and demoralising a garrison swollen to 3,000 but without adequate means of firing back.

Leros looked a natural fortress. Coastal batteries on the high headlands protected the almost land-locked harbour; inland, the scrub-covered switchback of hills and boulders offered cover to defenders while limiting the movements of attackers but, even as the first casualties were counted, Major-General Ronald Scobie briefed war correspondents in Cairo to expect the worst: "We intend to do all we can to hang on to both Leros and Samos, but it would be idle and useless to pretend that the position is in any way secure."

In fact, the island fell faster than anyone had imagined. Surrender was agreed only five days after the main German assault on November 12, 1943. Messerschmitts strafed the defenders and dropped anti-personnel bombs while seaborne troops tried to land behind a smokescreen. The decisive thrust was the seizure of the island's narrow waist by paratroops landing on successive days.

Tony Grech, an RAF officer, watched with Lassen as the

parachutes floated down: "Andy and I had a beautiful view and it would have been like potting sitting ducks. I had just been given a carbine and I was tempted but Andy – and this was hardly the remark of an alleged killing-machine – told me: 'Don't do it. You'll only attract them to our head-quarters.' "

Defensive tactics on the first day put an emphasis on weakening the paratroops by capturing or destroying their containers of heavier weapons and ammunition. Nature did much of the killing on the second day when two of the Junkers 52 troop carriers went down in the sea while a small gale dragged and battered other jumpers against walls and rocky outcrops but, bloodily, the Germans prevailed with their dive-bombers, mortars and landing parties against a garrison ever shorter of sleep, supplies, anti-aircraft shells and effective communications.

Jellicoe and some four dozen of the SBS were among the 250 Allied servicemen to escape the trap at Leros, as did Stowell and Grech. They were preceded by Lassen who had been sent with a patrol of stalwarts – Wright, Holmes, Nicholson and Jarrell among them – to the more northerly but, as General Scobie had feared, equally untenable island of Samos. Lassen set up headquarters in Bathy, a port once thronged with wine-shippers and buyers and ox-carts trundling great tuns of Muscat along the quays. It was now deserted. The people had moved into caves or sought whatever shelter might be offered in the olive groves and vineyards.

Lassen's mission with a lighter and a tank landing craft was to evacuate wounded servicemen to Turkey and then as many refugees as possible. He found the Italian garrison pleading to come, too. The Italians knew the fate in store when the Germans recaptured Samos; two months earlier they had heard of 5,000 Italians being shot in the Ionian island of Cephalonia for resisting the Germans.

Jarrell:

At the end, we were left with only one caique which could carry no more than forty people. Andy told us: "Make the Italians and Greeks line up to come aboard from each side,

183

one at a time." Well, we were outnumbered by hundreds. They rushed us and the boat sank. One Italian was in such a hurry that he dropped his pack which burst open, revealing nothing but boot soles. I wondered if he intended setting up in Turkey as a cobbler.

The mainland was a mile away but looked closer, as distances do across water. The frantic Italians begged Lassen to float a rope from shore to shore, claiming they could then cross the narrows without boats. Lassen accepted the plan against his better judgment and the advice of his men, a decision that seems to indicate the strain of a situation where he felt he had to be seen to be doing something.

Holmes recalls: "He kept saying: 'We'll do it, we'll do it'. He wouldn't give way. We spent the whole afternoon tying on petrol cans to buoy up the rope, but the first Eyetie to use it sank after 50 yards. Ferrying was the only way." The ferrying was resumed in the safety of darkness and the SBS, using a rowing boat and a small schooner, carried 150 refugees to safety on that final night. The last three off Samos were Sergeant Nicholson, Lassen and his new pet, a mongrel dog he had picked up on Leros.

Somewhat to Lassen's annoyance, a picture of him on Samos appeared in *Parade*, a magazine for British forces. He, Nicholson, Wright, Holmes and a few others are seen sheltering in a rocky ditch during a Stuka attack. Lassen objected: "What sort of photo is that? Me hiding?" The answer ought to have been that it's an historic photograph, the only one of him showing normal fright. His face is tight and ghastly pale; once again, as on Simi and Leros, he was being bombed while powerless to strike back.

Wright: "We had no ack-ack but only Bren guns which were practically useless against planes." Holmes said:

The slit-trench was about 50 yards from a house that we were using. We were dive-bombed in it by half a dozen Stukas. I was shit-scared but Lassen was petrified. His head was down and shaking. I heard him sucking in his breath.

He hated aeroplanes and he hated parachuting. It must

have taken a great deal of courage for him to overcome those fears and complete the course for his jumpers' wings. He never jumped after training. And he was frightened when enemy planes were in sight, as many of us were . . . but that day on Samos he couldn't conceal it.

Grech agrees:

He had been hit on the head by a falling beam in a bombed house and, as a result, seemed to lose his nerve for about three days but he came round again. When we next teamed-up in 1944, first in Athens but mainly in Crete, he was the old Andy who knew no fear and who was the embodiment of patriotism. He believed in "gloria est pro patria mori". As I got to know him well, I found that he was also extremely kind and not vicious in any way.

Lassen and Nicholson were the last off Samos. Their departure marked the end of the Dodecanese campaign or, rather, the end of its first act. Temporary internment lay ahead. The British were penned on a beach near the small Turkish town of Kasadasi until being herded on a cattle train that chugged slowly to Aleppo in Syria, a 600-mile journey that took three nights.

Holmes remembers:

There was only enough room in the wagons to lie down in our sleeping bags. I was in the same wagon as Lassen and Pipo, a little monster in my opinion. Pipo pissed on a couple of sleeping bags and Lassen thought it a great joke; I saw him grinning when the dog then stopped by my gear so I warned him: "If that bloody animal soils my bag, I'll kick his arse right out of the door." We were all disarmed, we had no weapons of any kind: Lassen looked at me, saw that I meant it and did nothing – except for giving a half-hearted grin.

The train ride, although cramped and tedious, was jollier than that exchange suggests. The men disguised as civilians –

which, in practice, meant not wearing badges, stripes or flashes – jumped off at every stop to scrounge hot water from the engine driver for a brew of tea, or to bribe him with processed cheese into allowing them to use his boiler-plate as a grill. They were in good spirits because leave was due and the next action seemed far away; in fact, two months went by before the SBS could strike a second blow at the enemy.

The Germans used this lull to tighten their grip on Greece and the islands. The Italians, their erstwhile allies, were offered the bleak choice between fighting for Hitler or being sent to prison camps. Civilian resistance was crushed, wherever possible, with brisk brutality; tanks sometimes steamrollering houses and their occupants, too – if they weren't nippy. A wholesale reprisal was inflicted on a small, mainland town in December 1943. This was Kalavrita on the hills above the Gulf of Corinth. The church clock in the square is still stopped at 2.34, the hour when the Germans executed every male over the age of fifteen. There were 1,346 of them, grandfathers to schoolboys.

Chios, an island with a population of 62,000 in 1943, can serve as a typical example of life for the Greeks under the Germans. The occupation years of 1941–44 have been documented in the most careful detail by Philip Argenti and show that, exactly as happened after Appleyard and Lassen's raid on Sark, the threat of further attacks was met by withdrawal to a central strongpoint combined with severe restrictions on civilians.

Caiques not required for regular fishing were beached, riddled with rifle fire or stripped of planks to make them unusable. Boat-owners were formed into watches and threatened with punishment if their vessels were stolen for crossings into Turkey. Terror was spread by random arrests of hostages, German patrols would walk into cafés and pick out men to be taken away; as they did so, the streets emptied in minutes. Wealthier hostages were selected from the telephone directory; from time to time, the Germans would fan out quietly by car at night and encircle a town for identity checks at road-blocks.

"Treachery was not a problem in any of the Greek islands,"

186

says Colonel Sutherland. Everyone who served with him and with Jellicoe and Lassen agrees heartily with that statement; the Greeks would rather die than talk. Yet Argenti shows that Germans on Chios "relied heavily on informers, paid or spiteful"; these traitors talked to the Geheime Feld Polizei, the Secret Field Police, an organisation headed on the island by two former theology students, Locker and Wisbar. In the background, there was a mysterious intelligence and counter-espionage service – "the true Gestapo", wrote Argenti – disguised as economic advisers, the Wirtschaftkomission, but known to the Germans as AST, the Abwehrstelle.

Locker, Wisbar and their fellow Nazis treated suspects roughly and badly after softening them up by imprisonment without food in rat-infested cellars where human bones were scattered on the floors. Interrogation embraced any, or all of these methods: pistol-whipping of the head and face; flogging with a three-stranded whip of ox-sinews; firing a pistol behind the prisoner's neck as a reminder of his nearness to death and, a further torture, forcing him to lie face-down with roped feet while a rifle was twisted to tighten the rope unbearably.

The Germans were desperate men striving to hold Greece against growing unrest and the increasing strength of what the British loosely lumped together as "Andartes" (guerillas) but who were, in fact, from groups often nearly as opposed to each other as they were to Hitler. The Communist-organised National Freedom Front had its military wing in ELAS; the Greek Democratic National Army (neither democratic nor national, but extremely right-wing) fought as EDES. Smaller in numbers, but high in prestige, the Hieros Lochos (Sacred Company) fought for the British as special service troops, each of its members a Greek officer who had undertaken to serve in the ranks. The name commemorated a unit of Thebans who had died to a man fighting in 338 BC against the Macedonians. The Sacred Company (or "Squadron", as the British had it) were royalists, a minority cause; King George II was welcomed into exile by Britain as "a very gallant ally" although seen by many of his subjects as something of a Fascist sympathiser.

The essence of the Greek political situation was distilled

187

into four words by Francis Noel-Baker, MP, in his book, *Greece – the Whole Story* when he wrote, "There were no moderates." This fragmentation of opposition availed the Germans nothing for their own position had been weakened seriously by transfers to the Russian front. In 1942, a year before the first British attacks on the Dodecanese, the garrison of Chios was down to a single company of the 11th Grenadiers and two dozen Volkdeutsche, half-trained Home Guards or Territorials, from Poland.

Disease and famine raged around the occupiers. Outbreaks of scabies, pleurisy, trachoma, a rise in malaria and a surge in tuberculosis were reported on Chios. Food shortages sent the death rate soaring; in 1942, deaths quadrupled in Chios, also in Athens and Salonika. Meat was scarce, so were milk, butter and cheese. The villages had no bread. Ration cards were useless, the commodities they guaranteed were non-existent because, although air-power had secured the islands, the Germans lacked the sea-power to supply them.

Scarcity of fodder forced a slaughtering of pack-mules, the peasants' basic transport. Cattle died, too. Barter replaced cash trading, even for medical attention; two pounds of corn, or dried vegetables became a standard payment to doctors. Help, though, was on its way. SBS caiques – canvas dodgers along their gunwales keeping them less wet, if never entirely dry – set out in 1944 on a form of milk round dropping off ration cartons and footwear around the islands. The footwear, according to Colonel Lapraik, was "Indian Army boots. I always kept a stock of 200 pairs. They were high and stapled, a very basic boot when compared to ours but they fitted the Greeks better than anything else."

Lassen was an enthusiastic participant – indeed, a pioneer – in these deliveries. Jarrell says: "We went back together to Simi after the evacuation because it was Andy's idea, which I encouraged, to take in food for the islanders." It was a visit which supported Jellicoe's view that Lassen had:

A great deal of humanity and got on incredibly well with caique skippers, fishermen and crews. He was a natural leader – of that, there's no doubt whatsoever – and I've

always felt that Andy would have played a not inconsider-
able role in Denmark if he'd survived. He had all the
qualities of the buccaneering Viking – extraordinary courage, physical endurance, devil-may-care and keenness on
the girls. But there was something much deeper – a real
feeling for people and situations. A certain gentleness, too.

Lassen was ordered to hospital before being cleared to rejoin
the SBS for a resumption of action in January 1944. This was
his third spell of prolonged treatment since enlistment. His
health, as indicated by the kidney trouble at school, was never
robust. Neglect, heavy smoking, tinned food, strain and
insufficient rest didn't help. He found a familiar face in the
next bed – Hugh Stowell from Leros who had become Staff
Officer (Special Operations) to Coastal Forces:

> We were alongside in the 8th General Hospital in
> Alexandria at the end of '43 or, perhaps, early '44. Pipo was
> with him. When the doctors came round, the dog was
> shoved into my bed and I had to keep him quiet. I left
> before him after three or four days and during that time we
> talked in general terms but he was still on – and very
> understandably – about wanting to kill as many Germans as
> he could. He was a tense fellow, very highly strung. Not
> raving, though, but in very good form.

Lassen had previously been in hospital at Nazareth some four
months earlier, shortly before the capture of Simi, Leros, Cos
and the other islands. The next bed was occupied by Canon
Arthur Walter, a chaplain to the Parachute Regiment, who
remembers:

> He had yellow fever, hepatitis – and at times he was raving,
> out of his mind. He had bad dreams with a certain amount
> of hysterical talk to which I lent a sympathetic ear although
> I can't remember the details. He was very tense, tightly
> coiled – a wild young boy. Very often, in my impression, he
> was not aware of all that he was doing.
> Without denigrating the bravery, I think he was one of

189

those people who act without foreseeing the consequences. Something had to be done, so they go and do it regardless of their own safety. I acted, more or less, as father confessor while he lay naked on the bed and poured out his inner pressures. In action, he would be physically alert but mentally relaxed; afterwards, it would be the complete reverse.

He would be fatigued but as taut as a spring, and then he would have to find someone with whom he could unwind as he talked over the men he'd killed. I don't know if the tension clarified the action as he tried to find faults in it; certainly, it didn't stem from guilt. A guilt complex was the last thing Andy had; his deep feelings were about getting one back at the Germans. He was very restive in hospital and wanted to be out doing something.

Action behind the lines – always outnumbered, often hunted and without hope of reinforcement – examined a man's morale to the utmost. For instance, Colonel Sutherland and a Marine called Duggan found themselves, after three nights of pursuit across Rhodes in 1942, hiding in the crevice of a rock on which an Italian soldier then sat, swinging his boot back and forth inches from Sutherland's face. Colonel Lapraik was on a Harbour Defence Motor Launch off Stampalia in the Dodecanese when he found himself hastily obeying one of the war's most amazing orders: "A German destroyer rounded the headland and our skipper ordered: 'Open fire. Abandon ship'. He swept the destroyer's bridge with Brens and every weapon he'd got before giving the 'Abandon ship'. My God, it was close because the HDML was entirely obliterated by the return fire."

Stress is a natural consequence of such escapes . . .

One young officer on his first raid was so stricken by nerves that he couldn't hold his map the right way up. I straightened it for him and got us away just in time to avoid capture . . . An officer came to us with a fantastic reputation as a hard man. We'd be marching along and, without warning, he'd drop a live grenade. He'd just say "Grenade" and we would have to jump quickly or be blown up. His hardness was eyewash. He stayed drunk on the one raid we did with him; one of us went to Jellicoe afterwards and said: "If he comes again, he won't return alive" . . . There's an expression about people "crapping out" which happens often in war when you can't take any more. One of our NCOs was the perfect example. He had a medal and never imagined that he could be afraid. When, at last, fear came to him, he didn't know how to cope. He couldn't face action again.

Those assorted instances are also rarities. SBS officers and men handled themselves well, as Sutherland said: "Getting steamed up a bit – before, during or just after operations – was part of the job. There was a lot of tension, but nobody had what you might call a nervous breakdown." That is true, but continual raiding pushed individuals towards their limit and many were aware of it as they set off in 1944 for almost a year of non-stop operations. They heartened themselves with the knowledge that no troops in the world could have been better prepared. The "Killer School" in Jerusalem had seen to that.

16

THE KILLER SCHOOL

Forty years on, a passage from a lecture at the "Killer School" is remembered word for word by Sammy Trafford. His instructor was Douglas Howard, a Royal Marine sergeant with a Military Medal. Howard is the tutor usually recalled by his SAS ex-pupils; not for him, the parroted rattle through "Naming of parts". He worked, instead, with colour and vigour at preparing men psychologically for the hair-trigger actions ahead.

Howard looked round the class that included Trafford and said: "When you burst into a room full of enemy soldiers, you must remember the drill evolved for such occasions. Shoot the first man who moves, hostile or not. His brain has recovered from the shock of seeing you there with a gun. Therefore, he is dangerous. Next, shoot the man nearest to you. He is in the best position to cause you trouble." Howard paused, eyeing his audience expectantly. The question he awaited came from the back: "But what about the others in the room?" The instructor's mouth snapped like a bear-trap: "Deal with them as you think fit!"

Trafford recalled: "The school was in the old police station at Jerusalem and Grant Taylor was there, as well as Howard. The usual intake was 30 men, taken equally from the SAS, the Military Police and the Palestine Police. We spent every day in physical training and shooting with submachine-guns and pistols of our own choice. My favourites were the .38 Smith and Wesson revolver and the Thompson submachine-gun, the tommy-gun."

Gangster films made the tommy-gun famous. Equipped with a 50-round drum and firing two .45 bullets a second, it was the weapon of old stars like James Cagney, George Raft, Edward G. Robinson . . . and, in real life, the weapon of the St Valentine's Day massacre in America's prohibition wars. It was heavy, weighing roughly 12 lb loaded, but popular with

British special forces for its reliability and stopping power. Trafford recalls:

We didn't use drums, they tended to jam. We used magazines and kept the gun set at automatic although, to save bullets, we fired single shots which required fast reactions and a technique of tapping the trigger, instead of pulling it. Anyone who fired two bullets, not one, was too slow for the SAS.

We were taught to fire from the battle crouch, rather like a boxer's stance when weaving forward. It was impressed on us that it wasn't necessary to delay fire until our weapon was in the correct, upright position; the barrel remains round and would hit anything it was pointed at, no matter which way the gun might have turned in our hands.

We worked hard on firing our revolvers with either hand because of the way that doors open. A door hinged on the right and opening inwards called for an entrance with a gun in your left hand. Hinged left and opening inwards meant firing from the right hand. As we left the room, we had to crouch right down and reload. I don't believe the scenes on TV of men entering rooms with their gun clasped in both hands while they stand upright like target-shooters. Our target was always the big one, captured in this slogan: "Aim for his guts, and he's surely dead." Not many men recover from a stomach wound.

The tommy-gun magazine holds 20 bullets but we were allowed only 10 shots for the passing-out test at the Killer School. Ten bullets, 10 targets – and each target popping out suddenly and unexpectedly from cupboards and corners, or on stair landings. And, of course, the gun was on automatic. But that wasn't all . . . each examinee was sent round an obstacle course three or four times so that he arrived for the test out of breath. I'll always be proud of my marks for shooting at Jerusalem because I finished joint-top with David Williams. We each had 286 marks out of a maximum 300; I'd been better with the tommy-gun, he had beaten me with the pistol.

Williams, who won his Distinguished Conduct Medal and Military Medal in the Korean conflict, liked a captured Luger as his hand-gun and once lost a week's wages on a bet about firing at a Palestinian coin – "the size of a British 10p" – placed on a tree 20 paces away. He hit it three times out of seven, one fewer than his opponent. Williams says: "Ammo was plentiful. We shot every day; anywhere there was space and a target – pomegranates and tins were favourites. From 100 yards with a .303 rifle, I could guarantee to hit a 1 lb tin of jam [about 4 inches high] seven times out of ten."

Dick Holmes speaks from experience about the value of the daily shooting:

It was never more evident than on the island of Nsiros in 1944. There were only four of us and we were in a cave with Alan Sanders guarding the entrance. A German looked over the wall and saw us, then turned to run away. If he had reached the next terrace, we would have been sunk. But Alan, firing a Schmeisser from the hip and not aiming, shot twice. Bang, bang and the man fell dead some 30 feet away with both bullets in his back before he could move a step. That's the training which saves your life.

Sanders shrugs off praise for his accuracy: "The guy fell off the end of my gun." He was not a specialist marksman but an all-rounder doing duty as a navigator, as a map-reader and as a stand-by wireless operator able to send Morse at 18 words a minute. Versatility is prized in special forces. Everybody in the SBS, for instance, learned some techniques of the frogmen. Sanders said:

We would swim with mines, very slowly and using a gentle backstroke motion of the hands without breaking water. Except with the head, water was not broken because of phosphorus giving away the swimmer's presence.

The mines were limpets. Powerful magnets attached them to ships' hulls. They had to be carried on a "sleeper", a sheet of metal fastened to a belt clasped round the swimmer's waist. We had to scrape a patch clear of barnacles and then position the limpet on the hull while being careful to keep our fingers hooked round the base of the mine. Unless we kept a firm grip, the magnets would jerk forward and arouse the watch by clanging against the hull.

Training in shooting, swimming, high-speed marching, unarmed combat and handling rubber dinghies known as "Jellicoe Invaders" continued unabated throughout a memorable Christmas for Lassen. On Christmas Eve 1943, the third anniversary of his arrival at Oban, he learned that General H. Maitland Wilson had confirmed the second bar to his Military Cross. Only ten days earlier, he had been promoted from acting to temporary Captain. Although welcome, these marks of approval presented him with dress problems.

Lassen's mother wrote:

His manner of dress was altogether so haphazard and careless that it was not always easy for outsiders to see whether he was an officer or a private, and it would sometimes happen that a young newly arrived officer, correctly dressed with shining Sam Browne belt but without battle experience, might allow himself to behave slightly superciliously towards Anders, only to discover later that it was a triple MC he had patronised.

The bars to a Military Cross are worn on the medal ribbon as rosettes and, even if Lassen had bothered to apply for them, there was probably no machinery for forwarding decorations to an officer who was usually behind the enemy lines. Lassen looked round for a substitute and the slightly burnished lid of a naval "Tickler" tobacco tin took his fancy as being of suitable sheen. Porter Jarrell cut two small, scalloped circles from it and sewed them on the ribbon. Lassen grinned and was heard to say: "Rough and ready, maybe. But, according to regulations, properly dressed."

One of these ersatz rosettes fell off later and was not replaced. This was in character. Lassen did not flaunt his

ANDERS LASSEN, VC, MC, of the SAS

medals. There is unanimous agreement that he seemed rather shy, even embarrassed, about them. As with the rosettes – none on, two on, finally one on – he was in a continual muddle with his shoulder pips and Sammy Trafford tells the story of Lassen's hospital visit, an anecdote probably distilled from a string of incidents:

> Andy walked up the ward with three pips on one shoulder, but only two on the other. Afterwards the arguments started. Someone across the ward called: "Who was that Lieutenant who came to see you?" . . . "No, he was a Captain" . . . "No, no. He was a Lieutenant" . . . "He was a Captain with three pips" . . . "No, he'd bloody two on" . . . And then enlightment dawned when someone else called: "Don't you know who he is? That's Andy."

A Christian name alone had become the only identification needed by Lassen after less than a year with the Aegean raiders. The foreigner once treated with reserve had turned into a star; as the footballer Ray Iggleden says: "He was the man, the one everybody talked about. He wasn't athletic, sports-minded or even military, but he was very brave. I think the SAS would have followed him anywhere."

Lassen's reputation continued to grow from mid-January 1944, when the *Tewfik*, the largest SBS caique, sailed with him to set up the first base in neutral Turkey. Commander Seligman, who planned the naval part of the move, explains: "The Turks were only nominally neutral. They wanted to keep in with the Allies. In principle, we didn't go ashore there but the Turks came down to our boats and swopped great biscuit tins of honeycomb for packets of cigarettes. Marvellous wild honey, Dorian honey. Famous from antiquity."

Gordon Hogg, Seligman's signals officer, remembers the Turks offering to barter a wild boar: "They wanted .303 rifle ammunition. We agreed and barbecued the boar on the beach as a change from herrings in tomato sauce. But as we rowed back from the feast, we saw ripples in the water round us. We were being fired at with our own bullets – just for fun."

Hogg continues:

From time to time we would receive a message that Franz von Papen, the German ambassador to Turkey, had heard of our goings-on and was coming to inspect the coast and the territorial waters. We always had sufficient warning – and we needed it. In the clear waters of the Aegean, you can imagine the cleaning-up required to remove every trace of our presence – especially the tins thrown over the side because we lived primarily on tinned food.

Tewfik, a 180-tonner, was the mother-ship for SBS squadrons that Jellicoe's staff changed every eight weeks "to keep them fresh like bomber crews." Each two-month tour was a packed schedule of raids, long-stay reconnaissance, food-drops round the starving islands, penetration of enemy harbours and, where possible, interception of their shipping. These tasks had been made easier by the caiques' modernised communications, as Hogg said:

> Standard signal equipment was cumbersome and heavy, and not really suitable for such small vessels. We needed something compact with the versatility to receive and transmit on a range of frequencies. I went to see Army Signals HQ in Cairo who were extremely efficient and who found some first-class American sets from Kittyhawk aircraft. These sets were remotely controlled by cable and could be sited anywhere on the boat; normally, we put them in the forepeak and ran the cables to the tiny cabins from where we could receive and transmit on admiral's wave, on destroyer wave and on submarine wave using one-time pads, still the only unbreakable cipher.

Friendly relations between the Turks and the forward bases were fostered by gestures such as a distribution of loot from the *Eugenia*, a German supply schooner captured with stores for the garrison on Leros. The fine French champagne was drunk by the officers from enamel mugs, and the Czech beer was confiscated by the SBS, but they were generous to the peasants with the hundreds of Wehrmacht blankets, towels and boxes of toilet rolls. Nick Benyon-Tinker wrote:

197

I don't think the mysteries of modern plumbing had yet reached the Turks in their remote fastness; they were certainly not toilet-paper conscious. The rolls, probably looked upon as being a new and large type of paper streamer, were seized upon with zest by the younger Turks and promptly thrown – long and snake-like, wreathing themselves in graceful arabesques – into the 'fir trees fringing our harbour . . . It is impossible to describe the bizarre effect produced by this.

Turkish flags and signs were erased in all photographs from the advanced bases while reports from Ankara warned repeatedly of Turkey's growing sensitivity to the German complaints. In January 1944: "The Turks have specifically withdrawn the privilege of crews coming ashore for exercise." In February 1944: "Operational caiques must not remain alongside base caiques longer than absolutely necessary." In April 1944: "Continued use of the facilities is dependent on our limiting their use to the absolute minimum and making our presence as unobtrusive as possible."

Spies were everywhere and Hank Hancock is sure: "The Germans were on the Turkish mainland as well as us. They lit fires to warn their people on the islands when our boats were going out. We were scared that they might raid our bases, so we kept thoroughly dispersed wherever we hung out."

Bodrum, a small mainland port looking south towards Cos, had German affiliations through being a U-boat base in the First World War. The SBS unmasked a Nazi spy there and – in the words of Colonel Lapraik:

He went missing. As a result, I was whipped into jail by the Turks after going ashore in Bodrum. They arrested me largely because I was in charge, but I had no weapon and I knew they couldn't produce a body; I'll not say how I knew, but I knew. I was prepared to stay in prison as long as my safety was assured, but not beyond that. So I let it be known through the British Military Attaché that I would tell my people to come ashore and take me if there was any question of my being polished off.

Lapraik was released after three weeks for lack of evidence and resumed the sequestered life of the bases where entertainment was what the men made it. BBC broadcasts to the Forces were difficult to receive. Lapraik said: "Anyway, we couldn't afford to listen because of the batteries which rationed us to one radio schedule a day between seven and eight in the morning."

Forward squadrons organised their own fun under the time-honoured title of: "Sing, Say or Show". Contrasting stars remembered by David Williams were Captain Walter Milner-Barry and Corporal Karl Kahane:

> After a few drinks, Milner-Barry, who was well into his forties and must have been the oldest officer in the SAS, would do a Rugby-club version of "Mother, darling mother, may I go to the fair? Yes, go with young Roger, young Roger Kildare".
>
> Karl's act was cleverer, he acted out a song showing how different nationalities asked a girl to dance. Karl was unusual. He had an Iron Cross from the First World War and had been a town clerk in Austria until, being Jewish, he fled to Palestine after the Anschluss. He came to us from the Special Interrogation Group, a unit that specialised at infiltrating German transit camps to pick up information. He taught our lads German and went raiding with us, but I had to carry him on my back off Santorini after giving his pack to a prisoner. Karl was exhausted, saying to me: "I can't run any more; I'm too old for this."

The Santorini raid at the end of April 1944 became known as "Andy Lassen's Bloodbath" but there were other terrifying attacks on the islands before that. Colonel Lapraik said:

> On two successive raids, the German commander lost his balls – shot off, or blown off. That put the fear of God into the men. It was just the luck of the draw, but nobody believed that; they thought we had some secret method of achieving it. The German troops in the Aegean weren't of the highest quality; the officers were good enough, but not

the men, a lot of whom were Russians. We kept them going
– it was probably our main achievement – to the extent that
two-thirds of them were standing-to all night.

The raids followed a pattern outlined by Lapraik:

> We operated largely in sticks of twelve – an officer, a
> sergeant, a corporal and nine men including a signaller. As
> a general rule, we would go ashore without guides waiting
> for us. We would collect guides later but didn't want to be
> met in case they had been followed or had given us away.
> As well as an assortment of guns and grenades, we carried
> an SBS invention to leave outside the wire of enemy
> barracks. It comprised two tubes just over a foot long on a
> triangular base and fitted with a time pencil, then loaded up
> with a grenade aimed at the windows. It used to do an awful
> lot of damage when we were on the way back to Turkey.

No first-hand account of the raids was published in British
newspapers, partly due to the usual official passion for
secrecy but also because missions behind enemy lines had no
place for non-combatant supernumeraries, even if fit enough
– and the majority of British war correspondents were ruled
out of active service themselves through age or medical
defects. America, though, sent a writer willing to carry a gun.
He was Donald Grant of *Look*, a long defunct New York
magazine much admired for its use of pictures.

A testy comment in green pencil reveals Cairo's reaction to
this innovation: "Who authorised US war correspondents to
go on these shows? Do British war correspondents go?"
Headquarters were too late. Grant had been, gone, written
and broadcast. In May 1944, he told listeners in the United
States:

> These British raiders are some of the finest fighting men in
> the world today and I'd like to say something about them
> and the job they are doing.
>   All praise is empty for a soldier who will put on the rags
> of a peasant and walk through a German garrison, knowing

that one false word or move will land him in the torture chambers of the Gestapo. I saw him do this with the calm poise of a man buying a pack of cigarettes at a corner tobacconists.

I lived with these men who hid by day and attacked by night, and who were hunted through the mountains like hares. I saw starving Greek men and women, and especially children, fed by British soldiers. Sometimes the food they gave had been taken – Robin Hood-like – in raids on German garrisons. I watched German soldiers looting Greek homes, saw them terrorise old men and women by firing submachine-guns close to them and heard the crude laughter of the Germans enjoying their cowards' game . . .

One cool morning with spring fresh on the mountainside, where nimble-footed goats stepped over wild flowers, a British patrol took me with them when they ambushed and killed the commandant of a certain German garrison walking with his bodyguard along a narrow gravel road. You might pity this fair German boy until you remember the dog kept by the Gestapo for the benefit of the stubborn Greeks. A great black beast with flashing eyes, he was trained to grasp the throats of his bound victims, while Gestapo agents tried to make them talk. Our patrols hunted the Gestapo dog, too, and finally removed that terror from the oppressed Greek people . . .

These raiding forces men would not be very impressive on a parade down the Mall in London. They pride themselves on their beards while on operations . . . While hiding in the mountains near a German outpost, no-one washes because the water is scarce and no-one ever takes his clothes off at night. There is considerable variation in uniform but all are dirty, greasy and torn. About the only common garment to all raiding force men is a strangely hooded jacket, which often makes them appear to be a band of Robin Hood's merry men stepped out of a story-book, complete with knives slung at their belts.

Grant's magazine piece opened punchily: "This is my story from one remote segment of a global war; a corner so remote that, until I was there, no war correspondent had ever visited it. I found it a strange kind of war, full of death and suffering as all wars are, but full of gallant and romantic heroism too." He touched on incidents omitted from the radio script: "I saw three young girls rescued from a German brothel by a British patrol . . . The time when a captured German officer was made to pay a 30,000 lire fine imposed on the local Greek populace for harbouring a British patrol . . . And the letter written by a British officer to a German commander on toilet roll, the only paper available." It was the first and last of Grant's dispatches from the Aegean because, on the very day of publication, the French port of Cherbourg fell to the United States 1st Army. The American public, sensing the break-out to come, focused attention on Normandy and could no longer be interested in a British sideshow, no matter how colourful. Grant was reassigned but is remembered in an SBS report for the distinction of wearing a tie throughout an operation.

This was a raid on Piscopi, an arid, limestone island with few wells or springs and where the people, as so often in the Aegean, depended for water on rain-barrels and cisterns. Grant, in spectacles, collar and tie, tagged along behind a party of six men, plus two corporals and two officers, the South African Lieutenant Keith Balsillie and the Greek Lieutenant Stefan Casulli. They were met by a shepherd who showed Casulli the German billets and gun positions as well as the best spot to ambush the morning patrol. Sammy Trafford was on the raid and remembers: "It was where there were walls on both sides of the road. We waited from the small hours until after seven in the morning – Balsillie on one side, and me, Guardsman Harris and Donald Grant on the other. And all of us eating goat cheese and hard-boiled eggs."

The road, which led to the village of Megalocori, had not been used by the Germans since a drunken disturbance that had antagonised the Greeks on Easter Sunday, some days earlier. A plot to entice them back was devised by Casulli with the village mayor and the shepherd, who answered to "Mike". At half past seven in the morning, "Mike" signalled that the bait had been taken. Four Germans were on their way – 2nd Lieutenant Urbanicz, his quartermaster, his personal clerk and, 100 yards behind, a private with a mule and a dog. Trafford:

> Casulli, dressed as a peasant, went into Piscopi with the mayor and told the German commander that the present of a big, fat pig awaited him in the village. When the patrol came alongside, Balsillie jumped up and shouted "Hande Hoch!" but they reached for guns and we began firing. The Germans that I shot were still living although down with the others on the ground. Balsillie said: "Finish them off", so I shot one twice through the head with my tommy-gun and the other through the back of the neck. It was the first time I had killed anybody. One of them had a pistol, so I said: "I'll have that" – and I sold it later in Palestine for £25.

Balsillie reported: "The casualties were four Germans and one dog killed. The mule got off without a scratch . . . We crossed over the mountain and returned to our hide-out. At midday the Germans (who had 160 men on Piscopi) fired twenty-four rounds from a gun at the upper slopes of Mount Cuzzoreglia, apparently mistaking some goats for us."

The action had moved too fast for war correspondent Grant. It was over before he remembered to slip his safety catch. After the escape through the mountains, he saw the difference between an American and a British operation. Everything stopped for tea. Trafford said: "I always carried the brew-can. I found some twigs and then, even though the water had to be chlorinated, we could have a cuppa."

Balsillie's patrol returned unscathed from their five days behind enemy lines. Not all the SBS were so fortunate. In that same week of April 1944 two caiques were intercepted and overpowered off Alimnia, a tiny island north of Rhodes. Ten prisoners were taken: Captain Hugh Blyth and his four-man patrol; Sub-Lieutenant Allan Tuckey RNVR, of the Levant Schooner Flotilla, his wireless operator and three Greek seamen.

Blyth, of the Scots Guards, was flown to Germany for interrogation under torture in the SS camp at Moosburg outside Munich. A transfer to a normal prisoner-of-war camp then saved his life. He was the only one of the ten to survive. The other nine fell into the hands of Army Group E whose intelligence staff at Arsakli, near Salonika, included Kurt Waldheim, later Secretary General of the United Nations and President of Austria.

Waldheim and his colleagues were aware that the Commander-in-Chief of Group E, General Alexander Löhr, was an enthusiastic supporter of the principles outlined by Hitler in a memorandum to the Commando Order:

While the Russians use land routes to smuggle partisans behind our lines, England and America land sabotage troops from submarines or rubber dinghies, or by parachuting agents . . . This kind of war is completely without danger for the enemy. They have been given orders to ruthlessly dispatch German soldiers or even inhabitants in their way, but are in no danger of suffering serious losses themselves.

The worst that can happen is that they are caught, whereupon they give themselves up instantly, believing that they are under the protection of the Geneva Convention. This represents the worst kind of abuse of the Geneva Convention . . . England and America will always find volunteers for this kind of campaign as long as these volunteers can be assured that they are not in mortal danger and can simply give themselves up when caught.

If the German war effort is not to be severely damaged by such methods, then it must be made clear to the enemy that every sabotage troop will, without exception, be cut down to the last man. That is to say, their expectancy of survival is nil . . . a troop sent to carry out explosions, sabotage or acts of terrorism is to be completely exterminated . . . If it is found useful to spare one or two men for questioning, these men are to be shot immediately afterwards.

Waldheim's colleagues carried out the Führer's wishes to the letter in expediting the "special treatment" of Blyth's nine

204

companions. The three Greeks seem to have been executed at Goudi prison in Athens; one of them, according to an inmate, with "his leg half-rotten from beatings".

Approval for the execution of the wireless operator and one of the Greeks was not received until the beginning of June 1944, but the death warrant of the other seven was sent by telex from Belgrade three weeks after their capture. The SD killers worked in secret; unlike the shooting of hostages, designed to spread fear, the disposal of Allied prisoners was a covert affair. They may have been machine-gunned en masse at Kaisarani, the SD's killing-fields in the Athenian suburbs. The exact date, place, and method remain unknown after more than forty years, but there is no question that one of the victims was Gunner Ray Jones.

German firing squads slaughtered three close companions of Anders Lassen between the summer of 1943 and the late spring of 1944. First, Graham Hayes of the Small Scale Raiding Force at Fresnes prison in Paris; then Philip Pinckney, the creator of "Palestine soup" who joined the SAS with Lassen when they flew together from England to North Africa after the break-up of the SSRF. Pinckney was executed after being captured in the Alps when trying to blow up the rail tunnel through the Brenner Pass from Austria to Italy. Jones, the third to go, had won his Military Medal when partnering Lassen in the raid on Kastelli airfield.

The fate of Jones was unconfirmed until 1987 but Lassen and the SBS did not need to trawl through archives to understand the probable outcome for a patrol listed as "Overdue". They had seen and heard enough of German reprisals against Greek civilians to know that, in Hitler's phrase, their own "expectancy of survival is nil". Lassen suspected the worst from the outset and was quick to take revenge. Two of his old Irish patrol went with him.

17

SANTORINI

Although the government of the Irish Republic remained intractably neutral throughout the war, the same was not true of its people. Some 80,000 Irish citizens volunteered for service in British uniform and, almost to a man, kept their word to return from home-leaves spent in Eire, in civilian clothes, beyond the jurisdiction of courts-martial for desertion. Yet they sang rebel songs – "Come out, you Black and Tan", for example – in British barracks and gnawed ceaselessly at their centuries-old grievances against the English. Hank Hancock, the first English member of the Irish patrol, says:

> They were clannish. They wouldn't speak to me socially for nearly three months. The ice wasn't broken until my covering fire got them out of a tight spot on a raid.
>
> They were always annoyed with the English, always running us down. As a joke, I'd say: "If you're so fed up, why don't you go and join the Jerries?" Whereupon they would turn on me, asking: "Whose side are you on, then?" The Irish patrol were "K" patrol, the first that Lassen joined. Apart from myself and the American "Joe" Jarrell, they were all Southern Irish from the Irish Guards.

The SBS created both rivalry and team spirit by forming a number of communal patrols – the Irish patrol, the Brum patrol, the Jock patrol, the Marine patrol and so on. Wounds, leaves, illness might cause temporary changes but each patrol tried to retain their basic personnel; in the case of the Irish, this meant Sean O'Reilly, Patsy Henderson, Mick D'Arcy and "Gyppo" Conby.

Conby was the hardest man of a formidable quartet and is described by Hancock as: "Very strong and relatively quiet, but you wouldn't want to cross him." Jarrell remembers

Conby for: "His ruddy face and baby-blue eyes. He wasn't very bright but a helluva decent guy, even though a semi-animal at times." Dick Holmes, forthright as ever, says: "Conby was cold, a killer who recognised a kindred spirit in Lassen. All the Micks, and they were good soldiers, admired Lassen. And Sean O'Reilly thought the sun shone out of him."

D'Arcy, a qualified chemist and the best educated of the four, soldiered in partnership with O'Reilly and Henderson right from the fledgling days of the SAS in the desert. When Lieutenant Jock Lewes acquired fifty surplus parachutes in May 1941 D'Arcy joined him and Lieutenant David Stirling in the very first SAS jumps for which they were quite unprepared, being without either helmets or protective clothing. On the first jump, they wore only short-sleeved shirts; on the second, they put on pullovers for some warmth. D'Arcy wrote:

We flew in a Vickers Valencia which was used to deliver mail . . . We were to jump in pairs and the instructions were to dive out as though going into water . . . I dived out and was surprised to see Lieutenant Stirling pass me in the air . . . he injured his spine and also lost his sight for about an hour. I was a little shaken with a few scratches. Next morning we jumped again when Lieutenant Lewes in trying to avoid some oil barrels, rather badly injured his spine . . . The intended operation was eventually cancelled.

D'Arcy and the other Irish settled happily under the command of Lassen; with their own feelings of being foreigners in an English army, they felt it appropriate to have a leader in the same situation. O'Reilly – at forty-two, nearly twice Lassen's age – gladly became the young Dane's man-at-arms and fought side by side with him from Simi to Comacchio. Jarrell recalls:

Andy led the patrol by force of personality. On operations, there's no time for debate. Someone has to take the lead and that's what Andy could do – he made decisions. And, where most of us worry about being brave or not, Andy always had courage. At the beginning, he was not a killer (I don't think he ever cold-bloodedly killed prisoners) but once the action started, he was out to kill. Basically, he was a sensitive, decent person whom the war made tough – and you had to be tough to gain the admiration of people like Gyppo Conby and Sergeant Sean O'Reilly. It must have been difficult for someone of Andy's social class to understand Conby, but Andy and O'Reilly always looked out for each other.

Lassen protected O'Reilly. His drunken absences were only admonished, and a blind eye was turned to a ploy that allowed O'Reilly to write some of his own leave-passes; when O'Reilly shot him accidentally in action, Lassen refused at first to report the wound. The two of them were lying in wait for a motor-boat crew of Germans who were being lured to a landing-place on the island of Calchi near Rhodes. The bait was an invitation to a drink with an Italian – who had issued it because Lassen's gun was pressed into his back.

O'Reilly told Lassen's mother: "I cocked my rifle and, as we tore round the corner, I stumbled and the gun went off, hitting Andy in the leg. Then he got really mad. 'You Irish dog! Do you want to kill me?' He kept shouting abuse at me and all the time he fired at the Germans, wounding two of them."

Lassen and O'Reilly, assisted by only two others on the raid, captured six Italians, the German crew and their patrol boat, as well as supplies that included four live pigs. They returned from Calchi in a caique commanded by Adrian Seligman to whom Lassen confided his predicament: "If I report this bullet hole (a mere fleabite, by the way) as being caused by enemy action, they will give me a wound stripe or something foul like that. But if I say it was caused by one of my own chaps, then he may get into trouble – they may even send him down to base and that would be a shame; he's one of my best men. What should I do, Adrian?"

Benyon-Tinker, author of that account, continued: "It was not until days afterwards that anybody knew how Andy had been shot. He was so vague when asked for details that people gave up asking him and the whole matter faded gently away. Typical of him, his sole worry was to ensure that one of his own men did not get into any hot water."

Flea-bite understates a wound that turned septic and required an operation in the military hospital at Alexandria, but Lassen's reticence about the cause removed the slight danger of losing O'Reilly and so the two of them, as well as Sergeant Henderson, were able to pay the enemy a murderous visit only five days after Captain Blyth's patrol had been logged officially as: "Overdue".

The place was Santorini, also known as Thira and the southernmost island of the Cyclades. A night reconnaissance by Lassen with a Greek guide before the raid confirmed the description in the SBS briefing: "Ten miles by three. Sheer, sombre cliffs of black, volcanic rock. Wine-growing, but sometimes needs to import water." The curve of the harbour reminded him of the *Maid Honor* raid on Santa Isabel; Santorini was also a flooded crater with the extra benefit for fishermen of permanently warm, sulphurous water to de-weed the bottoms of their boats.

Lassen's raiders landed around midnight on April 22, 1944, after a three-night sail from Turkey, lying-up camouflaged in daylight at three staging points. Lieutenants Balsillie and Casulli were with Lassen, plus fifteen men including his regular signaller Billy Reeves and an interpreter identified only as "John". These facts are known from a report signed: "A. Lassen, MC. Captain 'S' Detachment, SBS" and dated "29th April, 1944". It runs to about 1,000 words. The length is unique. Little survives that was written by Lassen or attributed to him, and his usual reports would be considered terse even by the standards of a postcard.

"Landed. Killed Germans. Fucked off" is how his men say that he described at least one raid. Sutherland admits to invariably needing to press for more detail of actions. In several important ways, Lassen changed in maturing as an officer in the SAS. He ceased to be wild with guns; he started, as Benyon-Tinker noted, to be more concerned about his men even to the extent, according to Porter Jarrell, of beginning to worry about them when they were on leave but, in the matter of written work, he remained the laggard scholar. If there had been no war and he had stayed in Denmark's merchant fleet, he would have been obliged to attend full-time at the School of Seamanship and sit examinations for Third Officer – but without a chance of passing until he changed his attitude towards writing. Lassen, man of action, detested accounting for himself on paper . . . "It's done. What else is there to say?" he would retort when asked for a fuller version of operations. Why, then, is "Operation Report No.13, Thira" so lengthy? Because Lassen himself didn't write it. "The ideas and views are all his. Someone else put them together," says Sutherland. The text, in fact, reads like the notes of a de-briefing and begins with the composition of his force:

"P" Patrol: Captain Lassen, Lt. Casulli, Sgt Nicholson, Sgt Henderson, Corporals Kahane, Sibbet, O'Reilly, Parachutist Harris, John the interpreter. "Z" Patrol: Lt. Balsillie, Corporals Hughes, Fowler, Parachutists Partridge, Babb, Wright, Reeves, Trafford, Williams.

Object: To destroy, capture or entice enemy shipping in Thira, near Taimeli or Tyracea islands. To destroy enemy communications and personnel on Thira islands. To attack other opportunity targets as they occur.

Narrative: We left Balisu Bay on board LS 1 and 2 on 19th April at dusk and arrived at Cyrena at dawn next morning where a slightly wounded English Flight Sergeant was picked up. We left Cyrena the same night and arrived at Anhidros at dawn, 21st April. This island is uninhabited and has good anchorages, although they are not all-weather. There is water but it is very dirty and only fit for cattle to drink. We left Utsera the same evening.

I landed with Lt. Casulli at a monastery south of Mesa Buono to collect information from the islanders. We stayed ashore two hours but did not manage to get adequate information. We returned to the ships which then proceeded to Nea Kameli arriving dawn, 22nd April. The ships were camouflaged but, as the island is volcanic with black rocks and the nets white-grey, the boats were dangerously visible. We were, in fact, seen by several local fishermen. Very little shipping calls at Thira; none arrived that day.

All men were landed on the east coast of Thira near Point Volvoulous on the night 22nd–23rd April. The boats proceeded to Kristiani to lie up. After landing, both patrols proceeded to the village of Volvoulous where we lay up in a cave. During daylight, we collected information from the islanders. It was decided to carry out three attacks. Lt. Balsillie and four other ranks to attack the wireless telegraph station, an outpost at Murivigli. Sgt Henderson to attack the German officer in charge and his corporal in their house, and Capt. Lassen, Lt. Casulli and twelve other ranks to attack the barracks. Zero hour fixed for 0045, 24th April.

On the first floor of the Bank of Athens at Thira was a reported billet for 38 Italians and 10 Germans. This report was partly false, there were less than 35 men in the billet. We succeeded in getting the main force into the billet unobserved, in spite of barking dogs and sentries. The living quarters comprised twelve rooms.

It was our intention to take the troops there prisoner. This idea had to be abandoned and will have to be abandoned in similar circumstances in the future until raiding parties are issued with good torches. Casualties were sustained during the general mix-up in the dark. Instead, the doors of the rooms were kicked in, a grenade thrown into the room and two to three magazines of TSMG (Thompson submachine-gun) and Bren emptied into each room.

Lt. Casulli was killed almost instantaneously and Sergeant Kingston [a medical orderly somehow omitted from the report's listed personnel above] was seriously wounded by shots fired either from the rooms or by the sentries outside. Two other slight casualties, Parachutists Trafford and Harris, were also caused in the same way. During the engagement, a German patrol challenged us from outside but were heavily engaged by Sgt Nicholson

211

with a Bren fired from the hip. One Italian jumped from the window, a drop of 40 feet.

At approximately 0245 hours, and when I was satisfied that all the enemy were killed or wounded, we left the building carrying Sgt Kingston. Shots were exchanged with stray enemy during this withdrawal. We returned to the cave to find Lt. Balsillie waiting for us with eight prisoners. He had completed a neat job.

Sgt Kingston was fully conscious when we left the building. He himself, as a medical orderly, considered that he was not dangerously wounded. The next day, the local doctor was called to attend him and, on his recommendation, we decided to leave him by the roadside for the Germans to pick up as he had suddenly taken a turn for the worse. He died before this could be done. Arrangements were made with the local doctor for him to be buried with full honours. The same request was made about Lt. Casulli and I have every reason to believe that this was carried out.

By checking up on the 24th April through the local Greeks, particularly the doctor, it appears that three Germans were killed and two wounded, nine Italians killed and nine wounded which, with Lt. Balsillie's eight prisoners, made a total of thirty-one casualties on the island. There may be more as the enemy next day tried to hide what really happened and only a few Germans and six Italians were seen by the inhabitants.

As our hide-out was getting too well-known to the Greeks, we moved to – and lay-up in – a house two miles away. In the evening both patrols moved to Mesa Buono where the boat was to pick us up, but it did not arrive that night. The next day, 25th April, whilst we were hiding up in two houses at Mesa Buono, the islands were searched for several hours by four Junker 88s, two seaplanes and an ME 109 at an altitude of 300 feet. That night, in spite of very bad weather, HDML 1373 with Parachutist Orr, a medical orderly on board, and LS 1 and LS 2 all arrived and took us off. We proceeded to Anhidros and lay up during daylight, 26th April, and that evening the HDML sailed to Mersinjek. The two caiques sailed to Cerina and then to base.

Intelligence notes: The whole east of the island, excluding Mesa Buono itself, is suitable for landing. There are only a few landing places on the west coast owing to cliffs. There are stepped paths up the mountain. It is difficult to lie up without discovery by the local Greeks but fairly easy to hide from the enemy as there are many caves and stone walls. In the Profetis and Buono areas there are mountains and rough country although a strong enemy force could clear Mesa Buono. Water is only found near houses, and on the west coast it is necessary to move inland two miles before finding any.

Population: The local inhabitants are very patriotic but are very simple-minded and inclined to talk among themselves. This is more noticeable than in any other island we have visited. To avoid possible shooting of hostages, a strong note was sent to the surviving German commander, then a Leutnant Hesse, reminding him of the allied views on hostages and war criminals. His name should be noted if any hostages are shot. That undoubtedly is a good policy and should be adopted by all future patrols.

Morale: The Germans were of a different type to those so far encountered and appear to be mainly Marine Soldaten, sailors not marines. OC Island was an infantry officer. Italian morale is said to be poor. They are badly treated by the Germans and have no officers.

Notes: There is no doubt that shooting up barracks at night requires a great deal of skill and experience, such as only the older men in the SBS have and which will not be found in reinforcements. Lack of experience must be made up by rigid training, especially in street and house fighting, and they should be generally taught how to look after themselves, not to stand in front of doors for example.

The standard of marching among the recruits was poor and, in many cases, not what should have been expected. As usual, Sgt Nicholson, Cpl Sibbet and Cpl O'Reilly did extremely well and were calm and efficient during the attack. Parachutists Reeves and Partridge, although lacking in experience, carried themselves well and proved to be most useful members of the patrol.

213

Official reports tell everything except what it was really like – and Lassen's is no exception, although the defect is understandable when describing an action fought in darkness and confusion, hampered by casualties and conducted by men so concentrated on their own role that they cannot take an overall view. So what was it like in the bank at Santorini? Sammy Trafford remembers first a kindly remark by Jack Nicholson, an NCO proud of safeguarding the lives of his men:

It was my first raid with Lassen – "Andy Lassen's Bloodbath", they called it afterwards because he killed nearly every bugger. Nicholson said to me as we were setting off: "Coming with the killers, are you, Sammy? Don't worry. You'll be all right."

Lassen halted us on the march to the town and made everyone swallow two tablets of benzedrine, watching them go down before taking two himself. He wanted us wide awake. He was a good organiser, a hitman and killer. He carried just his Luger pistol and a fighting knife, and it was said he could be a devil with the knife.

Fear didn't seem to bother him, although I suppose he felt some; I tried to imitate his fearlessness and easy-going ways in the face of danger. He walked on the balls of his feet, very quietly. Someone once described him silently framing himself in a doorway; Andy Lassen never stood in a doorway in his life. He'd been taught better. One moment he'd be outside, the next inside and beside us, saying, "I vant you". He never could say his vs and ws.

Sean O'Reilly and myself were pushed first into the bank by Lassen. Five doors faced us. I took the middle door and O'Reilly took one on the right while Lassen brought in the others, one at a time. O'Reilly shouted "Grenade gone" to let everyone know he'd thrown one into his room, but then his Schmeisser jammed and he began cursing: "Jesus Christ, where the bloody hell are the others?"

Suddenly Casulli was hit by fire from a door that I'd not seen. He staggered towards me, obviously dying. I was hit next from the same direction. The wounds were in my upper arm and left leg. I staggered, too. Next, Guardsman Jack Harris shouted: "I've been hit in the leg", whereupon he limped out on the terrace. Sgt. Kingston from the RAMC should not have been on the raid but had asked Lassen to take him. Lassen agreed but told him not to go inside the bank because he couldn't be both a killer and our medical orderly. Kingston died from shots in the stomach.

Some Greeks found Harris and myself wounded and gave us brandy, then we marched all night after Lassen had told the signaller to send for the boat. I carried a Bren for Harris on the way but my wounded arm began going numb and I couldn't manage the weight any longer, so I dismantled the gun and threw the pieces in the sea. I told Lassen what I'd done; he didn't object.

Signaller Reeves said:

Casulli and Kingston were exceptions to the rule that very few people got killed on Lassen's raids. He was a lucky officer. But the bank was different. There was only one outside door – where I got knocked to the floor – and the enemy were on the upper floor so we couldn't go in saying, "Hands up". I remember us shooting one of them who tried to escape through a back window. Lassen's motto on prisoners that night seemed to be "Don't take any".

He liked things kept simple. For instance, it was SBS practice for us signallers to make up codes from our own names – William Arthur Reeves, in my case. When there was an attempt to change to a Q-code, I showed the instruction to Andy who said: "I don't want that. Keep to what we've been doing." I was pleased because I didn't want to carry a code-book as well as a wireless set and the big tank battery encased in wood with which I had to climb rocks and cliffs, as at Santorini. It may have been there, although I cannot remember for certain, that he blew me up for showing myself by standing at a crossroads; he made me feel knee-high. After that, I was careful with Andy Lassen, it was always "Sir" to him.

Lassen, as ever indomitable, re-grouped his men for a second attempt after the casualties and return fire at the front entrance had forced the raiders out of the building to the terrace. They broke in next from the rear, smashing the French windows of the dining hall and then throwing grenades through doors and shooting off locks. The Italian, a sergeant, who jumped from 40 feet was killed. Five other panic-stricken defenders were seen jumping from a lower window to escape, although the drop was still 30 feet.

Sergeant Nicholson, in 1987, scoffed at the suggestion that the attack could have been conducted less gorily if the raiders had been equipped with good torches: "We didn't have torches, we didn't want torches. A man carrying a torch is a target. That was the only time I was in action side-by-side with Lassen and it's one of the reasons why I'm trying to forget the war. It's no fun throwing grenades into rooms and shooting sleeping men. That garrison could have been captured."

Lassen's virtual extermination of the enemy could be justified as a literal interpretation of his orders to "destroy personnel", but the true motivation was more probably anger at the death of his friend Casulli from whom he removed a gold chain, identity disc and diary for the sad task, later in Alexandria, of handing them personally to his widow while answering her repeated and distraught question with the words: "Yes, it is true. Stefan is dead."

The severity of Lassen's measures reduced the Santorini garrison to a rump of a patrol powerless to do more on the night than unleash some random shots and exchange taunts with the raiders . . . "Kommen Sie hier" . . . "Nein, Sie kommen hier", and still unable to intervene next day when Lassen, in full view of the Germans, began a march slowed by the wounded Harris, Trafford and, particularly, the dying Kingston.

The Germans saved their bullets for hostages. Ten were executed, including the mayor. Meanwhile, Kingston made halting progress over the rocky paths towards the rendezvous beach. First, he had been carried through Santorini on a door and then, when the streets became too steep and narrow, he had been manhandled out of the town. Finally, for lack of a stretcher, he was carried on a gate borrowed from a vineyard. The men who hauled and staggered with the burden knew in their hearts: "If Balsillie hadn't wrecked the wireless station and if Lassen hadn't wiped out the garrison, we'd never have got away."

The HDML that lifted them off also took a risk in sailing right into the beach when the sea was too rough for the use of rowing boats; the caiques followed the motor-boat's example and so the whole party escaped to nearby Anhidros and spent the day hiding under camouflage from the German air-search.

There had been neither time nor opportunity for that phase of raiding covered by the word "Entice", which meant bribing Greek skippers to put themselves and their caiques at the service of the British. Haggling was not permitted; the inducements had been formalised by Raiding Force head-quarters at an official rate per ton and per vessel: "£2.10 shillings in notes a ton, or 10 shillings in gold, on approach and again on arrival", so a 15-tonner fetched a total of £75 although most Greeks opted for the golden jingle of 15 sovereigns.

All patrols carried about 20 sovereigns which, in the words of Porter Jarrell, "were usually the first casualties of a success-ful operation". The coins, worth £5 each, were intended to reward guides and to pay for supplies, but leftovers ran the risk of being pilfered for high living on leave. One veteran confided: "Our soft leather boots made a good hiding place; I've rammed as many as 17 sovereigns between the double crêpe soles." Spare gold came in handy after Santorini for the men returned from the raid intent on a lot of drinking.

18

Yugoslavia and Salonika

Raiding Forces mounted 381 operations all told and Lassen's men sometimes wondered if he had volunteered for the lot. The slaughter on Santorini whetted his keenness and, from May 1944, he fizzed and exploded like a crackerjack. He struck in the Adriatic as well as in the Aegean, he scouted the outermost Greek islands and attacked targets in Yugoslavia and Albania; wearing a borrowed civilian coat and hat, he popped up prematurely in Athens towards which Jellicoe – "jacked up to Brigadier to give the impression of more British troops than was the case" – was riding on a bicycle.

Lassen, with 6 feet 3 inch Jim Henshaw, five other officers and some three dozen men, then captured Salonika, the second largest city in Greece. Before the year was out, he returned to Crete with orders to contain the Germans although outnumbered by hundreds to one. "A fever burned inside him. Life had become a race against death," says Porter Jarrell, but Lassen's actions spoke just as clearly of a race against the end of the war, with his full wrath against the enemy still unexpended.

Some men speak of a death-wish but Lassen showed normal prudence in a frustrating raid on Paros that May when Hank Hancock and Busty Sibbet inadvertently aroused the defenders. Hancock recalls:

Our Greek guide – dead brave the day before – began to get behind us so that we had to put him in front at gun-point, more or less. But then he jumped over a wall and disappeared, leaving us on our own but able to see the white church in the distance that was used as a bomb store.

We found heavy camouflage netting near the church. As we lifted it, a light gleamed underneath. It was then we realised that we were looking into a German pill-box and that the guys inside were asking: "What's going on?" They flung open the door and let fly with Schmeissers. Fortunately, I was kneeling down, so they fired over me.

Then Busty and I took off, the Olympic Games had nothing on it. We shot away and hid in a cornfield while watching the German flares light up the sky. The operation was sabotaged and we were scared of going back to face Lassen. The first thing he'd ask would be: "Why didn't you fire back?" A good answer would be needed to stop him going crazy.

We told him that we'd not returned the fire because we were sure the Germans didn't know that we were British raiders but thought we were straying shepherds . . . "If we had shot back, sir, they would have been certain that somebody was there." Actually, our only object had been to get the hell out of it. I don't know if he saw through our excuse, but no more was said. We were greatly relieved.

Lassen withdrew from his own planned attack on a gun emplacement when the alarm was raised; Jarrell, Henderson and D'Arcy were also forced to cancel their assault on a wireless station. Only two of Lassen's six targets could be hit and, by his standards, Paros was a failure. He reported: "The islanders have not been helpful. The airfield is well-defended and three additional companies are expected shortly to strengthen the defence."

The successes were the killing of four Germans during the destruction of another wireless station and, after shooting his bodyguard, the capture of a German officer by Nicholson and Williams – but that feat misfired when other SBS, mistaking the ring of the prisoner's boots for the approach of an enemy patrol, threw a grenade that killed him. Jarrell sums up:

Everything went wrong on Paros, including Patsy Henderson, Mick D'Arcy and myself missing the rendezvous. When the light streamed out of the pill-box, we were down the cliff and below another gun emplacement that reacted to the alarm. This cut us off and we couldn't make the beach. Dawn broke with the three of us on a hill above the main German barracks, not daring to stir and hoping that

219

no aircraft came over. We left there at night and reached the rendezvous, although with no great hopes of rescue because we were a whole day late. Then lights flashed from the sea and Andy was there to take us aboard. He had over-ruled the naval officer and insisted on the boat returning for us. I think I owe him my life for that. At best, I could have spent the rest of the war in a prison camp.

That's a reference not only to the disappearance of Captain Blyth's patrol at Alimnia but also to a new viciousness in the Aegean. Roger Wright recalls:

There were atrocities, and not only by the Germans. Many men know the truth but say nothing. On one island (a raid not led by Lassen), my task was to blast the Germans out of a school so that they would run for exits covered by other sections of the patrol. Alan Sanders was my No.2 on the Bren and I opened up on the building with incendiary, armour-piercing and tracer; magazines of everything I could get hold of, although it did the barrels no good. Afterwards, I saw the bodies and something about their positions told me they had been lined up after surrender and shot in cold blood. Sanders and I had nothing to do with it.

Sanders says: "The Sacred Squadron did it and then placed a notice by the dead: 'This is the fate of Germans who oppress Greeks.' I've often thought about this. It was wrong."

Nothing outdoes the horror of a hearsay account from Billy Reeves and Paddy Webster about Yugoslav partisans carry-ing out a summary sentence on four Germans accused of rape: "We were told that they were staked out naked on the ground while a girl moved among them, gently masturbating each man. Behind her, came the executioner with a razor-sharp knife. The penises were stuck in their mouths."

Peter Kemp, a comrade of Lassen in the Small Scale Raiding Force, was parachuted by SOE to serve in 1943–44 with the Albanian guerillas among whom he met a man proud of personally cutting seventy throats. Exhibits in the Military

Museum at Belgrade can be taken as typical of wartime savagery in the Balkans, a wicked catalogue of torture, reprisals, executions, deportations, lootings and burning of villages.

A small bread-oven is on display. It is said to have been used for the roasting alive of a four-year-old girl by the Ustashi, an army of Croatian Nazis who attacked Lassen on his first mission into Yugoslavia when accompanied by Holmes: "He asked for me to go into the mountains with him and blow up a bridge. He often asked for me, although I didn't like him. He was a fantastic soldier, a really determined, strong character and I wouldn't attempt to persuade anyone that he didn't deserve his medals. But I never found him likeable."

The bridge, which carried a railway over a gorge at Gruda near the ancient seaport of Dubrovnik, had been drilled ready for demolition and Holmes remembers:

We set it up electrically. A couple of us did the wiring while a Royal Engineers corporal made a junction box with a primer cord to each charge. The wiring from the plunger to the detonator was less than 150 feet, shorter than we would have liked for 500 lb of ethyl-ammonal.

The rest retreated while Lassen and I stayed behind. We pressed the plunger but nothing happened. Lassen told me to clean the plunger so I unscrewed the terminals, polished and replaced the wires. We pressed once more. Again, nothing. In the meantime, the RE corporal had lit the safety fuse. We sat there for a couple of minutes and still nothing happened. Lassen said: "We'll have to do something." I said that perhaps the safety fuse hadn't yet burned through. He wouldn't listen, he said: "It must have burned by now." Finally, I talked him into waiting just a little longer but he was restless and stood up . . . as he did so, the bridge exploded and a piece of masonry fully five-foot square whistled past his head.

We knew the bang would fetch the Ustashis to chase us because we had seen them moving about in the valleys. So we took to the hills. Our partisans had disappeared already; they didn't want to fight. I climbed a tree and saw two lines of Ustashi moving up the mountain; there must have been 100 of them with German officers blowing whistles, they were all well-disciplined and nobody's fools. I said that we'd better get out and he saw the sense of that, but our packs with spare ammunition hadn't been moved to our defensive position. So we were up in the hills for three or four days with no food; I had, as we all did, a mixture of oatmeal, sugar and chocolate – but, in this case, no utensil to put it in.

The patrol reached the supposedly impregnable headquarters of the partisans in the mountain peaks, but the Ustashis tracked them down and overran it, while Lassen threw grenades and Henshaw covered the retreat. Company Sergeant-Major C. Workman, of the Grenadiers, wrote: "They chased us from place to place . . . At night we had to lie huddled together like sheep and cover ourselves with branches of fir trees . . . I never saw Yugoslavia again and was not sorry."

Hancock saw the problem for British Special Forces in Yugoslavia:

> The country was a mixture of politics, religions, nationalities, ever-changing sides and partisans jealous of our presence because the locals were saying: "Why are these foreigners fighting our war? You've been sitting around, singing patriotic songs and eating us out of house and home but we don't see you fighting the Germans." Then the partisans would get niggled and might even tip off the enemy. In the end, we had to function on our own.

In Albania, Kemp identified a more sinister aspect of Marxist guerillas . . . "They were not building up their military formations in order to fight Germans or Italians, but in order to gain control of the country for themselves by force." Lassen's souvenir of Albania was a Wehrmacht runabout, a captured Volkswagen that he shipped back to the new SBS base at Bari in Southern Italy. His farewell to Yugoslavia was an ambush on a mountain road with some dilatory partisans and Sergeant Nicholson:

> The partisans were supposed to start the attack but nothing happened, yet the German column, some 300 yards long, was beginning to pass us by. I said to Lassen, "We must fire." He said, "Are you sure?" and I said, "There can't be any more of them." So we fired and, at last, the partisans fired. It was a terrible slaughter – mules, men and horses, thrashing about in blood and baggage.

A swift return to the Aegean proved more congenial for Lassen. He sailed into the Saronic Gulf, checking out the islands for German occupation and the sea-lanes to Athens for minefields. Once again, a retinue formed around him – Zeppi the barber, Dimitri the odd-job man, cooks, shoe-blacks and hangers-on. Lassen collected people, such as his one-time bodyguard Sammy Trafford:

> I wasn't a bodyguard in the accepted sense. He didn't need a minder, he could look after himself. No, I was more of a personal attendant, mainly as his driver and as pilot of his dory. He talked to me like a mate or an NCO, not as a captain soon [in October 1944] to become a major. He was always cursing, sometimes in real bad language.
>
> I wondered about his merchant service because his boat-handling was alarming. As a Royal Marine, I knew that vessels are supposed to approach each other bow to bow but he'd take the wheel from me and go hell-for-leather straight at the side of ships before chucking the gear into reverse. Then he would leave me holding the tiller while he jumped aboard like a cat.
>
> I drove a lot for him, especially on Crete. If one of our vehicles was in front, he would order: "Pass the bloody thing" to which I'd usually object: "Sir, I'm not that experienced a driver." He'd then say: "Stop this jeep, I'll drive it" which meant pressing the accelerator to the floorboards and driving like a madman until he'd got by. Then he would turn and glare at the blokes he had

overtaken . . . "That's how you bloody drive, Sam," he'd
say, laughing.

When I was wounded on Santorini, he said to me: "You
bloody go back." He meant to hospital, but that's how he
talked. Then he went to my pal Ralph Bridger and said:
"That bloody Sammy got himself shot. You be my bodyguard now" . . . and Ralph told me that he thought to
himself: "No fear!"

Trafford was required only once for true bodyguard duties
when one of Lassen's men burst drunkenly into an officers'
dinner on Poros, an island commanding approaches to
Athens: "I won't tell you the man's name because he still
comes to our reunions. He wanted to fight Lassen who
overpowered him and tied him up before sending for
Kitchingman and me and saying: 'If he moves, shoot him.'
Next day Lassen let him off."

Lassen had been dining with two naval officers, one of them
a particularly close friend. Lieutenant Martin Solomon was
jolly and chubby, and nothing in his looks or background
suggested toughness. His time at Cambridge University had
been devoted to amateur theatricals, an interest that he had
turned into a pre-war occupation by becoming the personal
manager of four rising stars, John Mills, Michael Wilding,
Hermione Baddeley and Hermione Gingold. Yet Solomon
had won the Distinguished Service Cross at Dunkirk and a
bar to the DSC when commanding an MTB at Tobruk. At
twenty-nine, he also had a Croix de Guerre.

Orders were exceeded – or, at any rate, stretched – when
Lassen and Solomon sailed two caiques, with a jeep and fewer
than forty officers and men, beyond the northern limit of the
Sporades and turned a reconnaissance of islands into an
exploit that could be done justice only by Hollywood. It was
the capture of the great seaport of Salonika on four fire
engines.

Lassen's little force moored unnoticed in the Potidia canal.
Richard Capell, a war correspondent with a First World War
decoration for gallantry at Vimy Ridge, wrote: "Andy
Lassen, that terrible Viking of the SBS, had audaciously

sailed right up when the Germans had no notion of any British within a hundred miles." The canal was 30 miles south of the city but Lassen had his jeep and petrol, a combination which, Solomon wrote: "Spelt chaos for the whole area. I knew what was coming and prepared myself all night with prayer and solemn reflection . . . We set off at seven at too high a speed and made an 80-mile tour in country which we had no reason to suppose was not infested by the enemy."

Greek civilians thought the SBS were the enemy. Children fled and peasants trembled as Lassen roared by, blue eyes afire and his blond hair flying in the slipstream. Colonel Papathanasion, commander of the Communist-backed ELAS guerillas, got a flea in his ear within minutes of meeting Lassen. It was the historic difference between local troops, concerned only with their own manor, and national forces who saw the war as a whole. The Germans were pulling out and the guerillas were content to let them go; it was not their business if the Wehrmacht went off to fight somewhere else.

ELAS wanted a quiet life, Lassen wanted an immediate assault and swept aside the colonel's objections. His words, as reported by John Lodwick, were: "Venn I wish to see ze German position, I vill do so . . . you understand? Vy are you not attacking them yourself?" Solomon affirms: "Lassen impressed the partisans so much that their tone changed considerably."

German demolition parties were working unhurriedly when Lassen landed. They were thorough. The 9,000 British troops sailing to dislodge them would find no way in. The harbour entrance had been blocked, more than forty ships had been sent to the bottom and all the dockyard buildings had been razed. The arrival of Lassen and his men disrupted this steady tempo of destruction; as Capell noted: "His jeep and handful of men were magnified by mobility into hundreds."

The German commander of Salonika had two tanks at his disposal, as well as some self-propelled guns and almost a full battalion of men, but he had no spies or reliable intelligence and could not be sure that Captain Henshaw was bluffing when sending him a written demand for surrender to "the encircling British forces". A negotiator sought out Lassen and played for time, a forty-eight hour break in hostilities while the Germans left quietly. The approach was rejected and Lassen wired Army headquarters: "We intend to take Salonika ourselves."

His attack looked innocent at the start. A street parade, headed by Lassen's jeep and the city's four fire engines, winding along the waterfront and passing the white, stone tower that guards the ancient harbour. Nosegays, bouquets of flowers and bunches of fragrant herbs were thrust upon the SBS perched on the ladders and clinging to the sides of the engines, which soon resembled floats in a floral parade. The numbers grew with every yard. Girls and guerillas, grateful older Greeks with gifts of wine, eggs, goats' cheese, honey and the inevitable tots of ouzo. The SBS rolled along singing, nothing national or warlike but a comic ditty that had caught the raiders' fancy: "Pistol Packing Momma". The best-looking or boldest girls were hauled aboard. Kisses were exchanged or blown to the waving crowds, and the fire-bells clanged exuberantly. The accompanying ELAS forces, criss-crossed with bandoliers and bristling with largely unused weapons, slowed as they approached a square where EAM party leaders were assembling, speech-notes at the ready, for a rally with their gallant Allies. Lassen ignored them. His fire engines rolled on.

Wehrmacht sappers had blown fifteen ragged gaps in Salonika's breakwater, although with little effect on the harbour's reputation as a mill-pond, noted for the flatness of its water and shelter from wind. Lassen's parade coincided with one of these typically calm days, a Sunday afternoon that was warm for late autumn. The relaxing weather and the city's ardent welcome contributed to the men's belief that, for once, their intrepid leader might be on a joyride, not a mission. His light-heartedness showed itself on setting off from a suburban school that the raiders had commandeered for a billet. "We want a scout," he declared, ordering the seizure of a horse grazing by the road while a volunteer rider was sought. Lassen's choice fell on Trafford, who had admitted to some riding experience acquired while working on a farm. Until Lassen tired of this stunt, Trafford rode ahead, signalling the SBS forward while feeling like a Red Indian on a steed without saddle or stirrups and only an improvised bridle.

Greeks watching the approach of the SBS must have been struck by the contrast of their healthiness with the wan, woebegone appearance of most other inhabitants of the depressed and ravaged city. Lassen's men glistened with fitness and confidence. They were sturdy and well-fed, full of an energy that showed how they, unlike the retreating foe, had not tired of war.

Not all the enemy, though, were retreating towards Bulgaria; many in Salonika had dodged the evacuation by desertion, simply slipping over the wall of barracks and labour camps. These were usually press-ganged Poles, Serbs, Russians and the rest, making a living from girlfriends or the black market while dodging both the field police and the partisans. Even the Germans staying true to Hitler's cause were beginning to put their own interests first as Richard Capell shows in recording the payment of £15 in gold as a bribe to spare a power station. The demolition team had begun by asking for £100.

Plumes of smoke from the airfield hangars to the north as well as occasional bangs from the furthermost quays were the only evidence during the parade of the Germans remaining organised and active. It could easily have been forgotten that they still outnumbered the unexpected British invaders by eight to one. Lassen remembered, though. He had received a personal reminder of the enemy's strength and presence through their capture of his prized jeep for a few hours.

Solomon and Henshaw lost it through bad luck after snatching two prisoners from a gun battery. Their path back to the jeep was blocked unwittingly by the arrival of a small armoured unit and several lorry-loads of German troops. These odds were hopeless as Solomon told Capell: "So we disappeared rapidly, still with the prisoners but leaving behind the jeep. I daren't leave it permanently, though, because of Andy. I'd have been too frightened to tell him."

Solomon then hid himself near the battery for the night, imagining Lassen, who spoke to officers as he did to men, threatening: "I'll slit your throat" if the jeep had not returned. The morning firing gave Solomon his chance, he skirted the gun-site and made off with the jeep under cover of the noise.

The jeep, with Lassen as upright at the wheel as a bus-driver, forged on as pathfinder for the fire-engines through the joyous afternoon of Salonika's liberation. On and on, until the throng who had been lining the pavements began melting away like guests who have sensed that the party could turn into a brawl. All those happy, giggling girls, escorted by mothers and brothers, slipped down from the engines and vanished into the web of back-streets.

Lassen's crossing of the line between festivity and violence was abrupt but not unforeseen by those who knew him well. From the moment that the speech-makers had been left behind, his eyes had fixed themselves on anything that could be reported as: "A target of opportunity." Sammy Trafford, gripping a Bren gun while squatting on the ladder of the leading fire-engine, sniffed trouble coming as soon as the little column entered a chaos of dockland roads.

Instead of cheering crowds, scattered heaps of rubble and broken glass marked the way ahead. Random breaks in walls revealed the destroyed buildings behind; death's-heads, drawn crudely on rough boards, denoted mined ground and houses. Here and there, rolls of barbed wire had been abandoned . . . and traffic signs in Gothic script directed Lassen towards a fuel dump that he knew instinctively would provide some action. A few badly aimed shots from the German sappers showed that he had found it, as Trafford recalls:

The demolition party, after trying to ambush us, ran to alert their guards as we opened up with every weapon we had. It's said now that Henshaw personally killed eleven Germans in the fight and that Lassen killed eight. Nonsense!

Who kept a count? Who knows who killed who? It was impossible to tell when some forty or more of us, as well as several partisans, were firing submachine-guns. But I do know that we suffered only one man wounded – my mate, Tommy Kitchingman, who was shot in the shoulder.

Roger Wright agrees: "Henshaw shot these, Lassen shot those . . . rubbish! The men shot them. I can still see that parade and the little fire-engines unbelievably crowded. We were covered in flowers and snogging with the girls for miles. It was a victory parade and nobody warned us that we were approaching the Jerries. But the Greeks knew and we guessed when we saw how suddenly they had gone."

The fuel installation was saved and the final British claim was twenty-two Germans killed but Wright adds:

We didn't do any fighting from the fire-engines. We dismounted and divided into two patrols, Lassen's and Henshaw's. I went with Henshaw who, with me and another lad, crept close enough to hear the Germans talking. They were lining up a convoy and ready to get out; we wanted to attack but Henshaw, a fine officer who had been my sergeant at Dunkirk, said: "No, not over such open ground." So we hid in an abandoned gun emplacement and fired everything possible at them, killing quite a few until starting to run out of ammo.

Next morning, some days earlier than intended, the Germans evacuated the city to the last man. Lassen wired Cairo: "Have taken Salonika". Capell wrote: "Had it not been for Lassen and his handful of men, the town would have been exposed to severe destruction." British flags began to outnumber the red banners of ELAS in the streets and Lassen ruled the city for a week from his quarters in a commandeered hotel where Solomon wrote: "I shall never again have so much power or enjoy anything so much. Dictators for a week . . . Andy and I prevent riots and murder, we pass laws, we pardon and pass sentences. If we had not come, much blood would have been spilt."

Lassen left for Athens where, a Danish lady told his mother: "All the women fell for him. He was so unusually handsome that it gave you a small shock." Sometimes he operated from Eddie's Bar, the unofficial SAS headquarters, and sometimes from the Danish legation; from either base, he took his pick but not always wisely. A jealous Greek husband, firing a pistol, burst into Lassen's room at the Hotel Grande Bretagne, but the great seducer, presumably tipped off by the wife, had slipped away.

Three weeks of parties, late nights and lusty ladies were enough for Lassen. He sought a resumption of the war and ran into his RAF friend Tony Grech:

> He went to my commanding officer and said: "I want Grech." Being Andy, he got his way and we went off for two months of operations in Crete. I spoke Greek, which was very helpful, and on the first night we toured the brothels.
>
> We had settled our prices and gone to our various rooms when there was a helluva hollering in the courtyard. As I was organising things, I went outside and saw some of the SBS boys climbing over the wall to get in although the brothel was closed officially and under curfew. "For Christ's sake, go away," I said, but I was new and they ignored me. I went for Andy who came out in the courtyard, bollock-naked in the moonlight, apart from knee-high leather boots. He said: "Chaps, can't you let your commanding officer fuck in peace?"
>
> They said: "Sorry, sir" – and went away.

Grech recalls: "It was in the Heraklion Hotel in Crete, not in the Grande Bretagne in Athens, that he used to leave his jeep in the lift. He'd drive it up the steps, through the foyer and straight into the big, old-fashioned lift." All personal transport – cars, jeeps and fifteen-hundredweight trucks – were intended by the army to be immobilised when parked for any length of time and the recommended method was removal of the rotor arm. Lassen had neither the patience nor mechanical knowledge to delve into engines; jeep thieves had robbed him in Athens and he defied them to do it again once he had a lift for a garage.

Lassen had been sent to Crete as commander of "Senforce" (from the last three letters of his name), a special service group formed to protect the British military liaison officers but, chiefly, to keep 13,000 Germans penned in the north-west corner of the island while also stopping the Greek irregulars from killing each other. Sutherland came to see him:

> I wanted to know if there was any point in attacking the bottled-up German garrison. We came to the conclusion that it would have been a waste of time and good lives because the Germans were very well-defended. We then spent Christmas Day near Hania [where the Germans were] having the most extraordinary party. Andy took over a hotel, brought in all his dogs and summoned the town band who crammed into what was really a very tiny room and proceeded to play martial music, carols and the Danish national anthems. A lot was drunk. He was a great example of how to live up to the limit, in all respects.

A liaison officer described Lassen in a letter home as: "Quiet and sure . . . in a shaggy private's greatcoat, his chin on his chest and his blue eyes taking in everything." The same writer was startled by Lassen's sudden and unheard arrival in his office despite walking along a gravel path, climbing steps and crossing a wooden floor . . . "It was so terribly silent and quick that I thought: 'By God, that must be the way you appear at the German headquarters.'" But Lassen could shoot only goats, not Germans, in his two months on Crete where the Greek factions, particularly ELAS, gave greater trouble than the enemy.

An ELAS sniper, said later to be insane, killed Captain Charlie Clynes and dispatch-rider Leslie Cornthwaite near Heraklion, as well as wounding Captain Charles Bimrose. Grech says:

> Charlie was shot in the stomach and died in hospital about ten days later. Andy sent signals to me and Ian Smith. He was very angry when we gathered in Heraklion to discuss it.

231

I urged a shooting-up of the Communist area but he, remarkably wise for a young man, chose only a show of force. "Let's just frighten them," he said and then, mounting two machine-guns on the front of his jeep and another on the back, he drove up and down the ELAS-held streets for a few hours.

Forbearance of that degree had not been prominent in Lassen's character and so it may have been more than coincidence that a long-awaited order to leave Crete arrived on the day of Clynes' funeral. Lassen and his squadron packed that night. He had volunteered again. They were off to Italy.

19

COMACCHIO

Lake Comacchio, the scene of Lassen's last throw, is a shallow sump for weedy streams and sluggish rivers unable to reach the Po delta a few miles to the north. Comacchio is the English Fens writ large, almost 200 square miles of mud and reeds that are home to millions of eels, mullet and bream, and where a man can walk dry-shod only along the causeways heaped high from the pale Italian clay.

This watery bastion behind the old Gothic Line had been expanded under General Vietinghoff by the common German tactic of inundation. Sea defences were breached on the Adriatic shore to flood all the land to the eastward save for a causeway, in parts little wider than a house driveway, and which was guarded by a chain of sunken machine-gun posts sited along the line of a disused railway. It was there that Lassen would attack, pitting seventeen men against eight Spandau machine-guns.

He knew nothing of this mission when re-joining the SBS at Monte St Angelo, their base on the remote and thickly wooded Gargano peninsula. "A horrible, primitive place," in the opinion of Fred Green, the squadron's interpreter. "Only old people were there. And the funerals at the abbey were scary because the mourners in white robes looked like the Ku-Klux-Klan."

Funerals were also becoming unusually frequent among the raiders; the deaths of Clynes and Cornthwaite on Crete were followed quickly by the loss of Captain Lees and Tommy Kitchingman, Trafford's friend, when attacking a German-held villa at Lussino in the Northern Adriatic. Eight of the SBS were also wounded in this raid, a heavy casualty rate for such skilled men. Captain Henshaw, so often Lassen's partner, was then killed with Roger Wright at his side . . . "Not by a grenade, as the report states, but by someone shooting at the flash of our Piat mortar," says Wright.

233

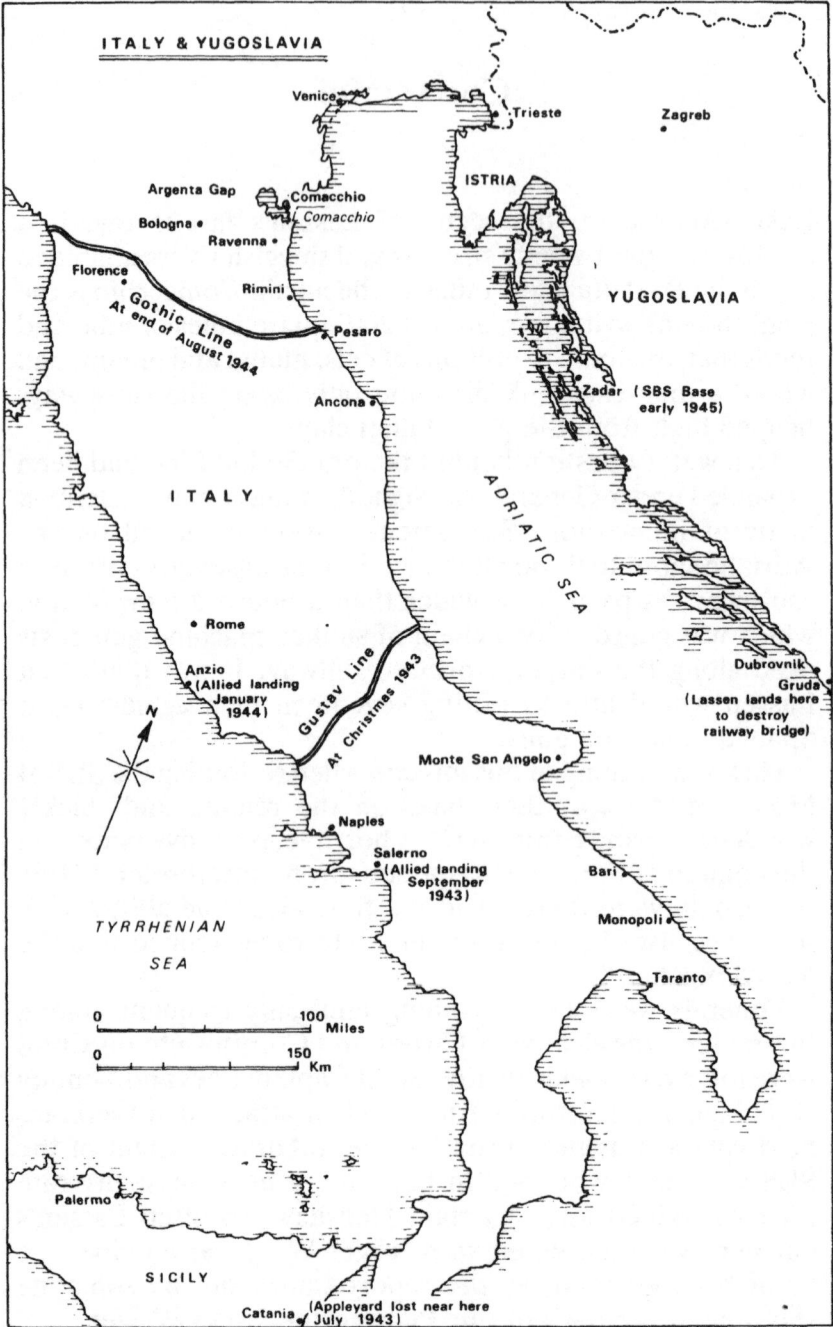

ITALY & YUGOSLAVIA

Venice
Trieste
Zagreb

ISTRIA

Argenta Gap
Comacchio
Comacchio
Bologna
Ravenna
YUGOSLAVIA
Florence
Rimini
Gothic Line
At end of August 1944
Pesaro

Ancona
Zadar (SBS Base
early 1945)

ITALY

ADRIATIC SEA

Rome

Anzio
(Allied landing
January
1944)
Gustav Line
At Christmas 1943
N
Dubrovnik
Gruda
(Lassen lands here
to destroy
railway bridge)

Monte San Angelo

Naples
Salerno
(Allied landing
September
1943)
Bari

TYRRHENIAN

SEA
Monopoli

Taranto

0   100
Miles
0   150
Km

Palermo

SICILY

Catania
(Appleyard lost near here
July 1943)

Deep sorrow never outlasted the combination of the survivors' relief at being alive and the massed wake on local wine procured by Green in a master stroke, when he rolled up with two motorised Army water-carriers filled with hundreds of gallons, one red and the other white. Hilarity extended to a parade honouring Lassen's dog, as recounted by Colonel Sutherland:

Andy said one day: "This dog has done many operations. He has his regimental badge [the SAS badge worn proudly on his collar] but don't you think he should have his wings as well?" I said it wasn't a bad idea and so we had a fantastic ceremony where the dog's operational wings were presented by the Commanding Officer. It was the only time I've seen Andy really clean up.

Lassen took a parade in Crete with torn trousers. On Cos, he mustered such a villainous-looking crew of raggle-taggle raiders that the inspecting officer blanched, especially when a squad, in assorted headgear and footwear, attempted to present arms with Bren guns, an impossible drill movement because of the Bren's tripod. According to Fred Green: "The inspecting officer asked sarcastically: 'Is *this* the British Army?' Andy, turning those blue eyes full-on, snapped: 'My fighting men, sir!'"

Hank Hancock, remembering an inspection shortly before Comacchio, said:

We were never appalled by Lassen's untidiness. We'd joined the SAS to get away from the military-type officers who looked askance at us and at him. This particular high-up visited our forward positions and said words to this effect: "Your men are in shite order, they are not even shaved. *You* are not even shaved. Get yourself shaved! What will the enemy think if they see you dead looking like this? They will think the British Army is demoralised." I don't know what he replied, but I know that he didn't give a monkey's.

Lassen spent a leave in Rome before the battle, staying at the five-star Hotel Excelsior in the Via Veneto and squiring an English girl from the WAAF round the bars and restaurants. He threw a party for his men during the week and Green remembered: "He was worried that we might not have enough money to enjoy Rome. I loved that about the SBS. When you went out socially, it wasn't your money, my money, his money but only our money. All for one, one for all . . . a spirit I've never found again."

Lassen's generosity impressed his sergeant-major at Comacchio, Les Stephenson:

> He talked about the capture of those ships in West Africa and said: "There's a lot of prize money, but the group entitled to it is shrinking. So don't worry about the end of the war because we'll share the money that's due to me." He spoke as one of us, not as someone in the high position of a major. He thought about us, the men with him. He didn't think: "Ha, I've got all this money for myself."
>
> I felt a bond from the time of a storm in the Aegean when, apart from the Greek helmsman of our caique, we were the only two not to fold or go below with sea-sickness. He saw that as a success. He was hooked on success and had a knack of recognising it in other people. I think he saw me as a success because I had escaped from a German prison-camp on Crete, where I met my wife; I wandered round the island for nearly two years living as a Greek, hiding in the mountains and in caves and ditches while cooperating with SOE and the resistance. That pleased him. He saw me as self-reliant, able to get by on my own.

Fred Green noted: "Andy Lassen put dangerous propositions to you in a way that made you forget danger. It was personality. You could not refuse but only feel 'I'll do anything for this bastard'." Stephenson also fell under the spell:

> I wasn't keen when he asked me to go to Comacchio with him from Crete. My field was Greece, I spoke the language

and knew how to live rough there. I didn't know Italy, but he was so persuasive . . . "You'll be a sergeant-major again" and that sort of thing. He wanted me with him and I knew that I'd follow him anywhere because I trusted him.

The SAS had good officers, no doubt about that. But he was unusual, a 100 per cent leader who, unlike some others, wouldn't forget about you after the operation. On or off the battlefield, he was reliable. If you had a request or a complaint, he'd go to GHQ or anywhere to press for it.

Some people didn't like him because he was too forthright and could rub salt in the wound. That was part of his leadership, there were no ifs and buts with him. He was a very positive man who had no trouble making his mind up and who didn't want you standing there arguing or hesitating. Provided you were truthful with him and carrying out orders, he was marvellous. It was a different story if anyone didn't do his best or tried to pull a fast one. You knew where you stood with him; he didn't hesitate and fuss, or shuffle his feet. You never doubted his ability to go where he said that he'd go and do what he said that he'd do. When he led, you had faith!

However, the problems of Comacchio, and the many other dislodging engagements of the Italian campaign, called chiefly for tenacious massed endurance rather than daring strokes of personal leadership. Italy had turned into a war for plodders and had been relegated accordingly to the bottom corners of the front pages, while the main headlines told of Montgomery and Eisenhower's men advancing into the Ruhr, of the Red Army besieging Vienna and of the Americans closing on Japan by invading Okinawa. In that late, damp spring of 1945, Italy had ceased to be news although remaining a costly drain of some 310,000 Allied killed and wounded as the Wehrmacht were winkled out of the mountains.

Order of battle, logistics, supply trains, siting of burial grounds, coordination of artillery and air support . . . this was not fighting that fitted either Lassen's temperament or experience. "I go now," he announced in the middle of a

colonel's address to an administrative conference. His un-
checked exit has been ascribed to sheer force of personality
but was more probably due to the organisers' recognition that
their day's work called for a Bradshaw, not a Hotspur. Lassen
would contribute little to the complexities of large-scale
planning but everything to his assigned task.

This was a diversionary attack to draw Germans towards
the Adriatic banks of Comacchio before Brigadier Ronnie
Tod threw a left hook to force a bridgehead on the west of the
lake, where his No.2 Commando Brigade had fought for days
to find a gap. The conditions frustrated them. Mud clogged
rifles and Tommy Heard, of the Heavy Weapons Troop, saw
an equipment-filled float go to the bottom – doubtless one of
many. Heard recalls: "Comacchio was a cock-up with unsuit-
able craft in a flooded area. It was a swamp, not a lake. I had
to hack paths for floats through a jungle of reeds and it was
freezing cold. Nobody had warned us about that, so we
weren't dressed for it."

Comacchio town and the adjoining harbour of Porto
Garibaldi were held by some 1,200 of the enemy, a combination of German riflemen and gunners and the Moslem
auxiliaries of the 162nd Turkoman Division. Hitler's forces
had been augmented from 1940 onwards by Spaniards, Finns,
Italians, Hungarians, Rumanians, Bulgarians, Yugoslavs,
elements of Dutch, Belgian and Danish Nazis and the
recruitment, either willingly or forcibly, of a million prisoners
from the Russian front. In 1944, it was estimated that nearly
fifteen per cent of the Wehrmacht were Soviet citizens and
few of them could have looked stranger, or felt more out of
place at Comacchio, than nomads from the desert republic of
Turkmenistan.

Yet their line yielded only slowly to the Commandos
despite many instances of great individual courage by the
attackers, especially that of 21-year-old Tom Hunter, a
Scottish corporal of the 43rd Royal Marine Commando who,
when his troop seemed nailed down on a canal bank,
"charged alone across two hundred yards against the fire of
nine Spandaus and mortars . . . personally cleared a group of
houses and drew fire until most of his troop had sheltered".

This was on April 2, 1945, a week before Lassen's venture, and Brigadier Tod, himself both a Scot and a founding Commando officer, had no hesitation about putting forward Hunter's name for a posthumous Victoria Cross.

Lassen moved up from Ravenna to the lake about this time with an assortment of Folbots, rubber dinghies, Goatley floats, flat-bottomed boats and some sixty men dressed for the part in wellingtons and woolly caps. He said farewell to the good life with an order to Fred Green for two of his favourite dishes, spaghetti and tomato sauce followed by a thin steak of veal. After that, it was back to Army compo rations and primitive living under shellfire on treeless islands in the lake.

The skyline of Comacchio has changed little to this day and the prominent feature on the northern horizon remains the campanile, the bell tower with a pointed roof in the Venetian style. From this vantage point, the Germans directed artillery of such accuracy that Lassen's men on the islands hardly dared stand erect in daylight and any of them wanting to urinate or excrete either waited for nightfall or did it in their clothing.

Jack Doyle, of the Royal Army Service Corps, experienced the German firing after a tedious crossing of the lake – "weed kept clogging the outboard motors" – in a flotilla of storm-boats laden with grenades and small arms ammunition which "we had to unload practically up to our shoulders in water because of the shelling." The island was Caldirolo, one of the few with a building – a small, stone barn used by Lassen for a headquarters. He shouted from it to the supply squadron, warning them to keep their heads down and then, after thanking them, paddled away in a Folbot.

His deep, quick and practised thrusts were no guarantee of progress, though. The SBS had scoured the lake for deep channels where navigation lights could be left to guide the Commandos, but the currents and shallows were for ever changing. Les Stephenson said:

In places you had to get out and tow the thing like the *African Queen*. As the first man in a three-man Folbot, I was the one who had to jump out and heave while, at the

239

back, Andy Lassen was cursing and blinding at every delay. He had a ship's box compass on his knee. I heard a splash, he'd thrown it into the lake in a temper. It wasn't correct, he said. He was commanding the Folbot like an old-time schooner. He said he'd navigate by the stars.

Lassen, unusually, was on edge at Comacchio. Almost all the survivors agree on that, but not on the cause. The lake itself was a strain – gurgling, stinking mud – and Lassen had the responsibility of hiding three large patrols for days under the noses of Germans not a quarter of a mile away. He was depressed about his missing pet. Dog Tom, Pipo's successor, had not been sent north from the new base at the seaside resort of Monopoli and Lassen's requests were brushed aside with the command: "Stop sending frivolous telegrams". The dog was dead, shot by a new sergeant-major maybe gambling on the non-return of the master. Lassen was worried, too, about the inevitable disbandment of the boat squadron when the war in Europe ended. He may have worried as well about some of the men with him, a scratch team, in the main, with only a sprinkling of such old reliables as Stud Stellin, Sean O'Reilly, Les Stephenson, Ray Iggleden, Billy Reeves and Freddie Crouch.

Lassen himself could have been infected by the general uncertainty about a mission to be conducted under this coded order: "Every reasonable risk must – repeat – MUST – be taken." This may explain his insistence on leading the attack personally in the hope of ensuring success although, as commanding officer, he could have stayed behind. As O'Reilly said after the war to Lassen's mother: "We respected Andy so much because we knew that he would always go in front." Bold leadership might just turn the tide for any of his men who might be getting war-weary, growing cautious or, like Freddie Crouch, in a miserable state of mind.

Hank Hancock remembers: "Freddie, a London policeman before the war, had a premonition of death and often told us of waking at night and seeing his body lying still with him outside it. We used to laugh and tell him that he was drinking too much but he stuck to his story. And then at

Comacchio, he was part of a write off. They all were. Decoys. The idea being to sacrifice up to fifty men, if necessary, to save thousands."

Crouch died at Comacchio as he foresaw – and horribly, but with iron discipline. Lassen's landing place was known to the British as "the Spit", a long neck of land stretching south from the town for three miles or more; it carried the causeway and was flanked on the west by the mouth of a deep channel. Fred Green says: "The water right at the edge seemed shallow but a man daren't walk there because the mud might drag him down and down. That happened to Crouch. He began sinking but would not call for help because that would give away our positions. He drowned before our eyes."

Absolute silence had been enforced throughout Lassen's approach; his men, mostly dressed like their leader in wind-jackets and battledress tops, rowed soundlessly through the midnight blackness to the causeway's steep and slippery banks. Lassen had split his force in three; he led the first patrol that landed almost two miles from the town and his rear was covered by a patrol under stocky little Lieutenant G. W. Turnbull, a new officer. The third patrol, due to set off some twenty minutes later under Stud Stellin, had been allotted the most spectacular task; their rubber dinghies were crammed with fused bombs and explosives, to be spread along the shore and causeway slopes for a fireworks display intended to create the illusion of a full-scale attack.

The flaw in the plan is explained by Les Stephenson:

There had been no proper reconnaissance. Trooper Crouch, my friend, set out with me in a canoe to do it but there was a high wind and we could make no headway; also his premonition troubled him and, although I tried to reassure him, he remained convinced, saying: "I don't like it. This job won't be right." We neared the Spit but ran out of time and had to go back. On a recce, attracting the enemy's attention is like forewarning them. Daylight was coming and on that flat lake, where you can see for miles, we would have been like flies on a screen.

Lassen was greatly disappointed when I told him we

241

hadn't been able to do the recce. It was pure bad luck, but it meant that we would be setting off on a blind date. I suggested to Lassen that the fishermen on the lake might help us. We were bound to be challenged somewhere on the Spit; if they could answer the challenge, we could be listening behind for where it came from. It's been said since that posing as fishermen was not a good cover because fishing on the lake was forbidden at the time, but fishermen don't take much notice of restrictions and a blind eye is often turned on them. I met one in the Aegean whose hands were stained yellow from sailing into a minefield daily and removing the explosive to use himself for stun fishing. In the same way, I saw fishermen on Comacchio in little boats on the flats, not fishing commercially but catching enough for their own needs. In fact, we got information from some of them.

The fishermen – or partisans, as they liked to style themselves later – apparently promised to help but went missing when Lassen needed them. Fred Green says: "At the last moment, they failed to show up and we had nobody to speak Italian if challenged. Andy Lassen came to me, saying 'How good is your Italian? You like Italian food, you know your way with Italian women. *You* are the fisherman!'"

Lassen walked side by side with Green for several hundred yards along the dark causeway while the rest of the patrol tagged behind out of sight. Stephenson, gun ready, joined Lassen behind Green when the challenge, "Chi va la?" (Who goes there?) came from in front and at ground-level. Green recalls:

Lassen whispered: "Forward you go. Do the talking." I wouldn't have gone without him there, I wouldn't have had the guts. I said: "Siamo pescatori di San Alberto" (We are fishermen from San Alberto). I said this three or four times. There was no reply and then firing began. Nobody at the checkpoint had spoken since the first shout. As soon as they fired, I was pushed to the ground and Andy went forward. I'm sure that something clicked in his mind at the sound of gunfire. He forgot who he was, he forgot about taking cover. He forgot every goddamn thing except going forward.

Stephenson says:

Fred had done his deed; it must have been nerve-racking for him to stand in front of a German machine-gun post for the first time in his life and try to pass himself off as an Italian. Anyway, we were grouped in our patrol positions and able to fire back at the slit trench that had challenged us but, in the darkness, some of the patrol got too far in front. That was dicey because we might shoot our own people but we overcame that problem and then saw that the next stage wouldn't be easy because we had no cover.

Two prisoners had been seized from the overpowered checkpoint and handed to Green for escorting to the boats at the rear. "I was told: 'Take them. Be careful – and wait.' They were Turkomans, short boys with a bluish-grey tinge to their skin." Meanwhile, the firing and a warning on the field telephone from the checkpoint had alerted the defences along the causeway; these machine-gun positions are variously described in the official reports as "pill-boxes" and "block-houses", terms which create an impression of substantial structures visible from a distance. In fact, the Spandaus were sited low down in firing-points built of stone, covered with sods and entered through an arch like the mouth of a small tunnel. Except for a direct hit by a shell or a bomb, they were invulnerable to long-range attack and probably only an aircraft like the rocket-firing Typhoon, then being used so abundantly in North-West Europe, could have strafed the causeway clear for Lassen.

In the absence of RAF assistance, Lassen did it himself. Stephenson remembers:

All our success had come from stealth but now we were being used for an infantry assault that, considering our type of soldiering, was a suicide mission. We were rushing along the road with him in front, blowing his whistle and shouting: "Come on. Forward, you bastards. Get on, get forward."

I caught up with him at a place where the machine-gun fire was getting heavier and pinning us down. Then it eased off for a while; the defenders would have been as much in the dark as we were. We had taken two of their positions and they were not to know we were only seventeen men. For all they knew, we could have been a couple of hundred.

Lassen was running out of grenades when I joined him in attacking the third German position. He was a grenade man . . . very fond of grenades. Some people hardly used them but he had a good throw and could put a grenade where he wanted. He said: "Have you any grenades, Steve?" so I passed him mine which I'd been keeping in reserve because we were supposed to go further along. He said: "You bastard, you haven't pulled the pin out!" You don't run round with a loose pin, so I let that remark pass over my head. It didn't bother me. He snatched at least one grenade out of my hand before I could pass it to him.

He shouted to the pill-box in German to surrender. Although a ruthless man, he wasn't brutal and, on occasions, would offer an opportunity to surrender. Somebody shouted "Kamerad", so he stood up from behind the small rise in the road that we had been using for cover. He told the rest of us to stay put while he went across in the darkness; as he neared the pill-box, there was a burst of machine-gun fire and then silence. We could barely see the pill-box, never mind what was going on. The silence seemed to last for twenty minutes but could only have been a few seconds and then I heard him call . . . "SBS, SBS. Major Lassen wounded. Here."

I wondered where he was and if there was anyone closer to him because the people from the rear should have reached the far side of the causeway by now. But I didn't hear anybody on that side, so when he shouted again I went across and found him lying by the right-hand side of the pill-box entrance. I tried to drag him away but he was a big, heavy man. He started talking: "Who is it?" and I told him:

"Steve". He said: "Good", and then: "Steve, I'm wounded; I'm going to die." He had been shot either through the groin or lower chest; I couldn't see which in the dark.

I fiddled round in my back pocket because we always carried morphine. I placed a tablet on his tongue. He asked what I was doing and I told him: "Morphine – and we're going to take you back to the boats." He said: "It's no use, Steve. I'm dying and it's been a poor show. Don't go any further with it. Get the others out."

I was still trying to pick him up but the two of us were entangled in a telephone line which was making it almost impossible to lift him – then he collapsed unconscious. I called: "SBS. Come over here" and eventually another chap came. When I asked for a hand to lift Lassen, he said: "No point. He's dead."

The result might have been different if we had carried on attacking. His decision to capture, not kill, had been the undoing of the whole thing. But I don't think he was killed by treachery. I think it was just bad luck. They had shouted "Kamerad" and were going to come out and give themselves up when they saw a figure rushing towards them in the darkness with a weapon in his hand. That could have alarmed them. Perhaps he shouldn't have gone forward so quickly to accept the surrender, but he was quick by nature and action. He didn't lead from behind, he was always in front. Besides, it wasn't an occasion for pussyfooting around. He wanted the pill-box silenced quickly and the initiative kept going.

Once he was dead, the action fizzled out. He was the leading light, the motivator. The driving force. We got back and told Turnbull of the order to pull out. He fired the red light to withdraw. Turnbull couldn't re-start the action, nobody could take over Lassen's role.

Bombardier T. C. Crotty and Company Sergeant-Major C. Workman were asked to provide the two eye-witness reports required to support recommendations for a Victoria Cross. The two accounts cover the same ground, although Crotty is more detailed:

Major Lassen, by himself, went forward and attacked the first position with hand grenades, putting it out of action . . . In the face of heavy fire from four enemy positions, he again went forward by himself to the second enemy position which he silenced with hand grenades . . . Our casualties, two killed and three wounded, weakened our fire power to one Bren gun and small arms. We were constantly subjected to heavy machine-gun fire but, in spite of this, Major Lassen quickly reorganised our force and went near enough to throw hand grenades into the third enemy position.

Turnbull's operation report revealed:

Each block-house was slightly larger than the one in front so that they could fire over the top of the position ahead . . . During all this time (after the capture of the second position), the two remaining positions were continuing with heavy fire of MG down the road, sweeping the banks and sending up illuminating flares . . . Owing to the magnificent leadership and personal courage of Major Lassen, MC, the force knocked out two enemy block-houses and one position. They accounted for six MGs, killed at least eight of the enemy, wounded some and took two prisoners. They also achieved their object of giving the impression that a larger force was in the vicinity.

The Germans retaliated at daylight with pinpoint shell fire on the islands, held then by Commandos as well as the SBS. Fred Green:

I remember that Stephenson and myself hid under a table with a goat; I don't know where the goat came from. Then there was the interrogation of the prisoners . . . German they did not speak, bar a few words. Russian they did not speak. English neither. We started gesturing until they were dead scared. Captain Bimrose came over, frightened we were going to finish off the two of them. I don't think I was normal; I had been speechless, shivering, crying, scared stiff and I was suffering the reaction that everyone felt from losing a commanding officer who had been our symbol.

Lassen's patrol had been all but wiped out with him. Four were dead – Lassen, Crouch, Wally Hughes, MM, from Stoneycroft in Lancashire, and Corporal Ted Roberts from Cheltenham. One was missing and the three wounded included Sean O'Reilly shot by a Spandau through his right shoulder. Seventeen men, eight casualties. The bodies were taken to Comacchio by the Germans and left temporarily in the loggia, rather like an old English butter market, beneath the red brick bell tower in the town centre.

The news reached Colonel Sutherland, who had succeeded Jellicoe as commander of the SBS, during an operation in Yugoslavia:

We were out in the wilds when the wireless operator produced this message and I went white. We all did, we couldn't believe it. We thought the man was totally indestructible after being through so much. Morale went down, absolutely rock-bottom. When I talked to the men with him on the raid, it struck me as being, even by Andy Lassen's bravery, something quite out of the ordinary. We decided to try for a Victoria Cross, the only posthumous award that we could put him in for in those days.

The SAS plan ran into a dead end at Commando Brigade, their controlling headquarters. Brigadier Tod, when asked to support the recommendation, said: "No, no. No question. Wonderful DSO but not good enough, in my opinion, for a Victoria Cross." The Commandos believed there was no chance of two posthumous VCs being awarded for a couple of comparatively small diversionary operations only a few miles apart – and Tod's approval had been pledged already to Hunter.

Sutherland says:

I decided to bypass the Commandos and go right to Corps, the headquarters of the Eighth Army commander, General

Sir Richard McCreery. I knew that would be the first place with a military secretary's branch handling honours and awards. I wrote what I thought was a very good citation backed by the necessary witnesses, then got in a jeep and motored up towards Klagenfurt in Austria. I had a friend, Tony Crankshaw, at Corps headquarters; we had been at Eton together and he carried a lot of influence with the General. I showed him the citation and he said: "My God, yes. You've got to do something about this"; I said: "What about you putting it in straightaway?" I wasn't going to miss a chance of getting a VC for the SAS and I was absolutely delighted when the Royal Marines got the VC for their man, too.

Three years after the war, I met Ronnie Tod who was rather affronted by learning how he had been by-passed. I said to him: "You must know that an SAS officer never takes No for an answer . . . but what counts is that both men, both marvellous men, got their VCs."

The decoration was presented by King George VI to Lassen's parents at Buckingham Palace in December 1945. Anders had been killed on the exact fifth anniversary of Denmark's occupation and his mother's biography of her elder son made him a national hero, but the Lassens decided against bringing the body home. Lassen, VC, rests in Italy, not fifty yards from the grave of Tom Hunter, VC.

20

LASSEN, VC

The war cemetery of Argenta Gap is screened by cypresses and hidden at the end of an unpaved byway skirting a farmyard. Here 612 British graves bake under the Romagna sun almost unvisited by their own countrymen. Lassen lies in Plot 11. His stone has been engraved with the VC and the SAS badge, and these words . . . "Major Anders Frederik Emil Victor Schau Lassen, VC, MC and two bars (of Denmark). Special Air Service Regiment. 9th April 1945. Age 24." A verse in Danish at the foot of the stone translates as:

> Fight for all you hold dear
> Die as if it counts
> Life is not so hard
> Nor is death.

Other memorials to Lassen can be found in Scotland, England, Denmark and in Israel, where two groves within the Danish Forest on the hills of Galilee were dedicated to his name after an appeal in 1986 by the Jewish National Fund. In Scotland, the headquarters of "D" Squadron of the 23rd Special Air Service Regiment near Dundee was named Lassen House in 1985; a metal plaque in the building commemorates him as "a revered officer".

In England, replicas of his medals were formerly held on display at the Duke of York's Headquarters in Chelsea. Photographs of him, although unflattering pay-book "mug-shots", hang in the Special Forces Club near Knightsbridge and in the Imperial War Museum. In Denmark, a memorial stone beside the little chapel of St Peter near his boyhood home is laid with wreaths and flowers on each anniversary of the liberation from the Nazis.

At Holmegaard, his brother's half-timbered and double-moated home, a bust of Anders Lassen stands on a small plinth in a quiet corner of the garden. In 1987, on the forty-second anniversary of his death, a new casting of this bust was mounted on a sturdy column and sited at the Freedom Museum in Copenhagen where, after the unveiling by HRH Prince Henrik, the gathering heard this from Colonel Sutherland:

> In my opinion, Anders caused more damage and discomfort to the enemy over five years of war than any other man of his rank and age . . . We know now that the sustained SBS attacks in the Aegean early in 1944, before D-day, gave the impression that a second front would be opened in the Balkans. In April, Anders' patrol eliminated the entire army garrison on Santorini. The German High Command reacted by reinforcing their Aegean positions. These troops stayed in place for the rest of the war when they could have been used elsewhere. Anders saved Salonika from demolition by the retreating Germans through the timely arrival of his squadron. In response to his ferocious attack at Comacchio on this day, 42 years ago . . . the Germans moved troops towards the Adriatic coast allowing the British Eighth Army to break out through the Argenta Gap shortly afterwards.

The Freedom Museum displays the full set of Lassen's real medals: Victoria Cross, Military Cross with two bars, the King Christian Honour medal, the medal of the Greek Sacred Squadron, and five British campaign medals – the 1939–45 medal, African Star, Italy medal, Defence medal and the War medal.

Plaques and museum exhibits and busts, no matter how lifelike, cannot catch a man as accurately as the mind's eye of friends and contemporaries. What picture flashes in their memories? Porter Jarrell: "I see him as in that picture used for the Anders Lassen Forest Appeal. Slim, brown, in khaki drill shorts. Also he's loping, he had a lope. And he's never relaxed."

Roger Wright:

> I see him in Crete where I'd crossed through part of the German lines to bring him wireless spares. The journey had

taken some days with a mule and I had passed through villages where the Germans had come at night with tanks and crushed houses to the ground while people were still inside. My destination was a mountain bungalow and Andy was standing on the verandah when I arrived. He had one foot forward and his left thumb was hooked in his jacket while he looked far below to the winding road filled with German lorries and troops and motor-cyclists. There were 13,000 of them and hardly more than thirteen of us, but Andy's stance and expression said: "I rule this valley."

Sammy Trafford: "He's always on his own. Preoccupied. And very much as when I first saw him on the poop deck of a caique, looking as if he stood on top of a hill. He'd walk about there smoking, thinking and staring out to sea."
Colonel Sutherland:

A Viking raider! I often said to him: "Just as well we weren't living a thousand years ago or you would be landing on the coast of Northumberland and scaring the daylights out of us." He looked a Viking, tall and thin, and he had that dreadful dog. I'm sure Vikings had dogs to nose around and make certain their master wasn't surprised when asleep.

Had Anders Lassen survived the war, could he have settled into peace-time life? Might he, as Lord Jellicoe believes, have played a significant part in Danish public affairs? It is possible because diplomatic service was in his heritage, as was the long line of Pastor Lassens. Sergeant-Major Stephenson knew nothing of that clerical ancestry but had seen the caring aspects of Lassen's character and wondered if the warrior might have found a new fulfilment in charity work.

Others say bleakly that Lassen would have become a mercenary, a gun for hire by any trouble-spot. One old comrade imagines him assisting Martin Solomon in smuggling Jewish refugees through the British blockade of Palestine after the war.

The boldest speculation pictures Lassen amassing a peace-time fortune by leading a raid to net more millions than the Great Train Robbers of 1963. Conversations about Africa are remembered . . . "He knew of a place with diamonds on the beach"; possibly a reference to Namaqualand, and the 300-mile belt of coastal diamonds, past which the *Maid Honor* had sailed in 1941. "He said: 'It's nearly impossible to land there but, with an ML and our experience, we bastards can get in.'" And he was probably right.

Now, instead of diamonds or wanted notices or a desk or fresh medals, there are only guesswork and legends . . . and the memory for the author of Frants Lassen in his garden on a summer day quoting General Robert E. Lee: "It is well that war is so terrible or we should get too fond of it." Then Frants, stretching an arm towards the bust, said: "But he loved it – and there were others like him!"

That is so, and there always will be. You will find them in the SAS, the Commandos, the Parachute Regiment and similar special units in every country – but in a world where whole continents can be obliterated by button-pushers thousands of miles away, nobody may ever again be able to fight such a personal war as Andy Lassen.

SELECTED BIBLIOGRAPHY

The principal sources Mike Langley consulted during his research for the first edition of this book were:

J. E. A., *Geoffrey: Major John Geoffrey Appleyard, DSO, MC and bar, MA of the Commandos and Special Air Service Regiment* (Whitehead & Miller, Leeds, 1945)

Argenti, Philip P., *The Occupation of Chios by the Germans, 1941–44* (Cambridge University Press, 1966)

Beamish, Derek, (with Harold Bennett, John Hillier), *Poole and World War II* (Poole Historical Trust, Poole, 1980)

Benyon-Tinker, W. E., *Dust upon the Sea* (Hodder & Stoughton, 1947)

Bleicher, Hugo, *Colonel Henri's Story: The War Memoirs of Hugo Bleicher*, ed. Ian Colvin (William Kimber, 1968)

Capell, Richard, *Simiomata, a Greek Notebook 1944–45* (Macdonald, 1946)

Clark, Alan, *The Fall of Crete* (Anthony Blond, 1962)

Durnford-Slater, Brigadier, DSO and bar, *Commando* (William Kimber, 1953)

Fairbairn, Captain W. E., *Get Tough* (Paladin Press, Boulder, Colorado)

Fairbairn, Captain W. E. and Captain E. A. Sykes – *Shooting to Live, with the One-hand Gun* (Paladin Press, Boulder, Colorado)

Fleming, Peter, *Invasion, 1940* (White Lion, London, 1957)

Foot, M. R. D., *SOE, the Special Operations Executive, 1940–46* (BBC, 1984)

Gander, Leonard Marsland, *Long Road to Leros* (Macdonald, 1945)

Gudme, Sten, *Denmark, Hitler's Model Protectorate* (Victor Gollancz, 1942)

Hampshire, A. Cecil, *Undercover Sailors* (William Kimber, 1981)

Howarth, Patrick, *Undercover, the Men and Women of the SOE* (Routledge & Kegan Paul, 1980)

Kemp, Peter, *No Colours or Crest* (Cassell, 1958)

Ladd, James D., *SAS Operations* (Robert Hale, 1986)

Ladd, James D., *SBS, the Invisible Raiders* (Arms & Armour Press, 1983)

Lassen, Suzanne, *Anders Lassen, VC*, translated by Inge Hack (Frederick Muller, 1965)

Lassen, Suzanne, *Anders Lassen, Somand og Soldat* (Gyldendal, 1951)

Lodwick, John, *The Filibusters* (Methuen, 1947)

March-Phillipps, Gus, *Sporting Print* (G. Bell & Sons, 1937)

Marrinan, Patrick, *Colonel Paddy* (Ulster Press)

Marshall, Bruce, *The White Rabbit* (Evans, 1952)

Marshall, Michael, *Hitler invaded Sark* (Guernsey Lithoprint)

Messenger, Charles, *The Commandos, 1940–1946* (William Kimber, 1985)

Noel-Baker, Francis, MP, *Greece, the Whole Story* (Hutchinson, 1946)

Pitt, Barrie, *Special Boat Squadron* (Century Press, 1983)

Ramsey, Winston G., *The War in the Channel Islands – Then and Now* (Battle of Britain Prints International, 1981)

Read, Captain G. W., *Raiding Forces – the story of Independent Command compiled from official sources and reports* (Ministry of Defence Library)

Seymour, William, *British Special Forces* (Sidgwick & Jackson, 1985)

Smith, Peter C. (with Edwin Walker), *War in the Aegean* (William Kimber, 1974)

Verney, John, *A Dinner of Herbs* (Collins, 1966)

Warner, Philip, *The SBS, Special Boat Squadron* (Sphere Books, 1983)